# Licensed to Sell

The History and Heritage of the Public House

ENGLISH HERITAGE

For Dave Gamston
who has done so much to pioneer
the appreciation and protection of
historic pub interiors

# Licensed to Sell

## The History and Heritage of the Public House

Geoff Brandwood
Andrew Davison
Michael Slaughter

ENGLISH HERITAGE

Published in association with

CAMRA

CAMPAIGN
FOR
REAL ALE

Published by English Heritage, The Engine House, Fire Fly Avenue, Swindon, SN2 2EH
www.english-heritage.org.uk

English Heritage is the Government's statutory adviser on all aspects of the historic
environment.

First published 2004: ISBN 1 85074 906 X
Reprinted 2005 with minor amendments
Second edition published 2011: ISBN 978 1 848020 85 6
Product code 51603

*British Library Cataloguing in Publication data*
A CIP catalogue record for this book is available from the British Library.

Brought to publication by Jess Ward, Publishing, English Heritage
Edited by Janet Hadley
Page layout by Chuck Goodwin and Hybert Design
Printed in UK by Park Comunications Limited

**Front cover** Hand and Shears, 1 Middle Street, London EC1.
**Title page** Screens and front bar at the Kings Head, Tooting, London SW17.
**Back cover** Peveril of the Peak, Great Bridgewater Street, Manchester.

# Contents

## About CAMRA

The Campaign for Real Ale (CAMRA) was founded in 1971 to defend the very existence of Britain's national drink – traditional cask-conditioned beer. It remains an independent, volunteer-led organisation with over 120,000 members and has been described as the most successful consumer group in Europe. CAMRA also promotes consumer rights and the pub, fighting successfully for more flexible licensing laws and continuing to campaign for fairer pricing on all real ale.

The public house is a vital part of British culture and CAMRA aims to ensure its survival for future generations to enjoy. Members survey pubs all over the country for inclusion in CAMRA's annual *Good Beer Guide*, the UK's best-selling independent pub guide. CAMRA initiatives also include Local Pubs Week and other events held throughout the year aimed at promoting pub usage within the local community.

The preservation of historic pub interiors has long been a key issue for CAMRA. The campaign's Pub Heritage Group produces national and regional guides to the nation's 'Real Heritage Pubs' – unique listings of the most important examples throughout the UK. Full details of these can be found on the Pub Heritage Group website www.heritagepubs.org.uk.

For more information about CAMRA and to obtain Real Heritage Pub books, visit our website www.camra.org.uk.

Campaign for Real Ale
230 Hatfield Road
St Albans AL1 4LW

01727 867201

## About the authors

The three contributors all have a longstanding interest in and love of the British pub. They are also all members of the Campaign for Real Ale's Pub Heritage Group.

Geoff Brandwood is an architectural historian and a former Chairman of the Victorian Society. He has particular interests in the architecture and planning of historic pubs and co-authored *London Heritage Pubs* (CAMRA, 2008). He has also written widely about Victorian churches.

Andrew Davison trained as an archaeologist and now is an Inspector of Ancient Monuments in the north-west. He has a special interest in licensing and the regulation of the pub and has written on the buildings of Temperance.

Michael Slaughter LRPS has been visiting the last remaining historic interiors pubs since introduced to them in 1976 on a narrow boat holiday. A professional photographer since 2002, specialising in pub interiors, he is editor of *Scotland's True Heritage Pubs* (CAMRA, 2007) and joint editor of *Real Heritage Pubs of Wales* (CAMRA, 2010).

## Preface

Public houses (or pubs) are among the most ubiquitous of building types. Most villages still possess them, and although not as numerous as they once were, they are still scattered liberally throughout our towns and cities.

The pub is also one of the great English institutions. Like the parish church, the idea of it is cherished by many who hardly ever cross the threshold, while, for countless foreign visitors, a trip to a pub is a must on the list of things to do. The pub has a very long history and one which is closely bound up with English consciousness. It is woven into the fabric of some of our greatest literature. Chaucer's late 14th-century pilgrims meet at the Tabard Inn in Southwark before their storytelling ride to Canterbury. In the plays of Shakespeare, Falstaff's roisterings at the Boar's Head in Eastcheap provide one of the enduring images of the pub, subversive, anarchic and joyous. Dickens assigns key roles to pubs in many of his stories, where they offer hospitality to a myriad of characters such as Mr Pickwick and his fellow adventurers or to Joe Willett fleeing his tyrannical father in *Barnaby Rudge*.

Not surprisingly, the notion of the pub carries with it a mass of perceptions and associations. The idea of tradition is certainly one of them. Signs such as 'Ye Olde ...', '1189 AD', and notices put out by hopeful licensees advertising 'A Traditional English Pub', 'Home Cooked Fayre' and the like, make the point. But when it comes to the pubs people actually drink in or eat in, how traditional, how old are they really? And more specifically, how traditional and how old are the surrounding interiors in which the drinking and eating is being done? The building may be a half-timbered, thatched, one-time farmhouse or have genuine medieval stonework, but what of the pub interior itself? The overwhelming probability is that it will have been substantially refitted in the past fifty years.

Our purpose here is twofold. First, we explain how the pub emerged and, eventually, took on its now familiar form. Its early origins are shadowy, to say the least, but the pub has been shaped over several centuries by constantly changing social attitudes, commercial pressures, technological progress and fashions in drink – plus the ever-present, and usually suspicious, regulatory responses. Secondly, in dealing with the buildings, our focus is on the part that matters most, the inside, looking at pub interiors as they were before the great wave of refurbishment in the late 20th century. Despite huge amounts of re-ordering, opening out and theming, there is still much to be enjoyed and appreciated. Our photographs include many of the most interesting and impressive historic interiors in the country and are the largest collection of interior views assembled in any book to date. The concentration, for reasons of space, is upon England but we add a short section looking at Wales, Scotland and Northern Ireland to show some of the marked differences that exist in pub styles.

Much of what follows arises out of a major survey, begun in 1991 by the Campaign for Real Ale (CAMRA), to seek out and record those pubs among Britain's stock of over 60,000 which retained genuinely old (ie pre-Second World War) interiors. It could locate only 200 or so examples throughout the entire United Kingdom which might be regarded as intact enough to be of national importance. Even taking in rather more altered examples which may be regarded as of regional importance, under 2 per cent of our pub interiors can be considered of much historic value. Responding to this disturbing knowledge, CAMRA and English Heritage joined forces in 1998 for a two-year project to assess pubs with historic interiors and to ensure they were adequately protected through the listing process. This led to twenty-one listings and upgrades (three at Grade II*), and many new list descriptions which now properly emphasise the value of the interiors.

The first edition of this book was published in 2004. In the intervening seven years the pub has been subjected to a wide and significant variety of changes and pressures – a radical new licensing law, a smoking ban, and intense competition, not to mention stiff increases in the duty on alcohol and (at best) indifference on the part of government. Not surprisingly many pubs have closed their doors for the last time. This revised edition gives us the opportunity to catalogue these changes in a new chapter which makes for at once depressing and hopeful reading. Despite everything the pub remains a vibrant institution in our society and is something to be proud of and enjoyed. We hope this book will give you a better knowledge of its rich and varied history, and a fuller appreciation of its surviving heritage.

# Acknowledgements

Large numbers of people have helped us with the writing and illustrating of this book and their enthusiasm and encouragement has been most appreciated. It is a nigh-on impossible task to thank everyone who has made suggestions and offered ideas: many of them are acknowledged in the footnotes. We are particularly grateful to all those publicans who have allowed us to invade their premises to take photographs or have answered our questions.

Various Record Offices have been a rich source of information on historic plans and other records and we are particularly grateful for access to material in Birmingham City Archives, Hampshire Record Office, Lancashire Record Office, London Metropolitan Archives, Norfolk Record Office, Northamptonshire Record Office, Plymouth and West Devon Area Record Office, Sheffield Archives and Wolverhampton Archives and Local Studies.

Lynn Pearson gave us considerable help with ceramics in the pub and Victoria Gorman helped us give real cider its just due. Colin Valentine and Stuart Wallace gave us valuable advice about Scotland. The Brewery History Society kindly allowed us to reproduce material from its collection housed in Birmingham City Archives. We are also grateful to David Lawrence and Martin Cherry for their patience in reading through early drafts and making many helpful suggestions.

In producing the first edition of this book, it was a great pleasure working with the English Heritage publication team – Val Horsler, who encouraged us to embark on the project, Sue Kelleher, who steered us all the way to the printers, and John Vallender, who redrew the plans to a common style and scale. We are delighted that the book was sufficiently popular for English Heritage to wish to publish a new edition and we are most grateful to John Hudson and his team for their confidence in the project; we especially thank Jess Ward for her work in bringing it to press.

And finally, we record our gratitude to the hospitality of the Cock and Bottle, Needham Road, Notting Hill, a few doors away from our excellent book designer, Chuck Goodwin. Here we received, at the eleventh (actually our second there) hour, the inspiration for the title of this book – clear proof, if any were needed, of the manifold benefits that the public house bestows upon mankind.

## A Note on Terminology

Like any specialised building type or institution, the public house has a terminology of its own. However, in the belief (and hope) that most of our readers will be no strangers to pubs, we expect that they will be familiar with most of the terms we use. Any slightly problematical terms are explained in the text and/or the glossary.

However, 'bar' is one particular word that is liable to misinterpretation. It can mean a room where drinks are consumed, and the counter at which they are served. To avoid any doubt, we refer to the latter by its equally proper name of 'bar counter', and identify the former, as appropriate, by a more precise name like 'public bar'. It can also refer to an entire premises, especially in Scotland and Northern Ireland. To add to the complications, there is the matter of what to call the whole service area where the bar-staff work. We have opted for the term 'servery' which, though not much used in popular speech, at least conveys a precise meaning.

## The Vanishing Apostrophe

If you look at books on and guides to pubs, pub signs and advertisements, and even telephone directories, you will notice a literary quirk – the vanishing apostrophe. Almost invariably we have the 'Queens Head', 'Kings Arms', 'Travellers Friend', 'Shipwrights Arms' and so on. Hardly ever is there an apostrophe. Is it one traveller or several? One shipwright or many? When it comes to artisans, is it their armigerous status (pretty unlikely in the case of the coal porters seen at work on the sign at a Peterborough pub, the Coalheavers Arms!), or a punning reference to their limbs that is being referred to? We have adopted a simple convention: if the singular is likely we have used, say, 'King's Head', if plural is likely, say, 'Shipwrights' Arms': if we cannot make a sensible guess, say as with 'travellers', we have followed time-honoured pub custom and practice – we have forgotten about the apostrophe!

## Locating the Pubs

Readers may, at some stage, wish to visit some of the pubs in this book. To quote addresses in the text would be wearisome so we provide an index of all the pub names mentioned with sufficient details for them to be found.

Chapter 1

# The Emergence of the Public House

**1.1** Medieval refreshment. A tapster on a misericord at St Lawrence's church, Ludlow (c1415–25). Presumed to be an alehouse keeper: several of the Ludlow misericords have an alehouse/tavern theme. See also 1.7.

To us the pub is instantly recognisable on street corners, high streets and in villages. Yet, as the highly distinctive building type we know and (mostly) love, it is relatively recent. It emerged from the middle of the 19th century, having incorporated features from earlier building types which had provided drink, food and shelter for different levels of society for centuries. The ancestors of the pub – the alehouse, tavern and, to a lesser extent, the inn – appeared during the Middle Ages and by the 1400s were all familiar to English people. In addition to contributions from these forerunners of the public house, key features of the 18th-century gin shop and the early 19th-century gin palace found their way into Victorian and later public house design.

The term 'public house' too is fairly modern. It did not make its appearance until the late 17th century but, within two or three generations, was in general circulation. The convenient and affectionate abbreviation 'pub' had certainly arrived by 1812, and by the late 19th century was part of everyday speech.[1]

Apart from normal commercial forces, the public house has had to cope with official suspicion about the motives and behaviour of its owners, managers and customers. That suspicion – still widespread today – appeared with the pub's earliest ancestors. It manifested itself in laws and regulations intended to enforce standards of behaviour acceptable to the authorities, and minimise outbreaks of the drunkenness, disorder and anti-social behaviour which they feared were inextricably linked with the sale of alcohol, and gatherings of the lower orders.

The alehouse, the tavern and the inn, in the official view at least, were very different from each other, providing

1

different facilities and catering for different groups in society – the alehouse for the lower classes, the tavern and the inn for the middle and upper ones. Consequently, they were treated very differently by the authorities, the tavern and the inn being subject to far less regulation than the alehouse.

## Early brewing and the origins of the alehouse

The origins of the alehouse go back before the Norman Conquest in 1066. Anglo-Saxon laws and ecclesiastical canons have occasional mentions of them. The laws of Aethelred (reigned 978–1016), for example, set out fines for breaching the peace in an alehouse. If someone was killed, the fine was 6 half-marks (£1); if no-one was killed, the fine was lower.[2] However, there is no evidence that alehouses were numerous, or that they were in any way different from

other domestic buildings. It is simply not possible to identify the site of any pre-Conquest alehouse despite the claims of pubs across the land (see chapter 7).

The Norman Conquest brought in a new ruling class but in many ways life continued as before. The Domesday survey of 1086, which deals with value of land and identifies those holding it, has not a single mention of alehouses or other drinking establishments, although the handful of references to brewers suggests that some people were producing more than was strictly necessary for consumption by their immediate families. The Domesday entry for Chester lists local laws which included a visit to the ducking stool or a fine of 4 shillings for anyone making bad ale. Presumably the bad ale would only have attracted attention if a dissatisfied purchaser complained about it.[3] Thanks to extensive research we know something of the brewing and drinking arrangements in medieval Winchester, the Anglo-Saxon capital which remained one of the country's most important cities under the Normans. A survey of 1148 lists over a dozen 'breweries', mostly clustered around the High Street. The occupiers of these properties were no doubt producing ale for sale,

1.2 In this 14th-century representation, the projecting stake shows that ale is for sale. It has attracted the sinful hermit who appears in a tale from the *Smithfield Decretals* (Latin text possibly written in France 1300–40, illuminated in England about 1340). The alewife has served him from a flagon and he drinks from a broad bowl known as a mazer.

yet there is no evidence at this period of them providing premises in which to drink it.[4]

Chester and Winchester were important cities and the production of ale for retail is to be expected. Elsewhere brewing was widespread but as a small-scale, part-time activity. For example, in 1262 Highworth in Wiltshire had just sixty-one tenants, yet in the 1270s some thirty people were brewing every year.[5] It seems most unlikely that any of them provided facilities for drinking on their premises except for family and friends. Brewing was time-consuming but could be fitted in around other household activities, and, before the Black Death – a bringer of many social and economic changes – ale-selling was a widely accepted way for women (especially poorer ones) to augment the family income.

Not surprisingly the importance of brewing started to attract the attention of the authorities both to regulate it and as a lucrative source of revenue. A royal proclamation in 1196–7, known as the Assize of Measures, specified national standard measures for grain and liquids to overcome the wide variations that had

## Ale or beer?

The words 'ale' and 'beer' have become more or less interchangeable over the past couple of centuries but it was not always so.

**Ale** was a fermented liquor made from malt and water. It was a medieval dietary staple, drunk in quantity by all classes of society, and providing a safe drink when hygiene was poorly understood and water often polluted. It could be made using readily available household equipment, but its poor keeping qualities, its bulk, and the difficulty of transportation, ensured that production remained a largely domestic activity.

**Beer** involved adding hops to the malt liquor. They gave it distinctive bitterness and, importantly, improved its keeping qualities. However, it was more expensive to produce, requiring extra equipment plus the cost of extra fuel and the hops themselves.

previously existed across the country. Attempts were also made to regulate the price of ale by relating it to that of grain, its chief ingredient. The first Assize of Bread and Ale was issued by Richard I in the mid-1190s, and was restated at intervals, most importantly as the Assize of Ale by Henry III in 1266–7. It laid down procedures for testing the quality of ale, and, again, standardised the measures for selling it.[6]

Offenders could be hauled before the local courts and fined. Records of such proceedings are rare in the early 13th century, but soon they began to appear regularly. In Norwich in 1288–9, 290 brewers were fined for infringements. There are similar records for 1312–13, and proportionate numbers found themselves in trouble in other major towns. Many were otherwise respectable citizens, and it is clear that by the mid-14th century the

**1.3** A fitting end for the dishonest alewife. In this 15th-century wall painting at Bacton church, Suffolk, a devil wheels her off to Hell in a barrow, still clutching an ale-pot.

h omes mozs ⁊ naures ¦ contre terre gefir

g anc vermel coloure/ hozs des plaies i

**1.4** Mine host profers a mazer of ale at the sign of the Golden Cross. The building is too grand for a realistic representation of an alehouse unless the owners or their servants are simply selling off surplus production. Marginal illustration in a Flemish manuscript, the *Romance of Alexander*, finished by the scribe in 1338 (in French) and illuminated in 1344.

Assize of Ale had become effectively a means of licensing brewers (although formal licensing was not introduced until much later) and raising money from their product.

Most manorial courts employed ale-tasters or ale-conners to test the quality of ale to be offered for sale. Brewers had to give notice when a brew was ready for testing, typically by hanging out an ale-stake, a branch or a pole with a garland of leaves at the end. Direct marketing, with ale sold from the premises where it was brewed, was the rule, although in larger towns 'tipplers' – who bought ale from the brewers for resale in small amounts – began to appear. In contrast with the efforts to regulate and license ale production, there were no attempts to regulate or license alehouses, which suggests that their numbers were too few to attract such attention.

All this began to change in the later 14th century, due to two very different arrivals from the continent. One was the Black Death: this reached England in 1349 and, by 1351, may have reduced the population by nearly half. The effect of recurring outbreaks was to restrict population growth for nearly a century.[7] The labour shortage that resulted led to increased wages, and employment opportunities improved. The number of women who needed to supplement the family income by brewing dropped markedly.[8]

The second arrival was the hop, the effects of which took longer to become apparent but which were profound. The use of hops in brewing began in southern Germany in the 9th century, and spread slowly north and west. By the mid-14th century brewing with hops was well established in the Low Countries, and the close contacts between Flanders and the ports of eastern and southern England ensured that beer soon began to arrive on these shores.

## Brewing

The process begins with malted grain. The grain is steeped in water until it begins to germinate, and then heated in a kiln to kill off the growth. Malting aims to arrest the development of the grain at the point of germination, when the maximum amount of sugar is available for fermentation.

The malt is ground to break up the individual grains and facilitate the release of sugars, and then placed in the mash tun, where it is mixed with hot water to dissolve as much of the fermentable sugar as possible. The resultant liquid (known as 'wort') is then run into the 'copper', where it is boiled. At this stage hops are added, both for additional flavour and for their preservative qualities (before the arrival of hops, a variety of herbs or spices might be added to the brew in order to enhance its flavour and keeping qualities).

After boiling, the wort is transferred into a fermenting vessel, where yeast is added, and it is left for several days to ferment. Between the copper and the fermenting vessel it usually undergoes some kind of cooling process – in the past it would be run into a large shallow pan and allowed to stand, but today will normally be run through a more sophisticated cooling device – to ensure that when the yeast is added it is not killed by excess heat. Once fermentation is complete, the beer is transferred to casks to condition ready for consumption.

The grain used for brewing today is normally barley. However, during the Middle Ages brewing took place using whatever grain was available, and wheat, rye and oats were also used. In the south-west and in upland areas barley was not normally available, and the standard ale was produced from oat malt. The resultant drink was something of an acquired taste – Andrew Boorde, writing in the 1540s, described Cornish ale, brewed from oats, as 'like washe which pigges has wrestled dryn'.[9]

The shift from ale to beer can be traced through imports. For example, the records of Norwich show that one, Richard Somers was bringing in Flanders ale as early as 1288–9. By 1400 beer was being imported into southern ports. Hops as a raw material followed, and they were soon being grown in Kent and Sussex. Beer brewing was well-established in London by 1500, and spread gradually across the country. However, ale brewing took a long time to disappear completely, and in parts of the north and west was still being carried on in the mid-17th century.

The better keeping qualities of beer made it more economical to brew in bulk, but the process was more complicated, took longer, and required more specialised and expensive equipment. The additional cost of the hops, and the extra fuel required (much more boiling was needed than for ale) forced out many a small producer by the late 16th century. The era of the

**1.5–1.6** Home brewing at the Blue Anchor in Helston, Cornwall. Even this simple brewery is much more elaborate and well-equipped than its medieval antecedents. By the early 1970s only four pubs were still home brewing. The others were the All Nations, Madeley, Shropshire, the Olde Swan, Netherton, West Midlands, and the Three Tuns, Bishop's Castle, Shropshire; all of these are still brewing, but unlike the Blue Anchor, each has had a period of non-production.

'common brewer', who brewed on a large scale, and sold on to retail vendors, had arrived, with brewing concentrated in the hands of a relatively small group of increasingly wealthy men in major towns, especially in the south and east. In London, a formal trade association appeared in 1437, when Henry VI granted a charter to the Company of Brewers, and similar bodies appeared in other major centres, including Norwich, Oxford and York. Apart from setting standards and lobbying the authorities, these guilds attempted, as such bodies do, to enforce a monopoly. In Oxford, for example, it was decreed in 1525 that sixteen brewers were to carry out the trade, and no others.[10] Publican brewing began to decline but even so it only disappeared in the Midlands, the north and the West Country during the 20th century.

## Regulating the alehouse: the introduction of licensing

Alehouse numbers increased during the 15th century as 'tipplers' (or 'tapsters') opened premises for drinking ale or beer brewed by others. A reason for this trend may be that wages were rising and a visit to the alehouse would have been a congenial way of spending disposable income. Also the Assize of Ale offered the attraction of allowing higher prices for drink consumed on the vendor's premises than if taken away. The process

### Alehouses, taverns and inns – a summary

Before the 18th century there were three kinds of establishment in which alcohol was sold and consumed. The most common were *alehouses*, which sold ale (or, later, beer). They also provided simple food and basic accommodation for the poorer traveller. *Taverns* were found only in the larger towns, and catered for the richer customer. They sold expensive imported wine, as well as more elaborate meals, but did not offer accommodation. *Inns* were found in towns, and beside the more important highways. They provided accommodation and refreshment for better-off travellers, and stabling for their horses.

is graphically illustrated in Winchester's records. Before about 1360 tapsters are not specifically mentioned among those brought to court for infringing the Assize of Ale. Afterwards, a distinction is drawn between brewers and tapsters. Before 1380 about three-quarters of those selling ale in the city also brewed it, but from about 1410 the proportion of tapsters steadily increased, far outnumbering brewers by 1500.[11]

By the late 15th century alehouses were numerous enough, and (to the authorities) disreputable enough, to bring about the first attempts to regulate them. Up till then enforcement of the Assize of Ale had been the responsibility of manorial and civic authorities. Now, in 1495, an important Act handed powers over ale quality and its sale to the Justices of the Peace, an arrangement which is only just being rescinded with the implementation of the Licensing Act 2003.[12] It allowed the Justices (often also called magistrates) to 'reject and put away common ale-sellers'. They could also demand sureties for good behaviour, and punish ale-sellers 'for allowing dicing in their houses'.

The authorities were ever suspicious of alehouses as dens of idleness and gambling and potential disorder. In 1503 the brewers of Methley in West Yorkshire were forbidden to 'harbour any players' or allow unlawful games, on pain of a fine of 3s 4d, a considerable sum.[13] William Langland, the 14th-century poet, describes people playing a drinking game called 'new fair', and medieval carvings show games being played in drinking-houses. In 1598 John Collyn was reported by the vicar of Barling, Essex, for allowing unlawful games to be played in his victualling house. They included 'dice-playing, cards, tables [backgammon] shovegroat, scales [skittles], dancings, hobbyhorses [morris dancing], and such unreasonable dealings as well on the sabbath day as other holydays'.[14]

Concerns about such deplorable activities rumbled on. An Act of 1552 stated that 'for as much as intolerable hurts and troubles to … this Realm doth daily grow and increase through such abuses and disorders as are had and used in common alehouses and tippling houses'. To curb such manifest evils, licensing of alehouses was

1.7 Two men playing backgammon (or a predecessor of it) on a misericord at Manchester Cathedral (c1506). A woman (part of the figure is broken off) draws ale for them (right). To the left a woman is carding wool, emphasising the domestic nature of the medieval alehouse.

introduced for the first time. The chief concern of the Justices was the character of applicants and their fitness to run an alehouse, rather than any finer points about the premises. Applicants had to swear to keep an orderly house and not to allow unlawful games to be played. For their part the Justices were only to license as many alehouses as they thought necessary for the area.[15]  Originally the duration of licences was not specified and annual licences only came in in 1608.

In 1577 Elizabeth I's Government, faced with expensive repairs to Dover harbour, decided that a tax on licences for drinking establishments in England would be a convenient way to pay for them. The resulting survey returned a total of 2,161 inns, 339 taverns and 15,095 alehouses. Allowing for the incomplete nature of the returns, there may have been something in the order of 24,000 alehouses throughout the country. The following year, and perhaps prompted by this newly acquired knowledge, the Government put pressure on the

Justices by issuing them with a wide-ranging Book of Orders. Reissued at regular intervals down to 1631, it obliged alehouse numbers to be recorded for each district. Further regulation came in 1618 when licensing sessions were required to be held in April or May, with licences being issued in a standard format and a copy kept by the clerk of the court.

Despite official concerns, the number of alehouses continued to grow from the late 16th century until the outbreak of the Civil War in 1642 and they became an increasingly well-established part of English life. Seasonal selling was in decline, and more and more alehouses operated all the year round, although

**1.8–1.9** The Railway Tavern, Kincardine, Fife, is a rare and extreme present-day example of how ordinary pubs were once virtually indistinguishable from other buildings. Here only the licensee's name over the front door marks it out.

there were some who, as before the Black Death, turned to selling ale as a secondary occupation. Setting up as an alehouse-keeper (in contrast to brewing) did not require much capital and England's expanding towns offered tempting prospects. Many alehouses were unlicensed and the efficiency of the Justices in issuing licences and suppressing illegal ones varied enormously. There were practical difficulties in identifying unlicensed houses in the more remote and sparsely populated parts of the country, or indeed in the back streets of towns. Between 1600 and 1610 there were no less than four sets of laws passed with the aim of suppressing illegal alehouses, restraining drinking and punishing drunkenness. These, as so often, proved ineffective, and in 1627 a further Act of Parliament increased the fines on those caught selling ale and beer without a licence; those too poor to pay were to be whipped.[16]

By the time of the Civil War alehouse-keepers were beset with regulations. They needed an annual licence from the Justices, and had to sell ale and beer at the correct prices in legal measures. They were not to allow drinking during church services, drunkenness, unlawful games or the sale of stolen goods; they were not to sell tobacco, or serve meat during Lent or on 'fish days',[17] and were not to harbour beggars or 'masterless men'. To add to their obligations, they were to provide at least one bed for genuine travellers.

## Alehouse facilities before 1640

Early alehouses had no distinctive architecture or internal arrangements. They were simply houses which happened to sell ale or beer. They were only recognisable by a stake or pole garlanded with foliage to show ale was available. Many 16th-century keepers adopted names for their premises, advertised by a pictorial sign. The premises could easily revert to a purely domestic building simply by taking down the sign – which happened frequently when alehouse-keepers ceased trading, moved premises or if they still sold ale seasonally.

Most alehouses were small. Probate inventories usually reveal five rooms or fewer, including both public and private spaces. These overlapped, with the kitchen (with its near-permanent fire) and the parlour normally used for drinking. Other rooms, if the building was that extensive, were pressed into service if extra space was required. Examples of far larger alehouses are known; in Canterbury, some had as many as nine rooms. Drinking must have often taken place around the front door and out in the yard in good weather.

A few benches and trestle tables sufficed for all but the largest premises. Service was in jugs from barrels, which were normally stillaged in the kitchen or other more private parts of the building to avoid pilferage. Only the largest alehouses would have possessed a cellar at this period. Drinking vessels were leather, wood or pottery, with an official mark showing they contained a legal measure.

Despite the requirement to accommodate travellers, few had separate guest facilities, and those staying the night would have bedded down in the public rooms, an outhouse or barn. This was to be a long-lived source of revenue for publicans; just over half of those keeping beerhouses (as they were then known) in Bradford at the 1851 census were taking in lodgers.[18]

## The tavern

The tavern, like the alehouse, was largely a drinking establishment, but one selling almost exclusively wine. The earliest ones appeared in the 12th and 13th centuries and seem to have been associated with the import and sale of wine by vintners. As wine was much dearer than ale, beer or cider, the tavern catered for the middle and upper classes, offering them a more comfortable drinking environment than the alehouse. Unlike the alehouse, there was never any statutory requirement to provide overnight accommodation.

Unlike alehouses, taverns adopted names early on. Medieval Winchester is again a rich source of information. A tavern known as Helle, seized in 1414 for rent arrears, was surely a tongue-in-cheek reference to its location in a cellar. A nearby rival establishment had been known as le Taverne de Paradys in 1380 but by 1414 it had been re-named Hevene – proof that name changes and the adoption of less-than-serious titles are nothing new.

1.10  17th-century gentlemen take their ease in what may well be a tavern. There appears to be food on the table and possibly a wine glass in front of the second figure from the left. From John Bickerdyke's *Curiosities of Ale and Beer* (1889) which says it is an 'exact facsimile' of a drawing in the Roxburghe Collection, a series of 16th- and 17th-century broadsheet ballads formed by the Earl of Oxford (b 1661).

Early London taverns included one in Cornhill called le Popeshed in 1415 which by 1542 had become the Bysshoppes Hed, no doubt to avoid suspicions of Papist sympathies. Typically, tavern signs were garlanded with vine leaves to show that wine was for sale.

Taverns were never very common although they existed in some numbers in larger towns by the middle of the 14th century, and a statute of 1330 claimed they had recently become more numerous.[19] The 1577 survey recorded only 339 taverns; allowing for its partial nature, there were perhaps 500 countrywide, only a tiny percentage of the total outlets for drink. Although the tavern did not suffer the kind of suspicion that haunted the alehouse, an Act of 1553 attempted to limit their numbers. This only permitted them in towns, most of which were to have only two, although twenty larger towns were to have three, four, six or eight, while London was allowed forty. Licensing the taverns was to be the responsibility of the local authorities.[20] However, these restrictions failed, partly because the Company of Vintners had an ancient right to freely open taverns in London,[21] and partly because the Crown itself claimed a right to grant wine licences; many had been granted by the time Queen Elizabeth I established the office of 'Receiver of Wine Rents' as a royal perk. In 1623

**1.11** The Olde Cheshire Cheese in Fleet Street, London, is now perhaps our closest approximation to a 17th- or 18th-century tavern. This is the front bar where some of the woodwork may date back to the late 17th century when the building was rebuilt after the Great Fire. Across a corridor is a dining room of very long standing.

Parliament, concerned by abuses of the monopolies granted by the king, made it illegal for anyone except the Crown itself to grant wine licences.[22] The Wine Act of 1660 confirmed this but it was still all too easy for someone deemed by the Justices unsuitable to run an alehouse to obtain a wine licence from the Crown. It was not until 1792 that wine licences became the responsibility of the Justices,[23] and wine retailers were required to also hold an alehouse licence.

The 17th century was the golden age of the tavern. Catering for wealthy customers, it was a place to see and to be seen, for societies to meet, and businessmen to negotiate deals. After the Restoration in 1660 it was even more popular but soon faced competition from rival establishments selling coffee, tea or chocolate, all available from the late 1650s. The first coffee house was Pasqua Rosee's in St Michael's Alley off Cornhill in London which was certainly in existence by 1654. By 1700 they were a feature of all major towns; there were more than 2,000 in London alone. Typically, they did not just sell coffee, but, like the tavern, offered wines and spirits, as well as food. Many were, in fact,

converted taverns, whose proprietors sold coffee and spirits as well as wine. By 1800 the coffee house was the fashionable place to socialise and the tavern, in its traditional sense, had ceased to exist as a distinctive type of drinking house.

## Inside the tavern

Medieval taverns generally occupied the ground floor or even the first floor of a building (with a shop below) with accommodation for the owner's family above. Some had public rooms on the upper floors, particularly for dining. Six taverns identified in early 15th-century Winchester, however, were sited in undercrofts and entered by steps down from street level. Wine was stored at the rear, and the area nearest the street was furnished for drinking. The two different uses were reflected architecturally, the rear compartment being plain and unadorned, whilst the front part had decorative vaulting.[24]

The smallest and simplest medieval tavern differed little in architecture, scale and furnishings from the alehouse. The furniture of the Winchester tavern called Helle consisted of just four benches, two tables and a cupboard in 1414. However, the largest of Winchester's medieval taverns offered more comfortable facilities for eating and drinking than most of the town's inns, and were frequently used during the 14th and early 15th centuries for civic entertaining – for example, opening local court sessions or visits by royal officials.

Gradually taverns offered increasingly elaborate accommodation, with a variety of rooms for general use and private gatherings. Even the public rooms offered a degree of privacy through the use of internal partitioning; in London taverns, at least, division of public rooms into drinking booths was a standard feature by the 1650s. A 1627 inventory of the King's Head Tavern, Leadenhall Street, includes 'six drinking Rooms with particions with Benches at thends [sic] and sides of fower of the roomes and the other two with Benches at the sides with tables fitted to them of Elme Planck … Item in the Yarde … six drinking roomes covered with leade with twelve Benches and six tables of Elme Planck fitted to the same'.[25]

## The inn

The inn, as a house for accommodating travellers, probably appeared in the 12th or 13th centuries. The word itself was first used in this specific sense around 1400, but it had a variety of earlier meanings – the town-house of an aristocrat or wealthy merchant, a lodging house for students (as in London's Inns of Court), or simply a superior dwelling house. The earliest ones of the kind to interest us probably looked just like large private houses, but by the late 14th century (when the earliest surviving purpose-built inns can be dated with confidence) more distinctive buildings were evolving. Early inns had few public rooms, chief amongst them the hall, but by the 16th century they offered a variety of parlours and other rooms where meals could be taken or business conducted.

## The architecture of early inns

Two types have been identified – the 'block' or 'gatehouse' type, and the 'courtyard' type.[26] The first consisted of a major building on the street frontage,

1.12 The George Inn, Norton St Philip, Somerset. Believed to be the earliest surviving, purpose-built inn, it was erected in the late 14th century for those attending the fairs organised by the monks of Hinton Charterhouse. It was refronted about 1475–1500. It is still used as an hotel.

1.13 The Angel and Royal, Grantham, Lincolnshire. The carriage entrance is placed centrally between two bay windows and leads to a courtyard behind.

**1.14** The King's Head, Aylesbury, and its carriage entrance.
The building dates back to about 1450.

containing most of the public rooms and guest chambers, with a yard and subsidiary buildings such as stables behind accessed through a large gateway in the main block. The George Inn at Norton St Philip, Somerset (1.12), appears to be the earliest surviving example. It was built in the late 14th century for merchants attending the fairs promoted by the monks of Hinton Charterhouse, who obtained permission to transfer one of their two annual fairs from Hinton to Norton St Philip in 1345. Other surviving examples include the Angel and Royal, Grantham (mid-15th century: 1.13), the King's Head, Aylesbury (c1450), and the George and Pilgrims, Glastonbury (c1480).

The 'courtyard' type had buildings ranged around a central courtyard. The earliest surviving example, the New Inn, Gloucester, was built around 1450 by Gloucester Abbey under the supervision of one of its monks, John Twynnyng. It was three storeys high, with galleries running right round the courtyard on the first floor giving access to the bedchambers. There were more than twenty of these on the two upper floors; given that each could have held several beds, the New Inn could accommodate nearly 200 guests. The ground floor offered parlours and other public rooms, although on the street front it was divided into self-contained shops which were let separately.

The basic building types altered little over the centuries. The George Inn at Stamford, built around 1640, was of the 'block' type, whilst one of the most famous surviving inns, the George Inn at Southwark, was rebuilt in 1676–7 on a courtyard plan. Like its predecessor (dating originally from about 1550), galleries gave access to the guest chambers on the upper floors.

### The inn at work

Early inns provided accommodation and drink for guests, and stabling for their horses. Although innkeepers feature in the late 14th-century Winchester court records for overcharging on drink and charcoal (for heating braziers), there are no references to the sale of cooked food to guests by innkeepers during the 14th or early 15th centuries, and guests probably ate meals brought in from public cook shops. Few Winchester inns offered wine during this period but ale was widely available and several innkeepers were also recorded as brewers.[27]

By the early 15th century most places of any size had at least one inn, and larger towns offered a choice. In 1417 Winchester had at least ten; the largest, the George, on the courtyard plan, had been built as recently as 1412. Towns such as Canterbury, Norwich, Southwark and York also had numbers of inns competing for medieval travellers. By 1415 there were enough in York for the innkeepers to form a trade guild, and by 1577 the town had more inns than any other outside of London,[28] a reflection of

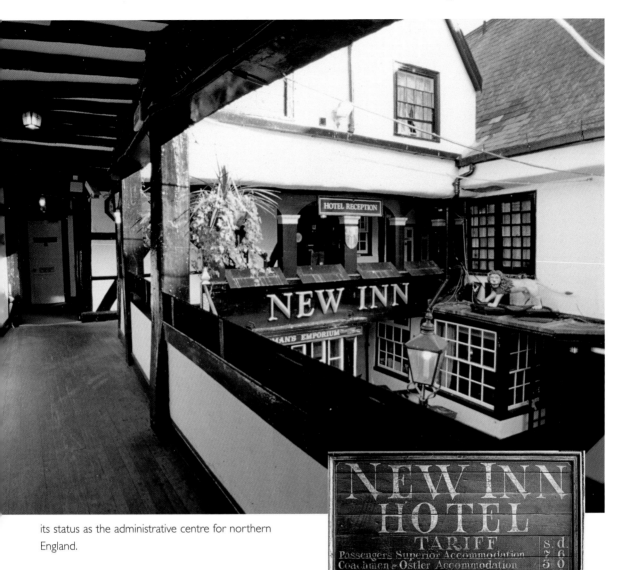

its status as the administrative centre for northern England.

Inns grew in size and numbers during the 16th and 17th centuries, mirroring a general growth in travel. More rooms were required since guests were becoming less inclined to share the rigours of communal sleeping. There was also, of course, a need for more extensive stabling. In the late 1570s William Harrison's *Description of England* claimed that some inns could lodge 200 or 300 people and their horses, with a specific room allocated to each traveller.[29] Such establishments were undoubtedly exceptional, but the inn was often the largest and most imposing building in a town after the parish church, and its proprietor a person of importance.

**1.15–1.16** The New Inn, Gloucester, begun about 1450. Galleries, leading to the guest rooms, overlook the central courtyard, where travellers arrived and departed.

From the late 17th century inns were boosted by the development of coaching networks which survived until the appearance of railways on a significant scale in the 1840s. New inns appeared in 'thoroughfare towns', that is those providing the main stops along the coaching

13

**1.17** The Three Swans, Market Harborough, Leicestershire (mentioned as the Swanne in 1517), was a coaching inn and advertised its presence by a particularly magnificent 18th-century wrought-iron sign. The two outer swans were added when the name was changed about 1780. It survived the demise of coaching by becoming a modern-day hotel.

**1.18** Although the coach had long gone, public houses remained hubs for carriers and their horses and carts. Postcard view of the Dun Cow Inn at Dersingham in rural Norfolk.

**1.19** (opposite) The Oxford Arms, Warwick Lane, City of London, in a sorry state in 1875. By then the heyday of the coaching inn had long gone. To the sadness of those who recalled their glory days, all London's galleried inns were swept away except for a portion of the George in Southwark. The parts of the Oxford Arms shown here went in 1903.

routes radiating from London. Until the mid-18th century, when a network of turnpike roads began to appear, even the best coaches could only achieve 25–35 miles daily, and the main coaching towns were those placed at this kind of interval; smaller intermediate centres allowed for a change of horses at mid-day. Thus the chief coaching towns on the Manchester road were Dunstable, Northampton, Leicester, Derby, Ashbourne and Buxton, with places such as Market Harborough and Loughborough providing intermediate stops. Inns were also important as depots for the network of carriers who conveyed goods around the country. Less romantic than coaching, the carriers outlived the coaches and the connection between the inn and the carrying trade was only broken after the First World War, when the army-surplus lorry (too large for the inn yard) replaced the horse and cart.

Inns were used for social gatherings and public performances in the 16th century and from the late 17th century they became focal points for the burgeoning urban leisured and professional classes. Dinners, balls, concerts and theatrical performances were held at inns; clubs and societies met at them and lectures were given there. They were also the venues for sporting occasions from meets of the local hunt to boxing matches and cock-fights, as well as for exhibitions and freak shows. Inns also accommodated official meetings, such as court sessions and inquests, commissions inquiring into enclosure proposals, and board meetings of canal companies and turnpike trusts. Increasingly, they acquired specialised rooms for such activities.

In her novel, *Felix Holt*, published in 1866 but set in the early 1830s, George Eliot looked back nostalgically to

### The early origins of the bar

An early 17th-century innovation at inns was the 'bar' – a room that served as a mixture of office and store for more expensive drinks such as wines or spirits, and from which service to the customer and the collection of payment was supervised by the landlord. It rapidly became a feature of both inns and taverns. As early as 1627 the King's Head Tavern in Leadenhall Street (see p 10), had 'a Barr with … Bynns and three shelves'. Later examples were divided from the public spaces by glazed panels, which improved supervision of the clientele; remarkably, an example still survives at the George Inn in Southwark. Inns and alehouses evolved into separate entities – the hotel and the public house – but, after the late 18th century, this was one feature of the inn which became a standard feature of the humbler building.

the great days of coaches and the inns that served them. 'Five-and-thirty years ago', she wrote

> the glory had not yet departed from the old coach-roads: the great roadside inns were still brilliant with well-polished tankards, the smiling faces of pretty barmaids, and the repartees of jocose ostlers; the mail still announced itself by the merry notes of the horn.

But not for much longer. The construction of public buildings, such as court houses, corn exchanges, assembly rooms and town halls took away much of its business, and the railway completed its eclipse. From the late 18th century the inn began to evolve into the 'hotel', a building which had a more specialist function. The first one in England was built in Exeter in 1768,[30] and they slowly appeared in seaside resorts, spa towns and commercial centres, but the term was still relatively uncommon even in the mid-19th century.

Whilst larger inns were closely related to modern hotels, only the amount of accommodation for overnight guests differentiated the small inn from the large alehouse. Nevertheless, there was a considerable difference in

regulation. Unlike the alehouse, the inn was regarded as a respectable establishment. Except for a brief period during the early 17th century, no licence was needed to operate an inn (although licences were still required for the sale of alcohol).

### The pub under pressure

In 1643 the Long Parliament imposed the Excise to raise funds for the war against Charles I. This was a duty levied on a wide range of goods, including both privately and commercially brewed beer. It was hugely unpopular and most products were gradually exempted, with the duty on domestic brewing being removed in 1653. However, that on commercial brewing remained. It affected all brewers, but smaller operators suffered particularly since the money was payable in advance. The Excise certainly contributed to the decline in the number of alehouse keepers who brewed and by 1700 very few did so in London alehouses.

Like many supposedly short-term measures, the Excise proved remarkably robust and, indeed, is still with us today. It became the Government's greatest source of revenue, and was to remain so until well into the 19th century when, as late as 1879–80, 43 per cent of all revenue came from taxes on drink.[31]

Disorder in the Civil War encouraged unlicensed alehouses as their keepers took the opportunity to avoid paying for a licence. However, order was restored after 1651, and more effective licensing over the next fifty years or so meant their numbers dropped. The Restoration settlement of 1660 placed local government firmly in the hands of the local gentry, who acted as Justices of the Peace and now had almost total control over licensing. By 1700 many counties, making full use of earlier legislation, had arranged special 'Brewster Sessions' where licence applications were heard.

Tightening regulation was not the only problem troubling 17th-century alehouse-keepers. They now began to face serious competition from alternative forms of alcohol. By the end of the century unregulated gin production and gin shops posed serious threats in London and some larger towns. The alehouse-keeper, however, suffered many impositions. Bitterly resented was the responsibility, in the absence of purpose-built barracks, for billeting troops. Private householders were exempt from 1628, and thereafter the burden fell squarely upon alehouses and inns. In 1689 billeting became compulsory under a new Mutiny Act, only taverns being exempt. The Act was for a year only, but from 1701 it was renewed annually, reflecting the growth of a standing army. The proprietors of gin shops were specifically exempted from billeting in 1720.[32] Billeting was disruptive to alehouses and inns since the off-duty soldiers' notorious behaviour could drive customers away and cause physical damage. Furthermore the allowances were hardly generous and were paid in arrears, with a long wait being a standard complaint.[33]

## The rise and (temporary) fall of gin

Distillation had a long history but until the early 17th century spirits were drunk largely for medicinal purposes. In the 17th century spirits began to be imported – brandy from France and genever (or 'gin') from the Netherlands. By 1684, 500,000 gallons of the latter were drunk annually in England. The Company of Distillers, founded in 1638, had a monopoly in England on production but this was a small percentage of the total consumed.

The accession of William of Orange as William III in 1688 made gin-drinking patriotic and its popularity was enhanced further when he led the country into war with France. An Act of 1690 swept away the Distillers' monopoly, giving every citizen the right to distil and retail spirits produced from English corn without a licence.

Disastrously for brewers, this liberalisation coincided with a rise in Excise duty on beer to pay for the French war. In 1689 it was raised by 50 per cent and doubled the following year. Inevitably shops selling spirits, known as 'dram shops' (the spirit was typically sold in quarter-pint 'drams', mixed 2:1 with water) or 'punch-houses', appeared in large numbers. An attempt was made to control them in 1701 when spirit retailers had to obtain an alehouse licence from the Justices.[34] But this was promptly weakened the

very next year by an Act exempting distillers selling their own spirits and also vendors whose main trade was in other goods; only a licence from the Excise Office, which was granted virtually without question, was required.[35] People began distilling in kitchens and outhouses, while gin was sold in every kind of shop, and hawked from barrows in the street. Worst affected by the 'gin craze' was London, where the major distilleries were based.

## Tied houses

A key feature of English pub organisation, at least until major restructuring in the 1990s, was the tied house system. The London brewers were in the forefront, buying up houses and installing their own tenants, or more typically by 'tying' the owners of independent pubs to their products through loans or other financial inducements. Indeed, the system of loan-ties became known as the 'London system'. There is evidence that some brewers in the capital were securing outlets in this way by 1600 or so. The trend towards tied houses can also be detected in the 18th century outside London: by 1764, sixty-eight out of eighty-two licensed houses in King's Lynn were owned or leased by the town's major brewers.[36] The brewers, complained a writer in the *Monthly Review* in 1773, were 'known to buy up paltry houses and settle retailers in every little parish, as well as in every town and city, and for fear there should be a place in the kingdom exempt from their advantage, we have scarce a village without some of their cottages and huts'. A House of Commons committee in 1816–17 found that over half of London's public houses were owned by the brewers, and in some places in the south-east the proportion was higher; in Reading sixty-six out of sixty-eight licences were owned or controlled by local brewers.[37] But the trend was less in evidence in the north. As late as 1820 the largest number of tied houses owned or leased by a brewer in York was twenty, and five years later no more than fifty of the city's 175 public houses were tied.[38]

**1.20** The misery and degradation of *Gin Lane* by William Hogarth (1751). A child falls to its death, family possessions are pawned, buildings fall into ruins (except for the pawnbroker's, of course), and death stalks the city. 'Kilman Distiller' (right) does a roaring trade and a child in arms (also right) soon acquires the habit.

Early attempts to control gin sales proved unsuccessful. A Gin Act of 1736 restricted spirit licences to those who already kept victualling houses. The cost of a licence was set at a prohibitive £50, and spirit duty rose to 20 shillings a gallon. The immediate

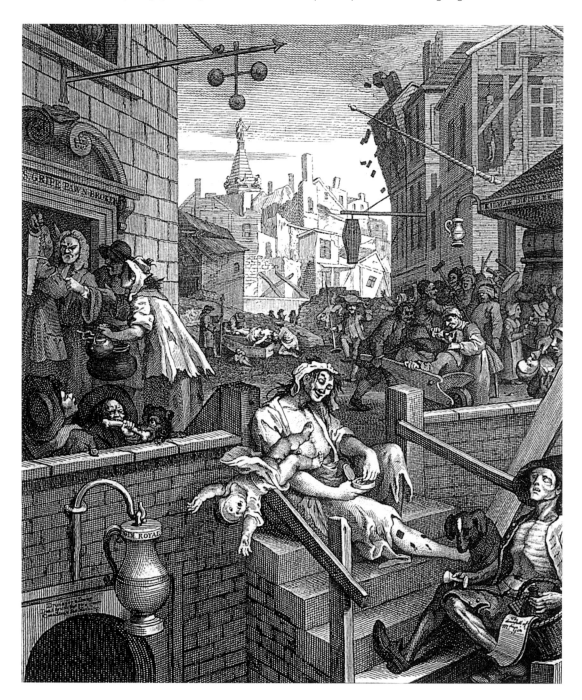

result was that distillers simply failed to declare their production and pay duty while few retailers were prepared to pay £50 for a licence. It was said that only two or three licences were ever issued, despite there being more than 8,000 dram shops in London. When

**1.21** Hogarth's *Beer Street* (1751), the companion piece to *Gin Lane*. A scene of well-fed contentment, hard work, and nothing for the pawnbroker to do but have a drink himself. His is the one house falling into disrepair. The new public house in the centre is apparently being topped out with beer. Note the large drinking vessels: until the 19th century the quart was the usual measure for beer.

the authorities attempted enforcement, rioting ensued. Finally, the authorities tried another tack, reducing the cost of a spirit licence to £1 in 1743,[39] and retailers once again began to apply. By an Act of 1751 the retailing of spirits was separated from distilling (distillers were not to retail, and victuallers not to distil): it also confirmed that spirit licences could only be held by people already holding an alehouse or wine licence, and so effectively brought the retail sale of spirits under the control of the Justices.[40] Over the next few years gin-only shops disappeared, and spirits production declined.

The 18th century witnessed a series of long-lasting reforms in alehouse licensing. From 1729 innkeepers, tavern-keepers and coffee-house keepers were required to take out licences if they sold beer too.[41] Until 1744, these were granted to individuals rather than to premises, but a new Act that year tied the licence to a specific house. Additionally, licensees could not be grocers or distillers.[42] A further Act of 1753 confirmed that licences were only to be granted at Brewster Sessions, required licensees to provide sureties for good behaviour, and barred brewers and distillers from serving as licensing Justices; it also set a minimum rental value for premises where spirits were to be sold.[43] With these reforms in place, licensing would not be tackled again for some seventy-five years.

These seventy-five years were a period of astonishing change in English society. The Industrial Revolution transformed a small and rather backward country into the most powerful economic, political and military force in the world. The process was accompanied by migration to the towns, as people sought work in mills and factories, and by a rapid rise in population. For many, working long hours at boring and repetitive jobs, and living in crowded and unsanitary conditions, the public house (as the alehouse was increasingly called) offered an opportunity for escape, as well as facilities unavailable at home.

The Industrial Revolution hastened the concentration in the brewing industry which had begun in the late medieval period. The London brewers led the way,

and from the 1780s were amongst the first industrialists to adopt steam engines to power ever larger breweries. Ownership of one of the larger London breweries offered not just 'a parcel of boilers and vats, but the opportunity to grow rich beyond the dreams of avarice', declared Dr Johnson on the sale of his friend Henry Thrale's brewery in 1781.

From the 1780s the public house came under renewed pressure, both from the gin shop and the authorities. Gin had lost popularity after the reforms of the 1740s and 1750s, but in 1786 duty came down greatly, production doubled and continued to increase steadily. By 1800 it had reached 4.1 million gallons, and by the late 1820s around 7 million – the level which had caused so much concern during the gin craze.

To make matters worse, malt and hops were hit by significant duty increases to fund the American and French wars and this undoubtedly contributed to a steep decline in the number of domestic brewers. Beer prices rose steadily, whilst spirits (which for lower-class drinking meant almost exclusively gin) became relatively cheap again. Hence the number of gin shops rose, although the requirement for spirit vendors to possess an alehouse licence meant that numbers never approached those of the 1730s and 1740s. Earlier in the century gin shops had been largely a London phenomenon, but now they sprang up in the industrial towns of the Midlands and north.

Competition from the gin shop was unwelcome but pressure from the authorities in the late 18th century was altogether more threatening. Faced with growing social unrest the official reaction was to clamp down on any organisations and institutions that were seen as actual or potential sources of disorder. Radical groups were broken up, trade unions outlawed by the Combination Acts, and moves made to bring the public house, regarded as a focus for the disaffected, under close control. Many magistrates believed that too many licences had been granted in the decades after 1750.

The crackdown effectively began in 1787 with a 'Royal Proclamation against Vice and Immorality'. In each county

in Masquerade; blowing a cloud & taking their heavy Wet at the Black-diamond merchant's free & easy King Charles's crib. Scotland Yard.

**1.22** Led by 'Tom and Bob', London coal porters enjoy themselves during 'their heavy wet', about 1800: this rowdy scene was scarcely the sort of thing to endear itself to the authorities. Customers' debts were often a problem to landlords, hence the 'No Trust' notice.

magistrates decided independently how to act, but the effect was that of a co-ordinated campaign. Across the country, constables were ordered to be more vigilant in enforcing the laws, particularly those against gaming and disorderly conduct in public houses, and against serving drink during Sunday services. The definitions of gaming and disorderly conduct were widely drawn, and included seemingly innocuous pursuits like billiards, skittles, cards, and musical instruments in addition to more brutal ones such as cock-fighting, bull- and bear-baiting.[44] Clergy and churchwardens were urged to take greater care in recommending people for licences. Many benches of Justices even resolved to issue no new licences at all. Others imposed new conditions on those they issued; in some counties – Berkshire, Gloucestershire and Oxfordshire among them – closing time was set at 10 pm in summer and 9 pm in winter, whilst the Leeds Justices demanded closure at 10 pm all year round. Sunday drinking was a particular focus of attention: the most extreme restriction was in Berkshire, where publicans could only sell a drink to *bona fide* travellers. The Wiltshire Justices not only required the customary certificates of good character from applicants for licences, but insisted on brewers providing sureties for the good conduct of their tenants.

The measures adopted, and the enthusiasm for their enforcement, varied widely. Relatively little action was taken in London, for example, even though it contained by far the largest concentration of licensed premises. Nevertheless, the overall effect of the Justices' campaigns reduced existing licences, and restricted the issue of new ones. No accurate figures exist for the number of alehouses in England and Wales in the early 1780s (variously estimated at between 40,000 and 100,000) but by 1810, when official statistics begin, the number of alehouse licenses issued was around 48,000. It remained at this level until about 1830, despite rapid population growth. Statistics of the number of spirit licences issued go back further, and show that from 36,675 issued in 1787, the number dropped to 32,850 in 1790, and about 30,000 in 1799. Thereafter the numbers rose slowly again, to reach 38,472 in 1825.[45] These, of course, were the official figures; unlicensed houses, known as 'whist shops' or 'hush shops', were also on the increase in the 1820s.

The Justices' zealousness lost momentum after peace came in 1815 with the defeat of Napoleon. One factor was that Parliament itself took a renewed interest in licensing in relation to the growing debate over free trade. Following the war, the economy became increasingly depressed, with rising unemployment and social unrest. Minimising regulation and encouraging free competition, it was believed, would lead to a boom in business and employment, and the ready availability of cheap, quality goods of all kinds. The growth in the number of tied houses, and the Justices' attempts to regulate the public house were seen by many as restricting free competition, and in the 1820s Parliament passed a series of Acts intended to widen access to the drink trade, and limit magistrates' powers over it. In 1824 home brewers were allowed to retail beer for consumption off the premises without a Justices' licence,[46] and this was followed by the far more sweeping and important Alehouse Act of 1828.[47] This combined all previous statutes, and laid down the

procedures for licensing Justices. General Annual Licensing Meetings and regular sessions for the transfer of licences were instituted, but most importantly, the power of the Justices to suppress alehouses was abolished. The 1828 Alehouse Act was to govern licensing for the next fifty years or so, even though yet more radical changes were still to come. In 1830 the Beer Act effectively threw open the trade, and heralded the era in which the public house developed more rapidly than it had done in centuries.[48]

## The revival of gin – the gin shop, the counter, and the gin palace

The 18th-century gin shop or 'dram shop' was just that – a shop selling gin and perhaps other spirits. Facilities were few and the aim was to serve customers quickly, clear them out, and get new ones in. Many carried their drink away in a jug or bottle, but others stayed. Seating was minimal so 'perpendicular drinking' was the norm to maximise the customers in the available

space. By the mid-18th century most gin shops also sold beer or wine (it was, after all, a legal requirement to have an alehouse or wine licence in order to obtain one for spirits). As we have seen, the increased spirits duty caused official numbers to decline by the later 18th century. They only slowly recovered to reach 38,472 in 1825. That year, duty was drastically cut in a further attempt to stimulate trade. Not surprisingly production doubled between 1824 and 1830, and the number of gin shops increased markedly.

A feature of the gin shop that enabled efficient, rapid service was the counter. It separated the customer from the server, provided a surface for pouring drinks, formed a barrier behind which drink, glasses and takings could be securely stored, and placed the onus on the customer to seek service. It was, of course, a feature of a shop rather than traditional alehouses, but by the 1820s it was beginning to appear in public houses as well as gin shops. The counter also provided

a secure base for fixing hand-pumps (or beer-engines). Invented by Joseph Bramah in the late 1790s, the hand-pump was a labour-saving device removing the need to fetch drink from the cellar. It was probably proprietors of gin shops, ever eager to speed up service, who initially saw the potential of the hand-pump, but in this case public house keepers were not far behind. By the 1820s the hand-pump was a regular feature of both the gin shop and the public house. The ultimate development of the gin shop, the 'gin palace', appeared in the late 1820s, the earliest examples being Thompson and Fearon's on Holborn

**1.23–1.24** The bar counter was a feature derived from gin shops and greatly increased the efficiency of serving. As at 2011 fewer than a dozen pubs lack a counter – mostly rural establishments such as the Red Lion, Ampney St Peter, Gloucestershire (1.23), where two hand-pumps are mounted against the wall. 1.24 shows an ornate counter of about 1870 at the Forresters Arms, Douglas, Isle of Man (demolished 2006).

1.25 No gin palaces survive, nor are any pubs lit wholly by gas. However, this scene at the mid-Victorian Viaduct Tavern in Newgate Street, London, captures something of the bright, glittering world of the gin palace that seduced drinkers in early 19th-century towns and cities.

Hill, London, and Weller's in Old Street. Designed to look like the shops that were appearing in the more fashionable districts, gas-lit, and fitted out in lavish style, the gin palace aimed to attract the crowds, and to serve them as efficiently as possible. Its appearance, and supposed vulgarity, caused outrage in polite society, but it also had an immediate impact on the planning and design of the public house.

The gin palace was a feature of late Georgian and very early Victorian England, yet the term has had undeserved longevity. The magnificent public houses from the golden age of pub building at the end of the 19th century are often casually referred to as 'gin palaces'. By then gin, and the places dedicated to its

consumption, no longer held their former importance (whisky became popular from the 1860s) but the survival of the term is probably simply because no better one has appeared to describe the finest examples of buildings dedicated to popular drinking.

**Alehouse to public house: the development of facilities down to 1830**

From the mid-17th century the alehouse offered enhanced facilities for its customers. Its changing nature was reflected in a new name – the 'public house' –, first recorded in 1669, according to the *Oxford English Dictionary*. Reflecting the muddying of the boundaries between different drinking establishments, the term was also applied to taverns and to smaller inns.

Unlike the purpose-built inn, the alehouse remained an ordinary house in which drink was sold until the end of the 18th century. However, there was increasing pressure from the authorities for alehouses to be 'fit for the purpose' (the 1753 Act, for example, required victuallers to have premises with a rental value of at least £12 a year to obtain a spirit licence), which meant a gradual increase in size and improvement in facilities. Before 1640, 60 per cent of Canterbury alehouses had fewer than six rooms, but after 1660 most Kentish establishments had more than this. By 1750 well over 50 per cent had eight rooms or more. In Leicestershire, only a tiny percentage had two or three rooms, the great majority having four or five by this time.[49] The increase in size was most marked in London, the south-east and the Midlands, however; in the north and the west small, simple alehouses survived in large numbers.

The increase in size was accompanied by an increasing amount of specialisation in the way rooms were used, with some being adapted specifically for drinking; distinctions were gradually made between public rooms and the landlord's private accommodation. Before 1640, drinking usually took place in the kitchen or, less frequently, in the parlour, but by the mid-18th century many public houses had several rooms specifically set aside for drinking, and using the kitchen for this purpose became less usual. By 1700, most alehouses had a cellar for storing drink, and during the century the 'bar'

became more common, imported from the inn and larger taverns.

Other specialised rooms and spaces began to appear. Alehouses had long been expected to provide overnight accommodation but these guests, usually poorer travellers, generally had to sleep on the floor, on benches, or in outhouses. But by 1750 larger establishments could offer sleeping chambers. Public houses became the headquarters for societies of various kinds and, consequently, club rooms started to appear. Provision for all sorts of games developed during the 18th century, and by 1800 many houses boasted skittle alleys, bowling greens, quoits pitches, or even billiard rooms. By the late 18th century there might even be a urinal whereas toilets for customers were conspicuously lacking in most earlier alehouses. Public houses increasingly displayed lamps to light the customer's way in, and to draw attention to the premises (1.26). The provision of external lighting was occasionally demanded by the Justices; in 1805 the Devon Justices demanded that each 'inn' should have a lamp over its front door, and each 'tavern' two.[50]

External changes accompanied these internal developments. The pictorial inn sign was almost universal by 1700, and it was more normal for a building to continue as an alehouse despite changes of ownership or tenancy. A new landlord, however, still often meant a new name. For example, among the establishments recorded in King's Lynn in 1764, the

1.26 Lamps often advertised the presence of a pub and were sometimes required by the licensing Justices. An elaborate Victorian pub lamp at the Red Lion, Parkgate, near Neston, Cheshire.

1.27–1.28 Public houses usually boasted pictorial inn signs by the 18th century. This advertising medium later went into decline but was revived in the 20th century and is still one of the iconic features of the pub. These are at the Blue Ship, The Haven, West Sussex, and the Red Lion, Ampney St Peter, Gloucestershire.

Huntsman and Hound had been the Greyhound by 1623, had turned into the Dog in 1723, and was to become the Bird in Hand in 1775; the Lynn Pink had been the Shipp in 1690, the Three Coines in 1742, and was to become the Recruiting Officer in 1775 and the Recruiting Sergeant by 1835.[51] This practice continued well into the 19th century.

The public house of 1830 was primitive compared to what came later, but all the elements were in place to turn it into a very special and distinctive building type, and social institution.

## Chapter 2

# The Development of the Pub

In 1830 Parliament passed the Beer Act, a remarkable piece of legislation whose consequences, foreseen and unforeseen, were felt for decades. It was part of a wider trend towards freeing the economy from tariffs, duties and quotas. After the end of the Napoleonic wars in 1815, Britain experienced a deep economic depression, accompanied by serious social unrest, and many believed the way out was to permit unfettered economic competition. In addition, some saw the tight regulation of public houses since the 1780s as an unnecessary assault on liberty. They were joined by those deploring the growth of gin shops who believed, as Hogarth had so graphically shown (1.20–1.21) that beer was wholesome whereas spirits were addictive and damaging to health. There was resentment too over the power the large common brewers exerted on the drink trade through their tied estates. Yet another factor was a belief that cheap beer would reduce smuggling and unlicensed spirit-selling. Resisting the reform were those with vested interests in the status quo, the brewers and the publicans. The latter often owed large debts to the brewers, and feared the consequences of deregulation.

**2.1** A village pub interior that looks much as it might have done in the 19th century. The Square and Compass, Worth Matravers, Dorset: a stone floor, simple benches and tables. Service is from a hatch just visible through the doorway.

The Duke of Wellington's Tory Government, formed in 1828, was deeply unpopular and calculated that liberalising the beer trade would not only stimulate the depressed and potentially subversive agricultural sector, but would also, by reducing the price of drink, earn it popular approval. The Act took beerhouses outside existing controls. But, as so often with the history of alcohol in this country, intentions and results were not the same thing.

### The 1830 Beer Act: a retail revolution

The Beer Act allowed any ratepayer to sell beer after paying an annual Excise fee of two guineas. A Justices'

2.2 (left) Many of the beerhouses which opened after the 1830 Beer Act were converted from workers' housing and almost indistinguishable from neighbouring buildings. Most of these simple pubs closed during the first half of the 20th century and their licences transferred to more modern premises. A rare survivor is the Big 6 (originally the Bowling Green) in Halifax which opened in 1857, occupying part of a row of back-to-back houses built in 1852; the beerhouse occupied one house and its brewhouse another.

2.3 (opposite) Plan of 1864 for converting a joiner's shop in Preston, into a two-room beerhouse. Brewing was on the premises. A large serving area ('bar') has been allowed for; fixed seating round the bar parlour walls was planned. Preston retained a large number of home-brew pubs until well into the 20th century.

licence was no longer required. Beer duty was abolished although that on malt and hops remained. The Act imposed just one restriction: the new beerhouses must close between 10 pm and 4 am on weekdays, and, on Sundays, could only open from 1 pm to 3 pm, and 5 pm to 10 pm. Public houses, however, under the 1828 Alehouse Act, had to close only during Sunday morning church service.[1]

Beerhouse numbers exploded. Within days of the Act coming into force on 10 October, thousands of licences were issued, mostly in London and major industrial towns. By the end of 1830, 24,342 new beer sellers had paid their two guineas. Numbers increased to 30,978 in 1831 and 33,515 in 1832, and continued upwards.[2] These new 'Tom and Jerry shops' or 'tiddlywinks' as they were called, were often found in alleyways and cellars, and almost impossible to police. There was certainly a short-term increase in drunkenness, as people took advantage of the sudden and ready availability of cheap beer. The problem was worst in the northern industrial towns, where gin drinking was less popular than in London. 800 licences were said to have been taken out in Liverpool alone in October 1830, whilst Friedrich Engels, writing about Manchester in *The Condition of the Working Class in England* (1845), claimed the Beerhouse Act had 'facilitated the spread of intemperance by bringing a beerhouse … to everybody's door'.

2.4 Many a beerhouse interior (and customer) would have looked like this. This scene of around 1900 is probably in Norwich. The advertisement is for Steward, Patteson, Finch & Co's fine Norwich ales. The stone bottle and the pottery tankard are also of interest – not all beer was bottled or served in glass, even though it came into general use from the mid-19th century, and pottery tankards for pub use were made up until at least the Second World War.

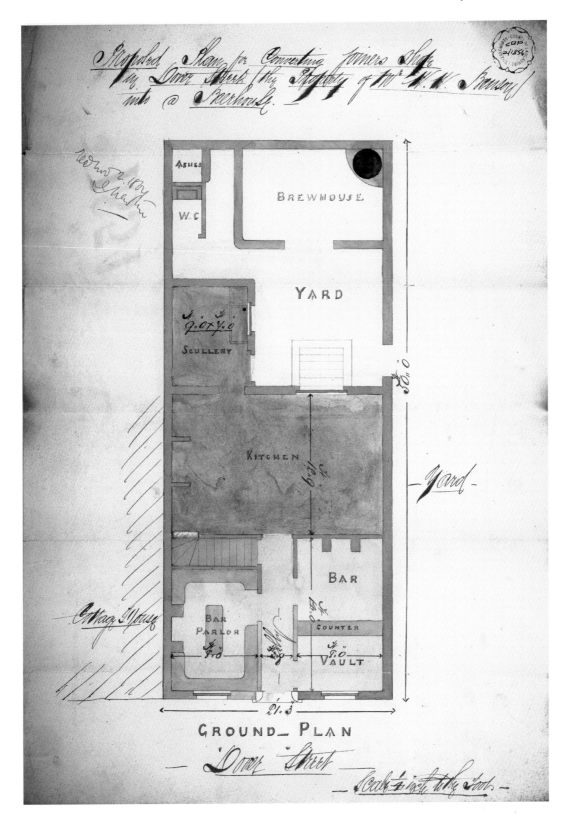

Proposed Plan for Converting Joiners Shop in Dover Street (the Property of Mr W. W. Branson) into a Beerhouse.

GROUND PLAN

Dover Street

## Time, gentlemen, please!

Traditionally, public houses could stay open round the clock apart from during Sunday morning church service. The 1830 Act, however, required the new beerhouses to close from 10 pm till 4 am in the week. Then the 1840 Beer Act ushered in slightly more liberal beerhouse hours, depending on population density with weekday closing at midnight in London, 11 pm in towns with more than 2,500 people, and 10 pm in rural districts. But time was starting to be called on public houses too. The Metropolitan Police Act of 1839 required London's public houses to close from midnight on Saturday to 1 pm on Sunday, and similar clauses were included in Police Acts for Liverpool (1842), Manchester (1845) and Newcastle upon Tyne (1846). The 1848 Alehouses and Beerhouses Act, however, gave some relief to Sunday drinkers by allowing all licensed houses to open at 12.30 pm (instead of 1 pm).

These restrictions, which appear light by later standards, met resistance but more was to follow as the Government responded to an increasingly influential temperance movement. The Forbes Mackenzie Act of 1853 closed drink outlets in Scotland on Sundays, except to *bona fide* travellers (basically, those having travelled over three miles). As for England, the Sunday Beer Act (or Wilson-Patten Act) of 1854 attempted to shut pubs on Sunday afternoons between 2.30 pm and 6 pm. Serious riots ensued, forcing a Government retreat, and Sunday afternoon closing was not imposed until 1872.

The 1830 beerhouses had to close overnight during the week, but there were no such restrictions on the older-established public houses until 1864. Then the Public-house Closing Act introduced weekday closure between 1 am and 4 am. It applied initially to London, although other areas soon adopted the restrictions.

## The struggle for control: 1830–72

After the Beer Act came into force, stories of mass drunkenness abounded and it was soon clear that spirit drinking had not been curbed in any way. Indeed, it may have even encouraged sales because public house proprietors, many of them beer-only licensees before 1830, fought back by obtaining spirit licences. Justices were often only too happy to grant these as it was the only way they could regain control over the premises. In Portsmouth, for example, the number of fully licensed houses rose from 238 to 332 between 1858 and 1870, all but three of the additional ones having begun life as beerhouses.[3] Many urban public houses were refurbished or rebuilt, as their owners attempted to distinguish them from beerhouses by adopting the features of the more ostentatious gin palace.

A House of Commons Committee on the Sale of Beer (1833) and a Committee on Drunkenness (1834)

2.5–2.6 The last beerhouse, where no wine or spirits were sold. The Seven Stars, Halfway House, Shropshire, closed in 2005. Apart from the Formica-topped table, the simple, one-room interior with its pair of settles, quarry-tiled floor and panelled dado, was of the kind that greeted drinkers in thousands of Victorian beerhouses.

reported on the near impossibility of supervising the new drinking establishments, and a massive increase in drunkenness and drink-related crime. A reversal of policy, however, was out of the question. Mindful of the mass unrest preceding the 1832 Reform Bill, and, realising that it would be blamed for any recession attributable to abandoning free trade principles, the Whig administration was disinclined to undo the work of its Tory predecessor. Control over the beerhouses, therefore, came but gradually. A second Beer Act of 1834 made a distinction for the first time between those selling beer for consumption *on* the premises, and those selling *off*. The Excise fee for an on-licence was raised to three guineas, and all beer sellers, except those in London, had to produce a certificate of good character signed by six ratepayers.[4]   A Third Beer Act in 1840 raised the rating qualifications.[5]

Successive governments were under sustained pressure from anti-drink campaigners. Closing times were only one aspect of this. Eventually Parliament bowed to pressure for greater controls. The Wine and Beerhouse Act of 1869 was introduced as a Tory private member's bill but was supported by both sides of the house. It returned to the Justices some control over beerhouse licensing. Henceforth the Excise could only grant or renew beerhouse licences with approval from the Justices.[6]   Existing licences could be refused on four grounds – that the applicant had not provided satisfactory evidence of good character; that the house or shop was of a disorderly character or frequented by thieves or prostitutes; that the applicant had had a licence forfeited for misconduct; or that the applicant, or the premises for which the licence was sought, was not properly qualified by law. The Justices were now able to crack down on more disreputable houses. The 1869 Bradford Brewster Sessions refused to renew more than one in ten of the town's 597 licensed premises – sixty beerhouses and one fully-licensed property.[7]

The 1869 provisions were incorporated into the Licensing Act of 1872, when the Justices regained powers to determine when drink outlets should close. By then, typically, pubs and beerhouses in London had to close between midnight and 5 am on weekdays, whilst in rural districts weekday closing time could be as early as 10 pm. Sunday hours were much more limited, and rural areas could see evening closure as early as 9 pm. The Act set minimum standards for public houses – there must be a minimum of two public rooms if spirits were sold. It brought in cheaper six-day licences (to encourage Sunday closure), and the requirement to display the licensee's name above the main entrance, together with details of the licence held. More importantly, it gave the Justices powers to transfer licences between premises. Although the 1872 Act was slightly modified in 1874,[8] its provisions remained in force for some 30 years.

The 1869 and 1872 Acts effectively returned control to the Justices, albeit with considerable constraints on their ability to actually affect the number of licences issued. These had continued to increase, so that the total number of on-licences, just over 82,000 in 1830, reached over 112,000 by 1870. According to some, this was 112,000 too many.

### Demonising drink – the temperance movement

Before the 19th century few suggested that alcoholic drink was evil *per se*. Beer was generally regarded as a wholesome drink, whilst wine and even spirits, in moderation, were not considered dangerous. Samuel

## The price of beer

The 1830 Beer Act had an immediate effect on prices. Porter, a dark beer which was by far the dominant drink in London and the south-east, had previously been selling for 5d or 6d a quart, fell to 4d by the end of 1830. Prices remained remarkably stable over the next 50 years or so, although the range of beers on sale changed markedly. Porter fell out of favour, to be replaced by lighter, clearer brews (the popularity of which was assisted by the general adoption of glass for drinking vessels from the 1840s, with a resultant preference for clear, sparkling drinks). No single drink replaced porter, however, and by the middle of the 19th century most brewers of any size were producing eight or ten draught beers, with a consid-erable variation in strength and price. Prices typically ranged from 3¹/2d or 4d a quart for dark, relatively weak mild to 8d a quart for the strongest ales.

During the second half of the 19th century the pint replaced the quart as the standard measure for the sale of beer (again, probably due to the adoption of glass for drinking vessels). Prices remained fairly stable until the outbreak of hostilities in 1914 when beer of medium strength was typically 2d a pint in the public bar. The war, and a Liberal Government hostile to the drink interest, led to a rapid escalation in prices; price controls introduced in October 1916 set the price of a pint of beer with an original gravity of under 1036° at 4d, and that of one under 1042° at 5d. The rise continued after the war, and by 1939 had reached 7d a pint for beer of medium strength. The price more than doubled during the Second World War, to reach 1s 3d by 1945, although prices dropped again afterwards. In 1960 a typical pint cost 1s 2¹/2d. Prices then began an inexorable rise; by 1973 a typical pint in London and the south-east cost 13p, rising to 40p by 1980, and today often costs more than £3. A new feature of the post-war era is the variation in prices across the country, with the typical pint in London costing almost twice as much as in parts of the north, although the gap has reduced recently.

2.7 Typical beer price lists from 1949. Mild sold for less than the stronger bitter, and prices in the (more basic) tap room were lower than in the better rooms. Beverleys brewed at the Eagle Brewery in Wakefield.

BEST ROOM & CONCERT ROOM PRICE LIST
FOR
BEVERLEYS' BEERS, WINES, SPIRITS ETC.

| | |
|---|---|
| MILD - | 1/1 per pint |
| TRINITY BITTER - | 1/4 per pint |
| GOLDEN EAGLE - | 10d. per small bottle |
| OLD WARRIOR - | 11½d. per small bottle |
| JUBILEE STOUT - | 1/1 per small bottle |
| GUINNESS - | 1/2½d. per small bottle |
| MINERAL WATERS | 6d. per bottle |
| CIDER - | 8d. per bottle |
| SCOTCH WHISKY | 2/- per small measure |
| GIN or RUM | 1/9 per small measure |
| GIN & VERMOUTH | 2/- |
| GIN & PEPPERMINT | 2/- |
| BRANDY - | 2/6 per small measure |
| PORT or SHERRY | 1/6 per small glass |
| BABY MOUSSEC | 2/4 |
| BABY BUBBLY | 2/- |
| EGG FLIP, COCKTAILS etc. | 1/6 per small glass |

OCTOBER, 1949.

TAP ROOM PRICE LIST
FOR
BEVERLEYS BEERS

| | | |
|---|---|---|
| MILD - - | 1/- | per pint |
| | 6d. | per half pint |
| TRINITY BITTER | 1/3 | per pint |
| | 7½d. | per half pint |
| GOLDEN EAGLE | 9½d. | per small bott |
| OLD WARRIOR | 11d. | " " |

OCTOBER, 1949

Pepys's diaries, covering the 1660s, give an insight into just how pervasive drinking was in the lives of Londoners at all levels. Pepys was frequently drunk and suffering the after-effects, noting, for example, on 22 September 1660 how his stomach was 'ill all this day by reason of the last night's debauch'. He was regularly remorseful but such behaviour attracted no serious moral censure and his friends and colleagues did precisely the same. Little changed in the 18th century. 'Drunkenness was considered a normal and satisfactory condition as much by Defoe or Sir Robert Walpole as it was later by Johnson or Wilkes.'[9]

The ruddy-nosed parson and gouty squire are stock figures of the time. As for the lower classes, the concern was that they should not idle away their time drinking when they should be working – not that they should be prevented from drinking in the first place. But the 19th century changed all this.

The time was ripe for change. Despite the proliferation of drink outlets, the actual *per capita* consumption of alcohol had been in decline for decades. Alternatives were available as a routine part of the daily diet – tea and coffee, both luxury products when introduced in the mid-17th century, were now cheap enough to be drunk by all classes. The water supply was also improving dramatically, with new waterworks guaranteeing pure supplies in many areas. Alcohol, robbed of any of its supposed health-giving benefits, was now a legitimate target for attack.

**2.8** Drinking to their doom. *The Gin Shop* by anti-drink campaigner, George Cruikshank, 1829, when the first temperance societies appeared in Britain. 'I shall have them all dead drunk presently. They have nearly had their last glass' exults Death (left). The gin-trap will soon spring and the corner captions give the destinations for drinkers. Old Tom was probably the best-known London gin.

THE GIN SHOP

The first temperance societies were established in America in the late 1820s and the idea soon crossed the Atlantic. In 1829 they appeared first in Belfast and Dublin, quickly followed by Glasgow. The first English society was set up in Bradford in 1830. The movement spread rapidly but, initially, was simply committed to moderation and was only really opposed to the drinking of spirits.[10] The heartland of temperance became the textile manufacturing districts of Yorkshire and Lancashire. A Preston Temperance Society meeting on 1 September 1832 proved a defining moment. The Society had been formed in March and was pledged to moderation. But, at the September meeting, seven members, later known as the 'Seven Men of Preston', led by Joseph Livesey, committed themselves to total abstinence. In March of the following year the Preston Society agreed by a majority to introduce the 'short pledge'. This was a pledge of total abstinence for a year, and by the end of the year more than 600 had signed. A new word soon entered the English language – 'teetotal' – which, according to the centenary history of the Preston Society, arose out of a meeting in September 1833, and the stammering attempts of the former fish salesman Richard ('Cockle Dick') Turner, to enunciate the word 'total'.[11] For a while the Society had some members pledged to moderation and others signed up to total abstinence. But in March 1835 the Society introduced the 'long pledge', a lifelong commitment of total abstinence which was soon to become a condition of membership. Other societies soon followed the Preston example.

The Preston Society's campaigning was typical of the movement. In June 1833 the first temperance procession was held in the town with over 1,000 attending. The following month saw a 'temperance crusade' when members flooded neighbouring towns with leaflets. Public meetings were held and, in August 1836, a petition was presented at the Brewster Sessions against increasing public house licences. The Society also despatched evangelising 'missionaries' to towns where temperance societies had yet to be formed.

There was a significant difference between moderation campaigners and those advocating total

**2.9** (above, top) Old Tom gin makes another appearance among other drinks in the more respectable surroundings of the bar-back of about 1870 at the Princess of Wales, Blackheath, London. Such advertising panels were commonly used in Victorian back-fittings.

**2.10** Sketch from *The Abstainer's Penny Pictorial Almanac*, 1857, published by the Scottish Temperance League, showing a baleful scene at a public house. The arch, with the name of the proprietor, 'D. Abolus', leads off who knows where?

MEETING OF THE TEMPERANCE SOCIETY.
*Chairman M<sup>r</sup> Drainemdry F. T. S. — Vice J. Ditch-Water Esq<sup>re</sup> F. T. S.*

abstinence. The former were often middle-class and regarded 'sensible drinking' (to use a modern phrase) as perfectly acceptable. But, for them, the drunkard was irredeemably wicked and beyond help. Teetotalism, on the other hand, became more of a working-class cause and was viewed with suspicion by many of the middle and upper classes. Its supporters believed nobody was totally beyond reclaim. Indeed, those who drank heavily were a particular target and reformed drunkards became some of the movement's strongest campaigners, addressing meetings and testifying to the benefits that signing the pledge had brought. However, the fellowship of the beerhouse or public house was not easily replicated when tea was the only drink on offer. Alcohol was such a key

2.11 The joys of water drinking. Not normally a subject to excite humour, here the temperance movement is lampooned by a very early Victorian cartoonist.

ingredient of English social life that those refusing it were widely seen as eccentric. By the late 1840s the temperance movement was running out of steam and its appeal to the working class was in decline. But, then, two powerful new elements entered the story.

The first was the Band of Hope aimed at 'catching them young'. Founded in September 1847 in Leeds by a Baptist minister, Jabez Tunnicliff, membership was limited to under-16s. Within months, 4,000 children in Leeds alone had signed the pledge. By 1889 there were over

**2.12** The Temperance Hall, Kirkby Stephen, Cumbria, one of many built up and down the country where the temperance message was proclaimed. Few halls were as imposing as this one.

*Now the liquor trade, and particularly the retail branch of it, is a public nuisance …physically, economically, and morally.* By its physical consequences it causes death to thousands, reduces thousands more to madness or idiocy, and afflicts myriads with diseases involving the most wretched forms of bodily and mental torture. Considered in its economical results, it impairs the national resources by destroying a large amount of corn, which is annually distilled into spirits; *and it indirectly causes three-fourths of the taxation required by pauperism and by criminal prosecutions and prison expenses;* and further it diminishes the effective industry of the working classes thereby lessening the amount of national production. Viewed in its moral operation, it is the cause of two-thirds of the crime committed; it lowers the intelligence, and hinders the civilization of the people; and it leads the men to ill treat and starve their families, and sacrifice domestic comfort to riotous debauchery.
(Quoted by the *Abstainer's Penny Almanac, 1857,* published by the Scottish Temperance League.)

Such arguments formed the backbone of temperance literature. This generally argued that people were poor because they drank, rather than that they drank as a means of escape from their wretched world.

16,000 Bands of Hope, loosely co-ordinated by the United Kingdom Band of Hope Union, with more than 2 million members – a quarter of the population under 16. It provided a vast array of improving reading matter from monthly journals to educational materials and novels. [12]

The second was prohibition. In June 1851 the State of Maine in America passed the first prohibition law outlawing all dealing in alcohol. Realisation dawned. Why try to persuade individuals to give up drink when the problem could be dealt with at a stroke by banning it altogether? Temperance societies pressed for prohibition of alcohol, and in 1853 the United Kingdom Alliance for the Suppression of the Traffic in all Intoxicating Liquors was founded.

The Alliance, however, found its initial campaign untenable. Not only was there nowhere near enough support to make it an appealing political aim, but also no Government was likely to be keen on banning a product which generated more than a third of national tax revenue. Most people rejected 'temperance by force', arguing that the battle could only be won through 'moral suasion'. In any case, prohibition had little support amongst most working people – the protests against mid-1850s Sunday opening restrictions were evidence the Alliance could not ignore. Nor could they ignore the fact that their original inspiration, the Maine law, had been hastily repealed in 1856. In 1857 the Alliance adopted the more limited policy of 'local option', under which ratepayers in each licensing district would vote every three years on whether liquor licences should be issued. Bills to establish the local option were submitted to Parliament annually from 1863 by Sir Wilfrid Lawson for the Alliance. They were always defeated but greatly enhanced the anti-drink profile and eventually found their way into Liberal Party policy.

The Alliance took encouragement from events beyond England, namely the Forbes Mackenzie Act of 1853 which brought Sunday closing to Scotland. The Alliance, founded the same year, campaigned for its extension to the rest of the United Kingdom. Societies

2.13 The economic arguments for temperance – or what to do with your beer money. A late 19th-century handbill.

2.14 The moral arguments for temperance outlined in a postcard produced by a temperance friendly society.

As often as this pint Jug is taken to the Public-house to be filled, Threepence is spent; Threepence per day is £4 11s. 3d. per annum. If filled twice per day, it costs Sixpence, and Sixpence per day is £9 2s. 6d. per annum; and this, in Five Years, comes to **£45 12s. 6d.**

Now, what could a Working Man do with this amount? Just listen!—He could put in

| | | | |
|---|---|---|---|
| The Savings Bank for a rainy day | £20 | 0 | 0 |
| Buy 5 Suits of Clothes at 50s. ℈ suit | 12 | 10 | 0 |
| A good silver lever Watch… … … | 5 | 0 | 0 |
| A good Overcoat for wintry weather | 2 | 0 | 0 |
| Two weeks' Holidays at the Sea-side | 6 | 2 | 6 |
| | **£45** | **12** | **6** |

READER, don't take the Jug to the Public-house any more, but save the THREEPENCES and SIXPENCES and "Go in" for good clothes, Banking account, silver watch, and two weeks' holidays.

w.

## Temperance and the power of statistics

Temperance workers were avid collectors and purveyors of data to show how vast was the expenditure in an excessive number of drink shops, and how it could be better used. Here is a sample from the *Temperance Journal* for 1879:

- 2 January. In 1877 £11 million was spent on cotton goods, but £142 million on intoxicating liquors. Yet we spend only £700,000 or £800,000 'for the evangelisation of the world'.
- 16 January. London's metropolitan boroughs have 8,923 drink shops or one for 333 people. Manchester has 2,337 or one for 164. The highest ratio quoted is Bristol with 1,306 drink shops or one for just 139 people.
- 1 February. In 1860 £86,897,683 was spent on drink whereas the amount voted by the Government for education was a mere £724,403. In 1876 £147,288,760 went on drink whereas the education budget was just £1,881,776.

with this specific aim came into being, a local one at Hull in 1861 and a national one in 1863. The movement scored a victory in 1881 when the Sunday Closing (Wales) Act extended the principle to Wales.[13] Subsequent bills to bring all-day Sunday closing to England were only just defeated, and to the sadness of some and the gladness of most, a Sunday drinking ban never materialised in England.

### The temperance pressure increases

The crusade against the drink trade was stepped up during the later 19th century. The Established Church became increasingly involved as its mission in poor urban areas brought it face to face with poverty and those who drank to secure temporary relief from it. This led to the formation in 1861 of the Church of England Temperance Society which grew into the largest adult temperance group in the country. By 1899 it had 7,000 branches and nearly 200,000 members. It enjoyed the support of many influential people, with the bishops forming a powerful lobby in the House of Lords.

Other groups adopted tub-thumping methods and viewed drinking as a sign of moral degeneracy. One such body, the Blue Ribbon Association, propounded this message energetically. Founded in 1877 in imitation of an American movement of the same name, it was initially a local mission, based at Hoxton Hall (a former music hall) in London's East End. However, the Association was revolutionised in 1881 by the arrival of an American temperance evangelist, Richard Booth. He was a consummate showman and, for ten years or so, led missions all over the country. These were carefully orchestrated: a committee was set up months in advance by local temperance groups, the largest hall in the district booked, and anticipation and excitement built up by posters and newspaper articles.

The Blue Ribbon movement burned itself out in the late 1880s, but not before a million people had signed the pledge. Other organisations had more staying power and learned from the methods of the Association. One such was the Salvation Army, founded by William and Catherine Booth in 1878, and organised on strict, military lines. By 1882 it had 521 local stations with 742 paid officers and 15,000 volunteer soldiers. Its opposition to drink was only part of its work and it became increasingly admired for its work among the very poor.[14]

### Liberal or Conservative? To compensate or not to compensate?

The 'drink question' was an important one in late Victorian England. There was general agreement that excessive drinking was harmful and all too prevalent, that the numbers of drinking establishments should be reduced, and that the trade should be better regulated. The issue was how. From the early 1870s the two great political parties took diverging paths. The Liberals were seen as the temperance party whereas the Conservatives, as the Tories had become known since the 1840s, were regarded as the friends of the drink trade. Their creation of peerages for some of the wealthy brewers led Liberals to talk of 'the beerage'. However, it was the Conservatives who brought in two of the more enlightened pieces of drink-related legislation – the Habitual Drunkards Act of 1879, which established sanatoria where people could obtain treatment for alcoholism, and the second Habitual Drunkards Act of 1898, which gave magistrates the power to commit drunkards who had committed crimes to these establishments for treatment. Another successful piece of Conservative legislation, passed in 1886, prohibited the sale of alcohol to children for consumption on licensed premises; then from 1901 it could only be sold to children in sealed containers to be taken away.[15]

The big difference came over licence reductions. In 1889 the Liberals went shoulder to shoulder with the United Kingdom Alliance and adopted 'local option'.[16] Licensing would be handed over from the Justices to local councils and a two-thirds majority of ratepayers would allow them to weed out or even close all licensed premises. And there would be no compensation. The reasoning behind this was 'that a licence was not a piece of property but something which was granted annually at the discretion of the licensing authorities'.[17] They introduced a local option bill in 1893 but it was postponed due to the Home Rule crisis. It was reintroduced in 1895 and would no doubt have become law had not the Conservatives won a landslide victory in the general election that followed an unexpected defeat of a Liberal motion in June. The Conservatives, while wishing to see a reduction in public house numbers, were totally opposed to the principle of no compensation.

### Taxing beer

1880 saw an attempt to promote moderation by making weaker beers cheaper than strong ones. In a move known as 'the freeing of the mash-tun' the Liberal Government under William Gladstone abolished the duty on malt and hops, and re-introduced duty on beer. This was initially levied at 6s 3d on a 'standard barrel' (a 36-gallon barrel of beer with an original gravity of 1057°) with more duty being paid on stronger beer, and less on beer of lower gravity. This system is still with us today.

**2.15** One of suburban London's grandest and most spacious pubs, the Salisbury, Harringay, 1898–9, was built as a pub-cum-hotel by developer, John Cathles Hill. He was a founder of the London Brick Company and laid out much of the surrounding area. The building makes the most of its corner site and is a free blend of Flemish gables, mullioned windows, structural polychrome, and wide depressed arches on the ground floor.

**2.16** The Prince Alfred, Maida Vale, London, was one of probably thousands of pubs refitted in lavish style in the late 19th and very early 20th centuries. The ceiling dates from the original build around 1856 but the woodwork, glass and tiling date from about 1898. This view is from a front bar to an entrance area.

## Boom and bust – the golden age of pub building

Because of the increasing difficulty in obtaining new licences, the 1880s and 1890s saw a scramble by brewers to acquire public houses. In 1886 Guinness, the Dublin brewer, became a limited company, raising a massive £6 million through the flotation. Although Guinness was not the first brewer to do this, it was the largest to date. During the next fifteen years dozens of brewers floated, and used the proceeds to purchase pubs. Old ones were refitted or rebuilt, and new ones put up, often in magnificent style. In large areas of the country, the 'free house' became a rarity. The competition for pubs was fiercest in London, where local brewers and entrepreneurs faced challenges from newcomers, especially the Burton brewers, seeking outlets in the capital. The price of licensed property rose, encouraging private owners to sell, and buyers to pay ever more inflated sums. The ensuing collapse from 1899 began in London, where it was most severe. Values were often more than halved, and owners found the loans they had taken out to fund purchases could greatly exceed what their property was worth. Bankruptcies multiplied and rolled on until the early 1900s. Outside London the story was somewhat less dramatic and lagged behind events in the capital. Speculation in licensed property never again reached the levels of the late 19th century.[18]

2.17 'The taproom at the Sieve' sketched by pub historian, Philip Norman, about 1900. Such basic premises were the sort of establishments likely to be targeted during licence reductions.

## Late Victorian licences

The 1872 Licensing Act classified outlets for alcohol in a variety of ways.

- **The alehouse licence.** Confusingly, this allowed the holder to run a fully-licensed house, selling all types of alcoholic drink for consumption on the premises.
- **The beerhouse licence.** This allowed the holder to sell only beer and cider for consumption on the premises.
- **The cider-house licence.** With this licence only cider could be sold for consumption on the premises.
- **The refreshment house licence.** This permitted the sale of wine to accompany meals in restaurants and eating-houses.

There were also several types of 'retail' or 'off' licence, allowing the holder to sell alcohol for consumption off the premises. Specific licences were needed to sell beer, table-beer (weak beer costing no more than 1½d a quart), cider, wine, spirits or 'sweets' (home-made wines – the 'dealer in sweets' sold wine, not confectionery). There were also restricted licences – six-day licences required Sunday closure, early licences required the holder to close an hour before 'normal' closing time. In all, magistrates controlled the issue of over a dozen different licences for the sale of alcoholic drink. They also controlled the issue of licences for billiard tables in beerhouses (the alehouse licence allowed the holder to keep one or more billiard tables) and for musical performances on licensed premises.

## Reducing pub numbers

Justices made increasing use of the 1872 Licensing Act to reduce public house numbers and to improve the quality of those remaining. The experience of the Star Inn at Wetherby in Yorkshire was typical. The magistrates refused to renew the licence in 1883 because it was 'superfluous to the needs of the district', and 'structurally unsuitable to be a public house'. The owners appealed to the Quarter Sessions, but were only allowed a renewed licence on condition that the house was rebuilt.[19]

The Justices' power to suppress public houses without compensation was confirmed by the landmark case of *Sharp* v. *Wakefield*. Susannah Sharp, owner of a public house in the Westmorland village of Staveley, fought against the licensing magistrates' decision not to renew its licence in 1887 on the grounds that it was too far from police supervision and was not needed. She pursued her appeal through every level of the courts only to have it finally dismissed by the House of Lords in 1891. This landmark case heralded renewed efforts by magistrates to reduce the number of licences.[20]

Owners seeking new or improved premises usually had to bargain with the Justices. York brewer W H Thackwray, for example, had to surrender the licence of the Fox Inn to obtain a spirits off-licence for the brewery stores in Goodramgate in 1895, whilst the Tadcaster Tower Brewery Company had to surrender four licences to construct the Jubilee Hotel in an expanding residential suburb of York in 1897.[21] In Portsmouth, an unofficial tariff governed the transfer of licences from old premises to new; the going rate appears to have been two old licences for a new one from 1879 until the mid-1890s, when the Justices began to demand the exchange of multiple licences (typically four existing ones) for the grant of a new one.[22]

**2.18** Too many! Part of the 'Drink Map of Norwich 1878' published by the United Kingdom Alliance to illustrate the excessive numbers of public houses. Similar maps were compiled for many towns and cities, and were a key part of the Alliance's campaigning tactics.

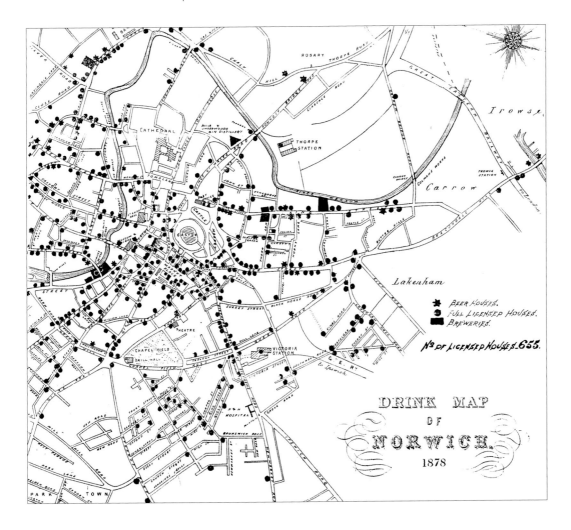

**2.19** The New Eight Bells, Robertsbridge, East Sussex, rebuilt in 1905. It evidently offered accommodation and was the kind of respectable establishment expected by the authorities – not to mention the type of clientèle who would have used the 'stabling, motor house (and) motor pit'. A private house since *c*2002.

The exchange of multiple old licences for new was at its most organised in Birmingham. Arthur Chamberlain, chairman of the licensing bench from 1894, instigated what became known as the Birmingham Surrender Scheme two years later, demanding the surrender of licences in the inner city for permission to construct new pubs in the growing suburbs. The brewers formed the Birmingham Property Company to negotiate the surrender of old licences, with compensation for those that were given up. About forty licences a year were given up until 1904, when Chamberlain lost the chairmanship of the licensing bench.[23]

Between 1896 and 1899 a Royal Commission (the 'Peel Commission') examined more than 250 witnesses in a thorough review of licensing laws. It led to the 1902 Licensing Act that, for the first time, empowered magistrates to approve alterations to public houses, and insist on alterations to premises they thought unsuitable.[24] Drawings for proposed alterations or new premises had to be formally approved by the Justices as part of the licensing procedure. The Act also made it necessary for off-licences to obtain a Justices' licence, and private clubs (the numbers of which were expanding) had to register. The act also made drunkenness in a public place an offence for the first time.

The other crucial outcome of the Peel Commission was the 1904 Licensing Act which introduced a fair mechanism for closing public houses deemed superfluous by the magistrates.[25] A fund, levied on all existing on-licences, would compensate owners for losing their licences (other than for misconduct of the licensee or because the premises were unsuitable as a public house). The amount of compensation was based upon the difference in value between the house with and without a licence (contrasting with the situation today, when pubs are closing because they are worth more as private houses).

Thus armed, magistrates embarked upon a systematic reduction of licensed premises. Nationally, more than

12,500 licences were compensated between 1904 and 1920. In York, for example, five houses were closed in 1906, four in 1907, three in 1908, three in 1910, and a further five before the First World War. In general, they were the most basic ones, situated in the poorest areas of the city, and were those identified by the police as the most disreputable.[26] In Bradford, 100 houses (all but two of them beerhouses) had been closed by 1920, most on the advice of the police. Portsmouth's magistrates divided the borough into a number of redundancy areas, one of these being dealt with each year; ninety-five houses were closed between 1905 and 1914, of which seventy-one were compensated, nine were surrendered in exchange for licences for new premises elsewhere, and eight were closed on the grounds of 'ill conduct'.

In 1906 temperance campaigners drew hope when the Liberals swept back to power. Two years later they proposed a Bill to reduce the number of licences by a third over fourteen years, as well as local option, and a ban on employing women in pubs. The proposals split the country. Ranged against them were the Conservatives – a minority in the Commons but a majority in the Lords – as well as brewers, publicans, drinkers and the barmaids who formed the Barmaids' Political Defence League to defend their jobs. Marches and rallies were held all over the country, thousands turning out to support or oppose the Bill. When the Bill was thrown out by the Lords, despite having passed the Commons, there were widespread celebrations. Hence, in 1910, the Licensing (Consolidation) Act, made no attempt to do more than tidy up the many licensing laws that Parliament had dealt with since 1828.

### The sober alternatives: the coffee tavern and the 'reformed' public house

Temperance campaigners widely believed that a key reason for the popularity of the public house was the lack of alternatives to it. Consequently an integral part of their campaign was to offer working men places to socialise, read newspapers, and play games much as in the public house, but without the accompaniment of alcohol. The first British Workman's Public-House opened in Leeds in September 1867, and was soon followed by similar establishments in London and other major towns. The People's Café Company (1874), the Coffee Tavern Company (1876) and the Coffee Public House Association (1877) were all

**2.20–2.21** The Ossington Coffee Palace, Newark, 1881–2, designed by Ernest George and Harold Peto in the Norman Shaw manner. An ambitious building with ambitious aims, it is the grandest architectural monument of the temperance movement but it lasted only a few years. The claim to be a perfect copy of a 17th-century hostelry is also a trifle ambitious.

## The Gothenburg system

Britain was not the only place where people worried about excessive alcohol consumption. In 1865 the Swedish city of Gothenburg took matters in hand by establishing itself as the licensing authority, fixing the number of licences, and granting a monopoly on them to a society of shareholders. Anything above 5 per cent profit on capital went back to the municipal treasury. The system was later followed in Norway. It involved what was called 'disinterested management' whereby managers had no incentive to promote alcohol sales. By 1892 some fifty Swedish towns had such schemes operating. The receipts from these ventures was said to be a hefty £75,000 in 1887 (about £45 million in present-day values).[28]

The model proved attractive to reformers here. The progressive Liberal mayor of Birmingham, Joseph Chamberlain, got support for an experiment but failed to secure the necessary Parliamentary sanction in 1877. However, the same year, the Boar's Head at Hampton Lucy, Warwickshire, seems to have become the first British pub to adopt Gothenburg principles. It had been bequeathed to the parish, and the rector, the Rev Osbert Mordaunt, introduced disinterested management. The manager got his accommodation free, and received the profits from non-alcoholic drinks, food and stabling. Profits on alcohol sales went to the parish, paying for, among other things, the church organist's salary. [29]

Several Gothenburg-inspired schemes were started about 1900 in England and Scotland and were a model for the 'Carlisle Experiment' when the State took over public houses around Carlisle and elsewhere. Three 'Goths' still operate in lowland Scotland.

founded as temperance alternatives to the pub. By 1884 there were 121 coffee taverns in London, and more than 1,500 nationwide.[27]

Most were modelled on the gin palace, with plate-glass, gas lamps and polished woodwork. Cheap, good-quality food was also provided. Despite these blandishments, the coffee tavern movement failed to entice many away from the pub. A tendency to patronise the customer, and the evangelical tone of much of the literature available, served only to antagonise much of the target market. Despite support from leading politicians, aristocrats, and religious leaders, the coffee-tavern movement had effectively collapsed by the end of the century. More successful was the 'reformed' public house, one of the first being the Tabard of 1880 in Bedford Park, Chiswick, designed by Norman Shaw. The reformed pub aimed to distract customers from intoxicating drink by offering a range of activities, hot and cold food, and various non-alcoholic beverages. Some were provided by paternalistic landowners, and in 1896 the

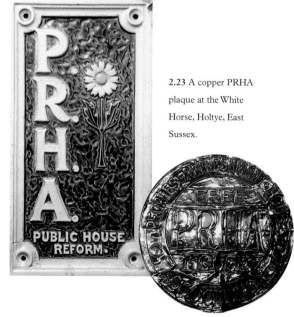

2.22 A Public Refreshment House Association faïence plaque at the Crown, Groombridge, Kent. The Aesthetic nature of the plaque with its flower typify the genteel aims of the Association.

2.23 A copper PRHA plaque at the White Horse, Holtye, East Sussex.

Public Refreshment House Association (PRHA), chaired by the Bishop of Chester, was founded to lease pubs run on reformed lines. It differed from the Swedish principle in that its public houses were not owned by the municipality but in other respects it was similar. Managers got no rewards from alcohol sales while shareholders had their dividends limited to 5 per cent with any surplus going to works of public benefit. The first PRHA pub was the Sparkford Inn at Sparkford, Somerset, which opened in 1897.

Another pub which was held up as a model of disinterested management and the civilisation of the public house was the Fox and Pelican at Grayshott in Hampshire, built by the Grayshott and District Refreshment Association and opened in 1899 (it sported a sign designed and decorated by the Arts and Crafts artist, Walter Crane). It was run by a local association whose shareholders' dividend was capped at 4 per cent with any balance going to improve the building and to public purposes. It was taken over by the PRHA in 1913 but sold to the brewers, Gale's of Horndean, in the 1950s.[30]

In 1901 Earl Grey proposed a public house trust company to operate inns and public houses on similar lines in every county. The first, the Grey Arms at Amble in Northumberland, opened later that year; it had two bars, two billiard tables, cycle houses, a tea room on the first floor, and a large hall and dining room.[31] Other counties followed suit, buying or leasing old coaching inns and renovating them to offer food and accommodation for cyclists and the motorists who were beginning to appear upon the roads. The county companies amalgamated as Trust Houses Limited in 1919, and then operated more than 100 inns and public houses.[32]

The True Temperance Association, formed in 1909, campaigned to make the provision of the features of the reformed public house – food, non-alcoholic drinks, games, newspapers and other reading matter, gardens and other recreational facilities – a statutory requirement in all public houses. The Association was actually a trade organisation, set up by the brewers to

**2.24** The Goth, Armadale, West Lothian, 1901 (tower, now leaning, added 1927), is still run by members of the Armadale Public House Society Ltd on 'Gothenburg' lines. Under this scheme managers were given no incentive to sell alcohol, and some of the profits were repatriated to the community.

split the temperance movement by aligning itself with the more moderate campaigners. In this aim it was successful, and its campaign for reformed pubs gained widespread support.

The influence of reformed public houses was considerable. They demonstrated how the standard of food in the nation's pubs could be improved, and the choice of non-alcoholic drinks on sale widened. Nevertheless by 1914, despite all these worthy endeavours, there were only a couple of hundred reformed public houses out of a total of some 87,000 licensed houses in England and Wales.

### The First World War and 'improvement'

The Great War brought further restrictions as the Government sought to regulate the supply and consumption of alcohol in the interests of the war effort. The Defence of the Realm Act (DORA), passed within a few days of the outbreak of war, gave the Government sweeping powers over all aspects of life, and on 31 August 1914 it was supplemented by the

**2.25–2.26** The Arcade Stores, Norwich, 1901. Designed by the distinguished local architect, George Skipper, this public house was developed as part of a very respectable city centre shopping development. A spacious bar and lounge/smoke room were complemented by sophisticated Art Nouveau tiling on the exterior by the artist W J Neatby.

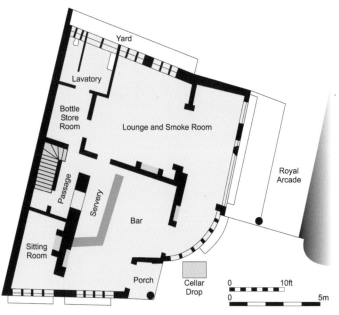

Back of the Inns

Intoxicating Liquor (Temporary Restrictions) Act, which gave magistrates the power to limit opening hours, or even to close pubs altogether. Within weeks opening hours were severely limited, with weekday afternoon closure being imposed for the first time. In October 10 pm closing was imposed, although many licensing benches insisted on an even earlier hour. In November beer duty was tripled. Restrictions were also imposed on spirit sales, and on the buying of rounds of drinks and other practices held to encourage alcohol consumption, such as the 'long pull', the practice of attracting customers by serving more than the legal measure at no extra cost. Some pubs near key military bases were closed completely. In May 1915 DORA No 3 set up the Central Control Board (Liquor Traffic) to regulate all aspects of the drink trade whilst the war continued.[33] As war dragged on and imports fell prey to U-boats, drinkers felt the effects in disagreeable ways. The pre-war gravity of 1052° was maintained until 1915 but was then reduced to conserve grain stocks: by 1918, 'Government ale', as it was known, had fallen to 1030°. Also, production virtually halved in 1917. The lack of beer, and the feebleness of what there was, were major factors behind the industrial unrest of mid-1917(2.31) – a lesson not lost on the Government during the next conflict with Germany.

In some places DORA's restrictions appeared to have little effect. These included the areas around the munitions factories at Enfield Lock, Carlisle and Gretna, and the naval bases at Invergordon and Cromarty. Each had vast temporary populations with few opportunities for leisure other than the public house. In 1916 the Central Control Board (CCB) took the public houses and other drink outlets in these areas into State ownership. In Enfield Lock this amounted to four public houses and an off-licence; around Invergordon and Cromarty twenty-eight public houses and hotels and eleven off-licences. The area around Carlisle and Gretna was entirely different in scale, and the Board took four breweries and 227 licensed premises into public ownership. The area was later extended to take in Maryport and district, which included another brewery and a further 136 licensed premises.

# FITZPATRICKS

**Fitzpatricks Unique Speciality Drinks**
**Popular since 1890**

## SARSAPARILLA CORDIAL

**For a delicious drink mix half & half
with ice cold soda water or sparkling
spring water, or hot/cold water**

### STORE COOL – SHAKE WELL

Sugar, Pineapple Ess., Sarsaparilla Ess.,
Sassafras Ess., Caramel, Citric Acid, Sea
Foamine, Sweetarin, Sodium Benzoate & Water.

**Best consumed within 10 days of opening.**

**Herbal Health, 5 Bank Street, Rawtenstall, Lancs. BB4 6QS**

**(Britain's Last Temperance Bar)**

**Tel: 01706 211152          Min. Contents 70 cl.**

2.27–2.29 Herbal Health in Rawtenstall, Lancashire, Britain's last temperance bar where sarsaparilla, as advertised on the bottle label here, takes the place of bitter. But the noticeboard outside has plenty of other non-alcoholic delights on offer. Much of the trade is for consumption off the premises.

THE ENEMY'S ALLY.

The CCB soon set about restricting the supply of drink. Between July 1916 and October 1918, fifty-three licensed premises were closed in Carlisle alone, and the ensuing reduction in beer sales made it possible to close two of the city's four breweries. Spirits sales were restricted by introducing 'spirit-less Saturdays', whilst complete Sunday closing was enforced. Pub managers received remuneration, on Gothenburg principles, from the sale of food and non-alcoholic drinks rather than liquor, and all alcohol advertising and window displays of bottles were removed.

More constructive initiatives included increased food provision in the CCB's public houses, the rebuilding of existing premises, and the construction of new, improved ones. The Gretna Tavern in Carlisle, opened in July 1916, typified the attempts to promote drinking in moderation, and was a model for the post-war improvement of the public house. A former post office, it discouraged perpendicular drinking, with a relatively small bar area but plenty of tables and chairs set out in large airy rooms. Waiter service was provided. The Central Control Board was wound up in 1919, and public houses in the Enfield Lock area returned to private ownership: those in the Carlisle, Invergordon and Cromarty areas district did not. State management was finally abolished in 1972.

Most measures introduced by DORA were abolished after the war, but the Licensing Act of 1921 set severely restricted pub and club opening hours. Earlier legislation had decreed when public houses should be closed (the so-called 'prohibited hours') but the 1921 Act substituted the concept of 'permitted hours'. It set

2.31 As the Great War ground on, many must have felt like the man in this postcard.

these at nine hours a day in London, and eight elsewhere, with compulsory afternoon closure (except on market days and in other specific circumstances). These restrictions were not eased until 1988. The Act also prohibited drinking on credit, except with a meal, and confirmed the prohibition of the 'long pull', although other practices outlawed during the war, such as the buying of rounds of drinks, were no longer illegal.

The 'Carlisle Experiment' had a considerable influence on the post-war thinking of licensing Justices and pub owners. As early as February 1918, a joint sub-committee of the Brewers' Society and the National

2.30 'Drink is doing us more damage in the war than all the German submarines put together … We are fighting Germany, Austria, and Drink; and as far as I can see the greatest of these three deadly foes is Drink.' Such was Lloyd George's famous assessment of the military situation in a speech at Bangor on 28 February 1915. He repeated it to a deputation of shipbuilders on 29 March. However, the evidence suggests drink was not responsible for significant lost production, but the restrictions on it caused massive public resentment.

49

Trade Defence Association recommended that 'arrangements [in new houses] should contemplate more general service of refreshments and practically in all houses provision should be made for the … service of non-alcoholic beverages. Facilities should be provided for recreation.'[34] As a result, the improved public house is closely identified with the inter-war period.

## Inter-war pub building

Between 1920 and 1939, there was major slum clearance, and also the construction of some 5 million new homes, mainly in new suburban estates. To service them, brewers sought licences for new public houses and, as before the war, they usually had to surrender several older licences to obtain a new one. The Justices, generally, were cautious in granting

2.32–2.34 The Cumberland Inn, Carlisle. A Tudor Revival pub built under the 'Carlisle Experiment' in 1928 to designs by Harry Redfern. It has a refined frontage, and elegant fittings in an upstairs bar. There are several gilded inscriptions, such as these from Omar Khayyam, in praise of civilised drinking.

new licences, and in most areas only a fraction of the applications were successful. Once the pace of housebuilding picked up in the late 1920s, those that succeeded offered a range of facilities in addition to the sale of alcohol. By 1939 the net result was some 12,000 fewer licences.

The policy was quite simply to reduce the number of licensed houses. In Birmingham, for example, magistrates and brewers revived the policy, now under the slogan 'Fewer and Better', to suppress poor inner-city public houses and build spacious new pubs in the suburbs. In Brighton, by the late 1920s, the brewers had agreed with the Justices that the pubs compensated each year for losing their licences should relate to the numbers owned by each firm. Often the onus was on the brewers to volunteer pubs for compensation, as happened in Portsmouth, where from 1932 the brewers put forward an annual shortlist for closure, from which the Justices would make their choice. A total of 154 licensed houses (all but thirty of them beerhouses) closed in Portsmouth between the wars, only ten licences being transferred to new premises.[35]

The brewers co-operated because it was in their interests to do so. Alcohol consumption, which had briefly revived after the end of the war, was in decline, and beer production effectively halved between 1920 and 1933. Beer strength increases were allowed at the end of the war but then went down again. This was a response to public demand. Society was becoming more sober and respectable, and taste veered away from strong beers. There were many competing alternatives for people's time and spending power: the cinema, rambling, cycling, sport and the radio all enjoyed huge popularity and the pub needed to improve its facilities to attract custom. The changing circumstances were reflected not only in new pub construction, and the reconstruction of existing ones (something like a quarter of the pub stock was altered or rebuilt between 1920 and 1939) but also in the dramatic concentration in the brewing industry. The number of brewers declined from 3,650 in 1914 to 885 in 1939 as companies merged with or took over their rivals.

The temperance movement, so strong before 1914, was no longer a threat by the late 1920s. Many of its

2.35 The Spinners Arms, Cummersdale, near Carlisle, 1930, in a very different style from the Cumberland Inn, this time Vernacular Revival, inspired by southern models.

7675    The Dun Cow, Dersingham

**2.36** Improvement in the countryside. This postcard shows the Dun Cow, Dersingham, Norfolk, rebuilt in 1937 on improved lines with spacious accommodation for both drinkers and the licensee, and a function room (right). What it replaced is shown in 1.18.

**2.37** The Pheasant, Wood End, Wednesfield, West Midlands, designed in 1935 by O M Weller of the Holt Brewery, Birmingham, as an improved public house to which respectable middle-class families might be attracted. Either side of the pub are children's playgrounds (beige); behind are two lawns and at the rear a bowling green flanked by two rose gardens. The blue area is a lily pond.

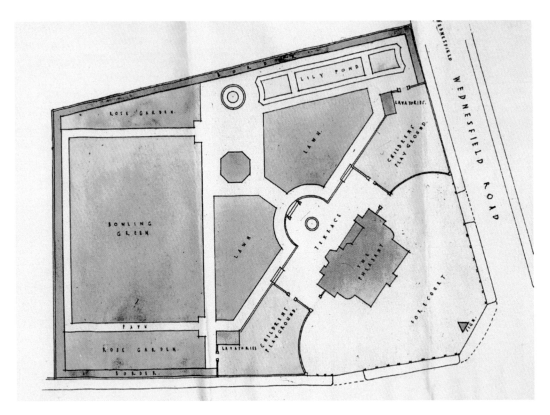

more moderate aspirations had been met, for example, the limiting of opening hours and the appearance of the improved public house as the model for civilised drinking. More hardline campaigners had lost almost all credibility as the result of events in America. In 1919 the Volstead Act had forbidden the production, sale and consumption of alcohol throughout the United States; the result was a disaster for the prohibitionists, as gangsters made vast profits from the sale of illegal alcohol and the running of unlicensed bars and clubs. The Act was repealed in 1933 – the 'noble experiment' had been a failure.

## The Second World War and its aftermath

Unlike the First World War, the civilian population was heavily involved in the second great conflict, and the Government recognised that maintaining supplies of drink was essential for morale. Pub closures, other than through enemy action – 106 licensed premises had been destroyed in Portsmouth alone by February 1942 – were effectively suspended. So, too, was the opening of new ones. In Northampton there were three schemes for pub alterations in 1940, then nothing for the rest of the war.[36] Scarce resources could not be diverted to pub construction.

Occasionally brewers were allowed to transfer licences from destroyed pubs to new premises which were conversions of existing buildings. A few prefabricated 'Mulberry pubs' were put up in south-coast towns to serve the troops assembling in late 1943 and early 1944 for the Normandy landings. After victory in 1945 pubs were a low priority: indeed, the Cambridge Hotel in Portsmouth was hailed as the first new post-war pub on the entire south coast when it opened in 1953. No new pub was planned in Northampton until 1954. Public house numbers continued to decline until the early 1960s and then remained more or less constant. The decline was due more to social change than action by the magistrates, who did not reactivate the inter-war campaign for the licence reductions.

The beerhouse and the improved public house were both casualties of the war. The beerhouse took a while to die. The 1947 Finance Act sealed its fate when it empowered Justices to accept the surrender of a single beerhouse licence in exchange for a new full licence nearby. For the brewers, this was a better deal than licensing benches had offered during the previous half-century and

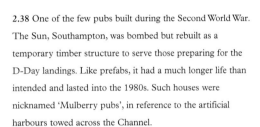

2.38 One of the few pubs built during the Second World War. The Sun, Southampton, was bombed but rebuilt as a temporary timber structure to serve those preparing for the D-Day landings. Like prefabs, it had a much longer life than intended and lasted into the 1980s. Such houses were nicknamed 'Mulberry pubs', in reference to the artificial harbours towed across the Channel.

2.39–2.42 They are no more. Many pubs retain the evidence of long-gone breweries. Mackesons of Hythe were taken over by Jude Hanbury of Wateringbury, Kent, c1920, Fremlins of Maidstone by Whitbread in 1967, and the Birkenhead Brewery merged with Threlfalls in 1962. Brewing on the premises, like Roberts of Ruthin, North Wales, has almost entirely gone, although the practice has undergone something of a revival in the past two decades.

beerhouses closed in large numbers. The odd beerhouse hung on anachronistically, but virtually all had gone by 1970.[37]

The improved public house was a victim of changing public tastes rather than legislation. The decline in pub going, already apparent before the war, accelerated. When building could begin again there was little demand for the large roadhouse or the wide range of facilities which it had offered. The growth of television from the 1950s meant that people were more likely to stay at home than visit the pub, unless to obtain a few bottles to enjoy on the sofa.

The brewing industry went through a phase of rapid concentration between 1955 and 1972, with the emergence of the 'Big Six' – Allied, Bass Charrington, Courage, Scottish and Newcastle, Watney Mann, and

Whitbread – who, between them, owned over half the country's pubs. The adoption by these companies of corporate liveries and of 'house styles' in interior design did much to make the character of pubs much the same.

This concentration of ownership led to inquiries by the Monopolies Commission (1966–9), the Erroll Committee (1972) and the Monopolies and Mergers Commission (1987–9). All criticised the tied house system for limiting competition and customer choice. The 1987–9 inquiry recommended that no brewer should have a tied estate of more than 2,000 pubs, that pubs in excess of this number should be sold, and that landlords should be allowed to purchase a guest ale from anyone they wished. These proposals formed the basis for the Supply of Beer (Tied Estate) Order 1989 – the so-called 'Beer Orders'.

2.43 The March Hare, Crowhill, Ashton-under-Lyne, Greater Manchester. A utilitarian, three-room pub of 1959–60 for a housing estate. It is much smaller than an inter-war counterpart (see 3.63–3.64) would have been.

As with the Beer Act of 1830, supporters of the Beer Orders were genuinely expecting beneficial results. Unfortunately, as in 1830, the results were very different from the predictions. The large brewers

either split their brewing activities and their tied estates into separate companies, or sold off their breweries to concentrate on their tied houses. In either case, the outcome was the same; the creation of pub-owning property companies which were not subject to the Beer Orders. The largest ones have come to control huge numbers of pubs.[38] The effect was to constrict customer choice even more, as the public house companies ('pubcos') sought large-volume, low-cost beers to sell in their pubs, whilst long-established breweries, cut adrift from their tied houses, closed in numbers. Many less profitable traditional pubs were shut down since the pubcos, unlike the breweries, had no interest in them as outlets for their beers. In December 2002, in a tacit acceptance that they were no longer relevant, the Beer Orders were rescinded.

Changes in the structure of the industry coincided with liberalisation of licensing laws. In 1971 the Erroll Committee had proposed that licences should be easier to obtain, that opening hours should be more flexible, and that children should have more access to pubs. Some of the  recommendations were tested in Scotland. In 1976 the Licensing (Scotland) Act introduced longer opening hours throughout the week, and restored Sunday opening for the first time in 120 years. In Wales Sunday closure of pubs had already been modified in 1961 by the introduction of a system of local referenda. As a result, Sunday closure gradually vanished, the last area to vote to go 'wet' being Dwyfor in Gwynedd in 1996 (local referenda were finally abolished by the Licensing Act of 2003). The 1988 Licensing Act allowed all pubs in England and Wales to open between 11 am and 11 pm during the week, and extended Sunday lunchtime opening by an hour. In August 1995 the requirement to close on Sunday afternoons was abolished altogether, although evening closing time remains at 10.30 pm, half an hour earlier than on weekdays.

2.44 An uninspiring, newly built interior of 1959. The public bar at Ind Coope's Hulstone, Crackley Bank, Newcastle-under-Lyme. 'Here', as the brewery publicity said, 'men from the surrounding estate of 1,000 houses can bring their wives and families in the evenings to enjoy a drink and a game of skittles, or darts.'

While the 1988 Act removed restrictions imposed in 1921, the Licensing Act of 2003 was far more revolutionary and about to come into force when the first edition of this book was published. The innovations it ushered in are discussed in chapter 8 (p173) where various other changes affecting the pub since 2004 – such as a smoking ban, the punitive increase in beer duty, and increasing numbers of closures – are described.

## Chapter 3

# Designing and Planning the Pub

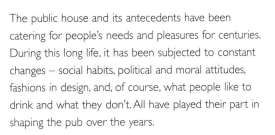

The public house and its antecedents have been catering for people's needs and pleasures for centuries. During this long life, it has been subjected to constant changes – social habits, political and moral attitudes, fashions in design, and, of course, what people like to drink and what they don't. All have played their part in shaping the pub over the years.

**3.1** The drinking lobby at the Swan with Two Necks, Stockport. The front door (at the centre of the picture) leads into a corridor which broadens out in front of the servery. There is space for half a dozen customers to sit although many will prefer to stand. The pub was rebuilt *c*1930 and the panelling is typical of its time.

In this chapter we look at various aspects of the architecture of pubs and the way they were planned. Thousands of them are buildings of considerable age and importance which were either not built as pubs or housed the pub element as a subsidiary activity. As suggested in the previous chapters, a distinctive architecture for pubs (as opposed to inns) did not really emerge until the early 19th century, and there are virtually no significant surviving internal fittings and layouts from earlier times. The emphasis here, therefore, is upon pub architecture and planning as they developed from the 19th century, and especially on those aspects which are still detectable and can be appreciated today, despite the avalanche of change since about 1970.

## The basic pub

At their simplest, early public houses were literally that – ordinary houses that happened to have rooms which were open to the public for the consumption of drink. Pub keeping was a family business and, especially in the country, was often supplemented by other strands of income to produce a livelihood. Apart from passing travellers, the customers (and what they drank) would have come from the immediate neighbourhood. This is quite unlike a pub at the start of the 21st century which is a highly specialised establishment for the supply of drink and food (perhaps in reverse order), aiming at a high throughput in a large trading area, selling non-local drink, and typically, run by a tenant or manager of a large pub company whose head office is far away.

The physical arrangements for these two types of establishments are obviously very different. The traditional one requires no more than a place to store drink, someone to serve it, and a room or two for the customers to consume it. Its 21st-century successor needs substantial space with all parts visible from the servery, cellarage below ground, bar staff, cleaners, a kitchen and people to cook in it, specialised equipment to keep drinks cool, a car park, and so on.

Pubs of the former kind existed in vast numbers and were once the typical pub type. Now they have nearly all gone as their owners have died or given up the trade. Visually, of course, such pubs tend to be extremely plain. At the extreme is a Scottish example, the Railway Tavern, Kincardine (1.8–1.9), where the existence of the pub is indicated only by a few letters on a keystone over the doorway in a row of terraced houses. Likewise the Sun Inn at Leintwardine, Herefordshire (3.6–3.7), is also part of a humble terrace but the pub sign at least creates a little more expectation of drink within. The Sun (extended 2011) originally had a single room, basically furnished, with drink being brought from the kitchen. Another simple survivor was until 2005 the last remaining beerhouse, the Seven Stars at Halfway House, Shropshire (2.5–2.6), where the single public room moved up a notch from the domestic simplicity of the Sun; bold lettering outside advertised its presence and a couple of high-backed settles focused drinkers on a fireplace in the middle of the wall.[1]

In urban areas, commercial pressures mean that very few of these small, simple pubs survive. An exceptional survival in the heart of Manchester is the Circus Tavern (3.8) which amounts to no more than two rooms with basic Victorian fittings; the servery is a tiny counter inserted under the stairs around 1930. A great many urban pubs, like shops, were sited on street corners to give prominence to their businesses. The simpler ones differed little from the adjoining premises but where the developer had extra ambitions and the money to support them, an extra storey might often be built and a little embellishment added.

3.2 Unmistakably a pub. The Crow's Nest, Salmon Lane, in London's East End. It is now a private house but the former purpose is clear from the advertising fascia between the floors, the recessed panel for more advertising, multiple entrances (corner one blocked) and touches of embellishment that mark it out from the rest of the terrace. This small pub was built in the early/mid-19th century but the ground floor was probably remodelled in the 1920s. It was a beerhouse until 1952 and ceased trading about 1962. It takes its name from William Crow who kept it in the 1870s.

3.3 Rural pubs were usually simple affairs. The Cider House, Defford, Worcestershire, is one of the last-remaining four cider-only houses. Service is at the hatch left of the barrel, and the main bar is the garden – at least in good weather. The alternative drinking area is the old bakehouse (far left). Sadly, after 140 years of family ownership closure is expected to take place in 2011.

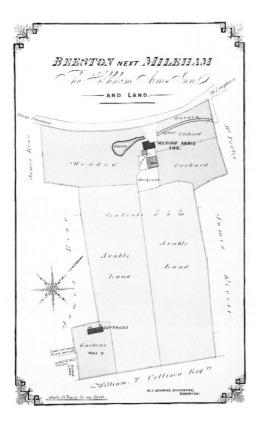

3.4 (left) The pub as part of a diverse business. The Holkham Arms, Beeston-next-Mileham, Norfolk, shown on a plan of c1880 with its surrounding farmland. This is taken from one of eight books of Bullard and Sons' estate plans in the Norfolk Record Office.

3.5 (below) Very few pubs now operate in tandem with another business. An exception is the Harrington Arms, Gawsworth, Cheshire, which is adjacent to and until 2007 part of a working farm.

3.6–3.7 The Sun Inn, Leintwardine, Herefordshire. Only a simple sign advertises the presence of a pub. The right-hand door is into the pub. The original public room is to the right of the doorway and very simply appointed.

## The rise of the Victorian pub

The distinctive public house architecture that emerged in the 19th century culminated in the great boom of pub building a few years either side of 1900. This brief period might be regarded as the golden age of the pub, at least in England. The larger pubs from that time, with their glitz and glitter, are still often spoken of as 'gin palaces' – a handy label, even though not functionally accurate. It is, however, a telling reminder that the Victorian public house in its most exotic form is a descendant of the true gin palaces, memorably described by Charles Dickens in chapter 22 of *Sketches by Boz* (1836). He found the 'handsomest in London' in the areas of greatest 'filth and squalid misery' and takes his readers off to the 'narrow streets and dirty courts' that divide Drury Lane from Oxford Street with their 'wretched houses with broken windows patched with rags and paper'. Dickens then goes on:

> ... turn a corner. What a change! All is light and brilliancy. The hum of many voices from that splendid gin-shop ... with the fantastically ornamented parapet, the illuminated clock, the plate-glass windows surrounded by stucco rosettes, and the profusion of gas-lights in richly-gilt burners, is perfectly dazzling ...

3.8 (left) The Circus Tavern and the Grey Horse are remarkable survivals of small urban pubs in the very centre of Manchester. The Circus still has its Victorian two-room layout and fittings.

3.9 (right) An Italianate façade was very popular for pub designers and owners in the 19th century. This is the Washington, Hampstead, London.

The interior is even gayer ... A bar of French-polished mahogany, elegantly carved, extends the whole width of the place, and there are two side-aisles of great casks, painted green and gold, ... and bearing such inscriptions, as 'Old Tom [gin], 549'; 'Young Tom, 360'; 'Samson, 1421' – the figures agreeing [denoting], we presume with 'gallons'.

Gin palaces, then, offered flashy, exuberant surroundings aimed at contrasting, as far as possible, with the drab, harsh world of everyday life. For a writer in the *Architectural Magazine* of June 1834, while most architects exhibited 'good taste', the 'gin-temple builders ... have shaken off all rules and trammels ... He who most lavishly bestows plate glass and gilding, together with a happy corruption or combination of all the three Grecian orders into one, is ... the most likely to insure [sic] success to himself in these gin-drinking times.'

**3.10** (left) The Palace Hotel, Bristol, and its mix of French and Italianate motifs.

**3.11** (right) The polychromatic Star of the East brings colour to Limehouse in London's East End. Built about 1865, the use of full-blown, High Victorian Gothic is most unusual in a pub.

Public houses – brash and convivial and (in the 19th century) essentially working class – were a far cry from the polite architectural world of the church or the country house. As Victorian industry and transport developed, a hitherto unimaginable variety of materials became available to pub builders and furnishers at prices which fell in real terms from the 1840s. Cut, etched and coloured glass, mahogany, teak, polished granite, tiles and mosaics all found their way into the Victorian pub. There were also unprecedented stylistic possibilities. Unlike previous ages, Victorian Britain had no original architectural style of its own, or rather, as the architect and critic, Robert Kerr observed in 1864, it had 'a very novel one' the style of 'miscellaneous connoisseurship'.[2] There was everything to choose from – classical or medieval, Renaissance or Baroque, Italian or French, or, for something a little more unusual, perhaps a touch of Byzantine or Scots Baronial.

For pubs which were meant to be more than a plain brick box, the most popular architectural dress was something sub-Italianate (3.9). But where money was available there certainly were some exotic flowerings, such as the French Renaissance-cum-Italian palazzo Palace Hotel in Bristol of 1869–70. Very occasionally Gothic made an appearance in the 1860s and 1870s as at the Hollywood, West Brompton, or the Star of the East, Limehouse, in London's grim East End. But such medievalising was rare indeed. This was no doubt due to the fact that, particularly since the polemical writings of Pugin, Gothic was inextricably linked with Christian religion, many of whose followers were vehemently opposed to the whole notion of alcohol and the pub. The secular architecture of the Italian palazzo transported to Britain's grey climes was much safer.

Pubs may not have been at the cutting edge of architectural progress but their design did broadly follow general trends in style and fashion. Second-rank architects could easily keep up with what was happening in the wider world through the abundant pages of the trade press, professional associations and the ease of travel. So it was that Gothic, little used for pubs in the first place, was abandoned as the style

**3.12** The extraordinary architectural confection that is the King's Head, Tooting, London, was put up in 1896 to designs by W M Brutton, a prolific pub architect.

**3.13** The Marlborough, Sparkbrook, Birmingham, 1900, one of the many brick and terracotta pubs put up in the city around this time: architect W Jenkins. The flanking working-class housing has gone, giving the pub an isolated appearance.

became one for religious buildings alone from the mid-1870s. The Italianate, palazzo-derived designs of mid-Victorian work were largely abandoned. Instead there developed a bold eclecticism in British architecture in general and in pub design in particular.

## The architects

Those who designed public houses were not the leading architects of the day.[3] The simpler establishments were, like ordinary houses, the work of local builders. Those that were architect-designed were by local men in general practice, whose output in a typical year might entail working- or middle-class housing, some shops, a factory extension and a board school. The names of those who designed even the greatest pubs of the golden age are unfamiliar to most architectural historians.

There were, however, firms and individuals who developed a speciality of public houses within their more general practices, especially at the end of the century, when the scale and quality of building pubs demanded particular talents. In Birmingham in about 1900, for example, the practices of James and Lister Lea and Wood and Kendrick were responsible between them for a series of imposing red brick and terracotta pubs which form such a distinctive feature of many a street corner. In Aston, the Lea practice built the most magnificent of all surviving West Midlands pubs, the lavishly appointed Bartons Arms in Birmingham (1900–1; job architect Mr Brassington: 5.25). At the same time, practices such as W M Brutton, Shoebridge and Rising, Eedle and Meyers, and Treadwell and Martin, were all busy designing for the great London pub boom. The designs are immensely varied: in a single year, 1896, they ranged from Brutton's extraordinary Franco-Italian-Indo-Saracenic confection at the King's Head, Tooting, of 1896 to Treadwell and Martin's restrained, refined Flemish façade at the Rising Sun, Tottenham Court Road. Pub design also started to come under the influence of the Olde English Revival. The style had been recreated to picturesque effect in the 1860s and 1870s, notably by Eden Nesfield, Norman Shaw and George Devey, and was widely used for houses both great and small. Surprisingly, it seems to have taken some time to appear in pubs, but its nostalgic use of half-timbering was ideally suited for conjuring up romantic notions of old English inns and Merrie England (3.47, 3.49). The popularity of what became known as 'brewers' Tudor' was thus assured, and pubs sporting carved barge-boards, half-timbered gables and bars lined with 16th-century-looking panelling were to appear in countless towns and villages. Its popularity was at its height in the 1920s and 1930s.

## Internal planning

Just as the architecture of the public house has gone through many changes, so has the way it is planned and fitted out. It is fair to describe the contemporary pub designer's normal brief as one demanding a large, single space with good supervision of all parts. There may be token differentiation between areas by means of, say, some booths for seating or a raised area but it will be minimal. The same price for drink applies throughout the pub and customers will mingle freely throughout it. Such a vision of a pub is completely at odds with that familiar to pub owners and their customers a century ago.

One of the simplest and earliest means of profession-alising the pub was the introduction of the bar counter. Early drawings of alehouses and taverns often show slightly chaotic scenes as bringing drink from a distance was an inefficient means of service. The bar counter, well established by the early 19th century and put to good use in true gin shops and gin palaces, provided not only separation of the customer side from the storage and serving side, but also swifter service. Drinks and glasses could be stored under it or behind it. Beer could now be efficiently served by hand-pumps mounted upon the counter, or drawn from casks stillaged behind it. However, the arrival of the counter did not entirely supplant the earlier 'bar', which survived in pubs where rapid service was not essential. The Cornish Inn (3.14) was one of several Sheffield pubs where as late as 1900 there was no counter.

The servery could take a number of different shapes but its essential purpose remained the same – to provide an easy and convenient way of dispensing drinks. In the simplest pubs it might involve just a

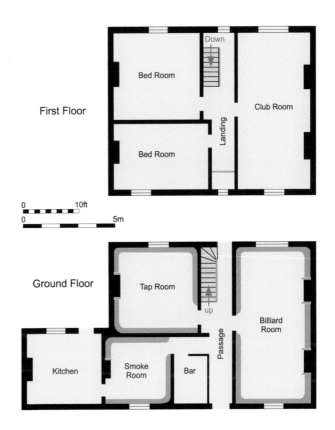

**3.14** The Cornish Inn, Sheffield, 1900. Service would have been from the 'Bar' but there is no counter. The billiard room takes up more space than the other two public drinking rooms.

**3.15** In this plan of 1896 for the Blue Posts, St James's, London, the central servery gives access to all the drinking spaces. The screens divide public bar areas from one another in this tiny pub. Such fragmentation was a particular feature of Victorian and Edwardian London pubs. The Red Lion (5.15) not far away in Duke of York Street still retains much of a similar plan.

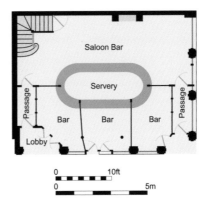

**3.16** This screen at the Nova Scotia, Bristol, separates the 'private bar' from the larger public one. Basic screens like this one, once extremely common, are now very rare.

**3.17** Plan for the King David, Bristol, 1892. Drinkers of lower social (and financial) status would have used one or other of the public bars which are separated by a screen. The smoke room was a better room, no doubt emphasising seated drinking. A lunch room was provided, again for the better-off.

straight counter across one end of a room. Where there were two rooms it might straddle both. Where the layout of the pub became more complex, it might be found at the core of a number of rooms. The staff could circulate from one room to another, drawing upon a central supply of drinks. In pubs in London and a few other major centres an island servery was sometimes to be found in the later 19th century. In the 1840s one was designed by Brunel for the refreshment room at Swindon station where large numbers of people had to be served quickly during a brief stop in their journeys. In a pub context such a counter was surrounded by a series of compartments and the serving area had at its centre a fitting or 'stillion' for glasses, bottles and other items. Many such features survive, especially in London, even though the compartments around the counter have invariably gone.

## Pub rooms and their uses

Although some very small, simple establishments may have had only one public room, a defining characteristic of pub planning as it developed in the 19th century (at least in England and Wales) was the provision of a number of separate rooms or divided-off areas. The requirement for several rooms or compartments implies a very different set of attitudes towards drinking and socialising from those prevalent today. There was a distinct hierarchy of spaces which

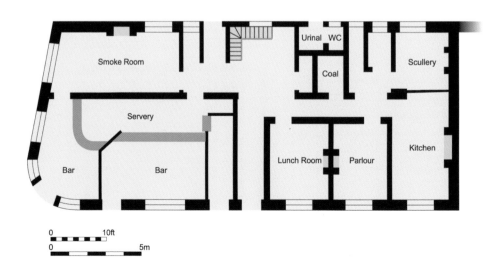

reflected subtle variations and affiliations in social groupings and status. Pubs were very largely patronised by men – of the working classes or, at best, the lower middle classes. The public bar would be the haunt of the poor and labourers, the better rooms, perhaps, of skilled workers, clerks, or shopkeepers sometimes even accompanied by their wives. Prices varied accordingly; such differential pricing was still normal in the 1960s but as pubs were opened up it disappeared and was almost non-existent by the end of the 20th century.[4]

The rooms had a variety of names. The cheapest, lowest status room and hence the most basically appointed was the 'public bar'. It was known by other names such as the 'vault(s)' or simply 'bar'. Sometimes there were two or even more public bars separated by screens or walling. A variant in the north, found in Sheffield, Bradford and Hull, is the 'dram shop'. Originally a room where people stood and drank gin or other spirits, it appeared in the 1830s as publicans sought to combat the competition from the growing numbers of beerhouses by concentrating on the sale of spirits. Norfolk inventories of the 1840s often refer to the bar as the 'shop', which again implies that it was used chiefly for stand-up drinking.[5]

A great many pubs had what was known as a 'private bar' where a casual visitor would no doubt have felt decidedly unwelcome. It was not necessarily any better appointed than the public bar but it implied exclusiveness, designed to restrict entry to all but a certain group of regulars. In East Anglia and parts of the north it was more commonly known as the 'bar parlour', and was typically entered by a doorway behind the bar counter, to underline the special status of those allowed access. In London, however, the term 'bar parlour' was more often used to describe an office or private room for the landlord behind the servery. A rare, if not unique, variant of the public bar/private bar terminology is near London's Fleet Street at the Seven Stars where the etched glass on the doors refers to 'General Counter' and

3.18–3.19 A variation on the public bar/private bar theme. Doors at the Seven Stars, Carey Street, behind the Royal Courts of Justice in London.

3.20 The Perseverance Tavern, Norwich: plan from the 1890s showing a porter room. The premises also included a bakery and a shop.

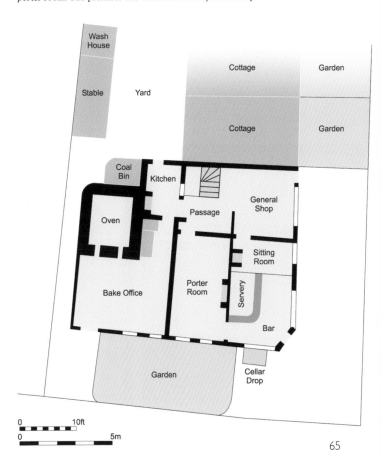

'Private Counter' (3.18–3.19). 'Tap room' is a term found in most, if not all parts of England a century ago, although the term 'porter room' seems to have been preferred in parts of East Anglia until the First World War (see, for example, the plan of the Perseverance Tavern, Norwich 3.20). The derivation of the name is unclear. It appears in the 18th century, and suggests a room where liquor was drawn off, but, by the mid-19th century, this was certainly no longer the case. Study of dozens of plans from across the country in the preparation of this book showed that the tap room or porter room was always at a slight, and often, considerable remove from the servery.[6]

Moving upmarket, we find 'smoke room' (occasionally 'smoking room'), 'lounge' and 'saloon' commonly occurring throughout England. They all imply somewhat more relaxed drinking and refined surroundings than in the public bar: indeed smoke/smoking room suggests

3.21 Door sign for the tap room at the Tucker's Grave Inn, Faulkland, Somerset. Dating from the early 19th century, if not the late 18th, this is surely among the earliest pub lettering in the country. It survived because, at some point, it was covered by a screwed-on sign.

the transfer to the pub of a term from grand houses where such a room was intended for gentlemen to take their ease. The saloon appears to have originated in the latter part of the 19th century and implied a large and fairly luxuriously appointed room, even perhaps with easy chairs and potted plants: such were the saloons at the grand London pubs-cum-hotels, the Crown (now Crocker's Folly), St John's Wood (3.32), and the Salisbury, Harringay (3.27). The names 'news room' and 'commercial room' also applied to better-class rooms, especially in the north-west. The latter is a vivid reminder that pubs with letting bedrooms used to be the most likely lodging place for commercial travellers and other business people on the move. In market towns there is sometimes a 'market room', no doubt for traders to foregather. Both the Lord Palmerston, Northampton (1895), and the Black Horse, Preston (1898), had such rooms and both are near their respective towns' marketplaces.

Coffee rooms sometimes make an appearance, for example, in window glass at the Holly Bush, Hampstead, London, the Romping Cat, Bloxwich, West Midlands, and the East Kent, Whitstable, Kent. Such rooms were intended to attract the more genteel customer with other things than alcohol on the mind. When the Lion in the Strand reopened in 1897 as the New Dublin House (a precursor to the Irish theme pub?), the smoke room offered clients 'pens, ink, and paper thrown in "free, gratis, for nothing" '.

Many pubs had a 'club room' or 'assembly room' – usually situated on the first floor for meetings or other private gatherings. Such rooms first appeared in the later 18th century, but soon became a typical feature. They are a reminder of how much the pub functioned as a social centre, and the headquarters for a huge range of clubs and societies, before the First World War. An alternative to the club room was the 'music room', 'concert room' or 'singing room', again normally on the first floor. The concert room first appeared in pubs in London and in Manchester in the 1830s, and by the 1850s had spread to other major urban centres. By this date some pubs were concentrating on providing musical entertainment to draw in customers; some of them evolved into that late Victorian phenomenon, the music hall (4.43–4.44).

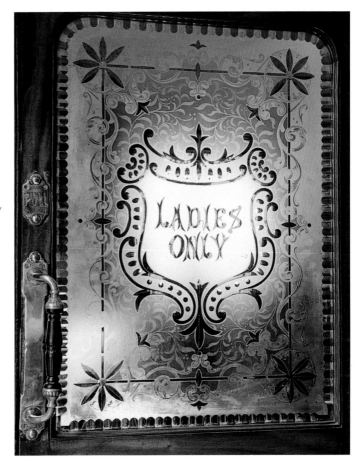

3.26 A few pubs had ladies' only rooms. This door glass is at the Mitre in Bayswater, London, and probably dates from the 1890s. (See also the plan of the Crown, St John's Wood, 3.32.)

3.22–3.25 Edwardian door glass naming rooms at the Victoria, Great Harwood, Lancashire. The public kitchen was probably just that – a place where families with poor kitchen facilities could have meals cooked.

Competition for customers during the 19th century was intense, with many more pubs than exist today competing for the patronage of a far smaller population. Publicans sought to provide facilities which would not only tempt in more customers, but also persuade them to stay longer (and spend their money). Billiard tables were very popular, despite the legal insistence that not only should billiards not be played on a Sunday, but that any room containing a billiard table should be locked out of use on that day.[7]

**3.27** The 'grand saloon' at the Salisbury, Harringay, London, 1898–9. This mosaic-floored space leads from a front entrance, past the counter on the left and drinking booths on the right to the former billiard room beyond the doors in the background. Note the spittoon trough in front of the counter for cigarette ends and other sundry waste. They were still being installed in pubs after the Second World War (see also 4.27).

**3.28** (opposite) The skylight over the former billiard room at the Salisbury, Harringay.

For this reason the table had a specific room allocated to it, the 'billiard room' (occasionally 'billiard saloon'), which again was often on the first floor. Few full-sized tables survive today but the large top-lit spaces are still recognisable in many late Victorian and Edwardian pubs. Games such as long-alley skittles (4.51) or quoits (4.61), required their own specialised space, usually separated a little way from the main pub rooms (for more about games in the pub, see chapter 4).

**3.29** A small snug at Ye Cracke, Liverpool, ideal for intense discussions about the conduct of the Boer War.

Over the years certain rooms or parts of many pubs have attracted nicknames from their regulars. Benches which attract the most elderly drinkers have, predictably, often been dubbed 'death row'; examples are at the Three Horseshoes, Whitwick, Leicestershire, and the Star, Bath. The small snug known as the 'War Office' at the Ye Cracke, Liverpool, got its name, it is said, from the deliberations by customers on the progress (or otherwise) of the Boer War. At the Waggon and Horses at Langsett, South Yorkshire, a tiny circular room where the regulars played dominoes and crib, acquired the lugubrious name of the 'Dog 'ole'.[8]

## Laying out the rooms and separating the drinkers

The disposition of rooms varied enormously. Representative examples are given in the plans presented here. As might be expected, there are some regional fashions, especially among pubs in Scotland and Northern Ireland, which follow very different traditions and are outlined in chapter 6. Here we can only highlight some key points about English pub planning. Generally speaking the public bar (or whatever name was used) is in the most conspicuous part of the pub, at the front and/or on a corner. The 'better' rooms, aiming at a slightly higher level of privacy and refinement, tend to be a little more tucked away. Also, and for the same reason, they were often planned with less of a prominent bar counter in order to reduce the amount of stand-up drinking, something generally frowned upon by the authorities. Many rooms of this type had no counter at all and were served via a hatch, or by waiters whose important role we will examine in the next chapter.

The separation of one drinking area from another was often by means of screens rather than a solid wall. Pubs in London had some of the most extreme compartmentalisation, being divided up by timber and glass screens into very small drinking areas. Nothing like it seems to have existed in other major urban centres. No ready explanation presents itself although it just may be a hangover from the coffee houses discussed in the first chapter, where small groups of people sought their own spaces.

### Numbering the rooms

Close inspection of many pubs will reveal numbers on, over or beside doors. '1' might be the public bar, '2' the smoke room, '3' the cellar and so on. Until recently it was a legal requirement for every licensee to make 'entry' of his premises with HM Customs and Excise, so that they could check that his premises complied with the law.[9] This involved listing all the rooms used for the storage or sale of alcohol. Whereas rooms might be marked by their names (public bar, cellar, etc), very often they were denoted by number, or, sometimes (particularly around Liverpool), letters.

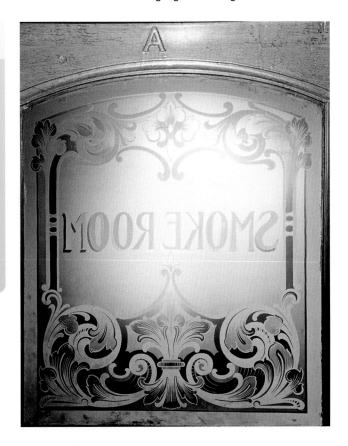

**3.30** Door to the smoke room at the Villa Tavern, Nechells, Birmingham, with a letter 'A' above the glass.

**3.31** Door to the vaults at the Coopers Arms, Nottingham, the room being identified to the Excise as number 4.

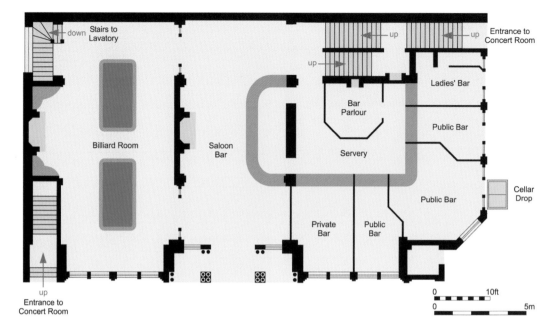

Stairs to
Lavatory

Entrance to
Concert Room

down

up

up

up

Ladies' Bar

Bar
Parlour

Public Bar

Billiard Room

Saloon
Bar

Servery

Public Bar

Cellar
Drop

Private
Bar

Public
Bar

0        10ft
0          5m

up
Entrance to
Concert Room

**3.32** Plan for the Crown, St John's Wood, London, dated 1897: architect C H Worley. Five drinking areas (including a ladies' bar) cluster round the right-hand part of the servery, divided from one another by wood and glass partitions, which have all now been swept away. The saloon bar is particularly grand with a marble fireplace and marble-topped counter. As so often with pubs around 1900, much space is devoted to billiards. The Crown doubled as an hotel and had a restaurant and concert room upstairs.

**3.33** Five drinking compartments radiate from the servery at the Prince Alfred in Maida Vale, London: this is the best-surviving example of an arrangement that was very prevalent in Victorian London pubs. Unlike the Blue Posts (3.15), where the servery is an island, here it projects, like a peninsula from the rear wall. The counter was refronted during a refurbishment in 2001.

The overwhelming majority of such London screenwork has been swept away on the tide of changing fashions. The best surviving example is undoubtedly at the Prince Alfred, Maida Vale (c1898), where screens divide the main body of the pub into no less than five compartments radiating from a finger-shaped servery which protrudes out from the back wall. Another remarkable survival is at the Argyll Arms near Oxford Circus (c1895) which has three compartments between a corridor and the parallel servery and divided from one another by impressive screens of timber and etched and cut glass. The smallest known drinking boxes are the two attached to the counter at the Barley Mow, Marylebone, and which look like an absurdly high version of box-pews in a Georgian church. They can accommodate four or five people at a squeeze and their miniscule size has led to an interesting explanation which we examine on p 170. Such 'snugs' tended to be viewed with some suspicion by the authorities and respectable opinion, and were certainly being cleared out, along with screenwork, before the Second World War.[10]

A feature found particularly in northern pubs on both sides of the Pennines (although it seems to have originated on the western side) is a 'drinking lobby' or a 'drinking corridor'. Dedicated to stand-up drinking with perhaps the odd table and chair, it takes several

**3.34–3.35** The two tiny drinking boxes at the Barley Mow, Marylebone, London, show how Victorian and Edwardian customers liked to drink in privacy and, evidently, in very close proximity to their companions.

**3.36** Outside London people seemed less preoccupied with small, separate drinking spaces. At the Mitre Tavern, Bristol, there were just short screens projecting from the counter plus one 'better room'. The parlour would have been part of the publican's private accommodation, although a few close friends might be invited in from time to time.

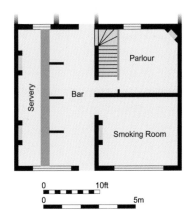

forms. It may involve an opened-out corridor in front of a servery, as at the Hare and Hounds, Manchester, the Swan, Clementhorpe, York, and the Swan with Two Necks, Stockport (3.1). Alternatively, it may consist of an L-shaped corridor wrapping round a public bar and being provided with several hatches through which drinks are served (excellent Merseyside examples are the Stork, Birkenhead, and the Lion, Liverpool, both from the very early 1900s). Even the mighty Philharmonic in Liverpool has what amounts to a large drinking lobby in front of the servery since most of the other rooms radiate off it. The lobby performs a similar function at the Three Pigeons, Halifax, a far smaller pub refitted around 1930 in Art Deco style.

3.37 (left) The Lion, Liverpool, very early 1900s. The L-shaped corridor embraces the public bar and is, itself, used for drinking. Service is at the hatches. The L-shaped corridor/public bar plan is found at several other street-corner pubs on Merseyside and it is thought to reflect a requirement of police supervision: officers had to be able to walk right through the pub, entering at one door and leaving by another.

3.38 The corridor at the Garden Gate, Hunslet, Leeds, seen at a quiet time of day. The only drinkers are gathered round a service hatch.

The drinking lobby remained a feature of pub planning in Lancashire and Yorkshire until the Second World War. All over the country there are much simpler arrangements of a corridor and a hatch which are pressed into service for a stand-up drink. Drinking in corridors or lobbies might seem a last resort, yet it is not uncommon to find a pub with the more comfortable rooms deserted and a cluster of men (it is usually men) in the drinking lobby or standing beside a service hatch. Such was the situation at the Garden Gate, Leeds, when the picture 3.38 was taken. Drinking lobbies are associated with northern pubs but they can be found elsewhere too. When the Old Green Tree in Bath was refitted in 1928 by the Lamb Brewery of Frome, it received a two-room-and-lobby plan just like the Manchester, York and Stockport examples. A fine southern example of a drinking corridor is at the Seymour Arms, Witham Friary, Somerset, of around 1866 where the area in front of the glazed screen always fills up first.

3.39 Corridor drinking in the south: the Seymour Arms, Witham Friary, Somerset, viewed from the main door. Drinks are served at the end of the corridor. Many customers will remain there standing or perched on the stools. The pub and its fittings date from c1866 when it was built by the Duke of Somerset (family name, Seymour) as part of his estate.

3.40 The outdoor department at the Coach and Horses, Salford, probably early 1920s. Customers would be served at the glazed hatch windows. They could make the most of the visit by enjoying a drink on the bench before returning home. Most of those on the bench would probably have been women.

## For consumption off the premises

An important difference between a pub today and one a century ago concerns off-sales. Nowadays people buy their needs at the supermarket, high street off-licences, occasionally a corner shop, and not infrequently, given the present duty differences between the UK and the Continent, from French hypermarkets – but hardly ever the pub. A century or so ago, although licensed grocers took a substantial share of the trade following the Gladstone government's legislation of 1860 to open it up, many people obtained their alcohol supplies from the pub. Large numbers of pubs had a dedicated area for this trade, most commonly known as the 'jug and bottle' (or sometimes vice versa). It was even called the 'family department' (Victoria, Durham, 1899), 'outdoor department' (Seven Stars, Oldswinford, Stourbridge), or 'retail department' (Queen's Head, Limehouse, London).

Occasionally some were equipped with a bench or two, presumably to allow purchasers to fortify themselves for the journey back – indeed, to excess, according to the presiding magistrate at Carlisle in 1905 who added disapprovingly that: 'These places seem to be used principally by women.'[11] There are benches, for example, at the Painter's Arms, Luton (1913), and the Coach and Horses, Salford (1920s). The Globe Inn, Chagford, Devon, had snob-screens to give customers a little privacy. A little later, large inter-war urban pubs were occasionally built with a detached off-sales which resembled a shop: two good examples in London are at the Railway, Edgware (1931) and the Doctor Johnson, Barkingside, Ilford (1937: 3.64). Off-sales compartments were still being built in the 1950s and even 1960s when the rise of supermarket sales suddenly and rapidly transformed purchasing practices, making these redundant spaces. Some were pressed into service for storage purposes but many more were swept away and the area used to enlarge an existing drinking room. Even where lettered glass does not proclaim a former off-sales area, a supernumary doorway may be evidence of this long-lost and little-remembered function of the public house.

**3.41** The 'out-door' (now removed) at the Star and Garter, Wigston Magna, Leicestershire. Note the bell to attract attention.

**3.42** The pub was not the only place to buy drink to take home. In 1880 the *Licensed Victuallers' Gazette* (p 104) claimed that licensed grocers sell 'far more alcohol than publicans dispose of by retail'. The location of this grocers may be in south or east Yorkshire.

## Into the 20th century

By about 1900 pub architecture and fitting had reached its zenith. Pubs like the Philharmonic (1898–1900: 3.43, 5.43, 5.47, 5.58) and the Vines (1907: 5.56–5.57) in Liverpool, the Bartons Arms (1900–1: 5.25) in Birmingham, the Garden Gate (1903: 3.44, 5.14) in Leeds, the Golden Cross (1903: 6.3–6.5) in Cardiff, and the Princess Louise (refitted 1891: 5.18) and the Salisbury (1898: 3.27, 3.28, 5.59) in London were among the grandest ever built and can still be seen and enjoyed much as they were planned. The date range shows that pub building on a grand scale did continue into the first decade of the 20th century. However, such ambitious projects were in decline. The Edwardian years were ones of depression: in London things went very badly wrong as the property price bubble burst and investment was dramatically curtailed after 1899. Elsewhere the pub building spree was slower to tail off:

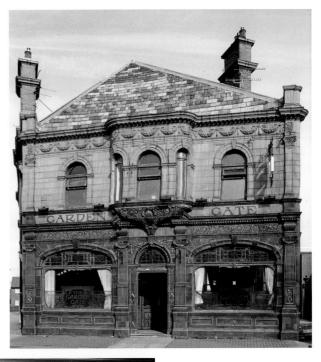

**3.43** (left) The Philharmonic, Liverpool, England's most magnificent public house, built in 1898–1900 for local brewer Robert Cain under his architect Walter Thomas. This vast inglenook leads off the mosaic-floored drinking lobby. Inscriptions name the figures in the glass as Robert Baden-Powell and Frederick Roberts whose military prowess was being much exercised in the Boer War as the pub went up. Cain built another spectacular Liverpool pub, the Vines, in 1907.

**3.44** (above) The Garden Gate, Hunslet, Leeds, 1903. The frontage is in brown faience below with terracotta above. The interior is a magnificent display.

77

3.45 The Forester in West Ealing, London, was built in 1909, several years after the great pub-building boom. It has a restraint that is not associated with the late Victorian years and points the way to what pubs would look like between the wars.

3.46 The Rose Villa Tavern, Hockley, Birmingham, of 1919–20 but still in the late Victorian and Edwardian tradition of Birmingham's tile and terracotta pubs.

building work on pubs peaked in York in 1903,[12] Northampton in 1908,[13] in Birmingham in 1909.[14] In terms of architecture and arrangements there is little to differentiate the pubs of Edwardian England and the years down to the First World War from those of late Victorian times. The tried and tested formula of hierarchically ordered rooms and spaces remained and, indeed, would continue to do so for a good many decades to come. There were, however, a few new decorative themes. The magnificent craftsmanship in the woodwork and metalwork at the Philharmonic and the Vines is clearly in the spirit of the Arts and Crafts Movement and can be understood in the context of the architect, Walter Thomas, having contact with the progressive Liverpool School of Architecture. Art Nouveau made an occasional appearance, most splendidly in the metal gates to the Philharmonic's Hope Street entrance (5.58), but also in glass decoration at various Merseyside pubs and ornamental tilework (as at the Cemetery Hotel, Rochdale, and the Stork, Birkenhead). The now closed Arcade Stores, Back of the Inns (2.25–2.26), Norwich, shared spectacular Art Nouveau tiling by Doulton with the adjacent Royal Arcade. These developments, however, are exceptional and the main trend affecting the detailing of pubs is the simplifying and refining of detail. The vigour and 'go' of the sprightliest Victorian architecture and decoration was rapidly falling out of fashion and by the 1920s it would provoke profound revulsion. A good example of this shift is the Forester built in 1909 by architect T H Nowell Parr in West Ealing which shows a distinct move away from Victorian glitz to something altogether more sober (3.45). This pub retains its major room divisions and, over a hundred years on, still shows how the public bar was much plainer than its immediate predecessors.

## Inter-war pub building

The dominant images of inter-war public houses involve great neo-Georgian or 'brewers' Tudor' roadhouses, large, 'improved' pubs for new estates, and the occasional sleek lines of Art Deco (3.53–3.55). These are by no means the whole story. Many pubs continued to be built on deeply traditional lines, albeit with modernised decorative detail. This is hardly surprising since most pub regulars were (and usually still are) deeply conservative about the places where they drink. Three examples from the West Midlands make the point. First, in the heart of Birmingham's Jewellery Quarter, the Rose Villa Tavern (1919–20: 3.46) by Wood and Kendrick is a stripped-down version of the same firm's tile and terracotta pubs of around 1900 while the extensive interior wall-tiling is very much a continuation of Victorian tradition, even down to the pictorial tile panels of young ladies. The planning involved a series of once hierarchically graded spaces (now with partitioning removed) round a central servery and with the public bar, of course, fronting the main street. Secondly, the Villa Tavern, Nechells, was rebuilt in 1924–5 in plain brick but still with three separate rooms which would have made any Victorian drinker feel at home. Finally, the Vine, Wednesfield, is a remarkable survival of a straight-forward, plain, working-man's pub rebuilt in 1938 (3.48). The detailing is all 1930s, but the planning with three rooms – two either side of a servery, one to the rear across a corridor – is wholly traditional. In similar vein is the Hand and Heart, Peterborough, of 1938, which has two rooms and an off-sales/small drinking lobby with a hatch to the servery.

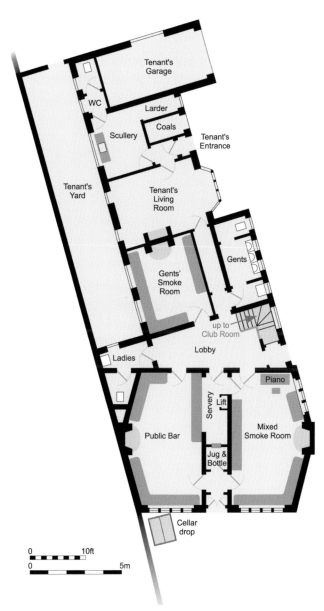

3.47 (left) Brewer's Tudor in Marylebone. The Lincoln Inn (renamed the Tudor Rose) was built c1930 for William Younger's, the Scottish brewers. The flat-arched windows, heavy window leading and applied half-timbering all create a sense of Olde England. This was very much the house style for Youngers' London pubs.

3.48 (above) The Vine, Wednesfield, West Midlands, rebuilt in 1938 as a small, working-man's local in the industrial outskirts of Wolverhampton. The rear smoke room was for gents only and there was a club room on the first floor.

**3.49** One of the largest examples of 'brewers' Tudor' ever built, the Black Horse, Northfield, Birmingham, is a massive roadhouse dating from 1929: architect Francis Goldsborough of Bateman and Bateman for the Birmingham brewers, Davenports. The first floor has impressive function rooms. At the rear the style turns into Cotswolds vernacular and there is a well-used bowling green.

**3.50** The Biggin Hall, Coventry. A 1920s interpretation of a Tudor inglenook fireplace.

The 'brewers' Tudor' style, born before the First World War, was extensively used after it. It was meant to evoke the old days of Good Queen Bess and a sense of comfort and ease which, no doubt, would have been rather more than a visitor to a real-life Elizabethan alehouse or tavern ever experienced. Progressive architects were disparaging and patronising about it. Basil Oliver spoke of 'pseudo half-timbering to which users of public houses have hitherto been supposed to be addicted and, judging by [its] prevalence, also attracted'.[15] Attracted they certainly were, and the style enjoyed a healthy life into the late 1930s. Good examples where the – again traditional – planning can still be found largely intact are the 1923 Biggin Hall, Coventry, which includes a fine rear lounge with original furniture among the three rooms; the Five Ways, Nottingham, built in 1936–7 by local

3.51 'Publican's rustic' at the Case is Altered, Eastcote, in west London. The pub was refitted, it seems about 1930, with adzed woodwork, reused beams, roughly textured doors, and chunky seating.

3.52 The Cittie of Yorke (formerly Henekey's) in Holborn, London, was built in 1923–4 and its rear room is an evocation of a great medieval hall. On the right is a series of small drinking booths (otherwise unknown in England before the late 20th century). A formidable array of now empty vats on the left: Henekey's concentrated on wines and spirits and the vats are said to have been in use till the Second World War. Dickens mentions huge vats like these in gin palaces (see p 60).

**3.53** Art Deco by the sea. The Ship, Skegness, was built in 1934 to designs by Bailey and Eberlin. Flat roofs, and rounded shapes characterise this building. The steps on the right lead up to a sun terrace. Much of the interior has been altered but there is still an impressive entrance foyer with its original staircase.

**3.54** The public bar at the Test Match, West Bridgford, Nottinghamshire, with its jazzy terrazzo floor. Built in 1938 it was the first new public house to be allowed in West Bridgford in the 20th century.

**3.55** The Art Deco entrance of the Vale, Arnold, Nottinghamshire.

architect A E Eberlin; and the 1926 Shakespeare, Farnworth, Greater Manchester, which still retains an intact off-sales compartment. The most extraordinary example, however, is in Birmingham – the Black Horse, Northfield, built in 1929 by Birmingham architects Bateman and Bateman for Davenport's brewery (3.49). It is built on a prodigious scale, like an enlarged half-timbered manor house lifted off the Cheshire plain. The separate areas at the front have been linked together now but at the rear is a room (originally the gents' smoke room) resembling a baronial hall. We will meet this mighty pub again when dealing with improved public houses.

From the same stable as brewers' Tudor is an aspect of inter-war pub design which has been little studied or recognised up till now. It is another exercise in nostalgia and might usefully be termed 'publicans' rustic'. It is not architectural but takes the form of chunky, rough-hewn woodwork which might have been crafted by a village carpenter. It is thus a distant relative of the Arts and Crafts Movement, an illegitimate child of its Cotswolds workshops. Two interesting examples on the outskirts of London are at the King and Tinker, Enfield, and the Case is Altered in Eastcote (3.51). Both are old buildings remodelled about 1930, no doubt with the object of enticing Londoners to motor out in their cars or charabancs for a little refreshment. They were fitted up with antique-looking woodwork, embellished by rustic ironwork details. A particularly interesting example can be cited from Scotland. When the Crook Inn at Tweedsmuir was refurbished in 1936, apart from the ultra-modern Art Deco toilets (6.11–6.12), it acquired, in total contrast, Willy Wastle's Bar, named after a Robbie Burns character (itself an exercise in nostalgia). It was fitted up with a rustic lapped counter and massively chunky furniture. So often the many country pubs which have received the trappings of rustic fittings and furnishings are assumed to have taken on this look between the 1950s and 1970s; but how many are, in fact, inter-war schemes? Such a treatment would be wholly in the spirit of those times as pub-keepers sought to entice people to what were much later to be called 'destination pubs'.

3.56–3.57 The destination pub arrives. Cycling became a popular recreation from the 1890s and would have brought new faces to many a rural pub. These cycles are outside the Hare and Hounds in the Banbury area (exact location unknown). The enterprising Mr Usher at the Bull, Colney, Hertfordshire, clearly saw the possibility of business from cyclists and motorists. The pub was evidently conveniently placed for Londoners taking the 84 bus.

## The 'improved' public house

Both before and after the First World War, there were great pressures to make public houses more respectable places. Magistrates and local authorities were keen to cut the number of licences in inner urban areas, and came to grant permission for building a new pub only in exchange for the surrender of several old licences. This policy is most famously

**3.58** The Red Lion, King's Heath, Birmingham, 1903-4, a pioneer of the 'improved' public house movement. The area was being developed by an estate company for middle-class housing and it demanded a very respectable public house for it.

associated with Birmingham, spearheaded by Arthur Chamberlain, chairman of the licensing magistrates from 1894 until 1904. And it was in Birmingham that there appeared in 1903–4 the Red Lion, King's Heath, designed for C E Bateman. It was built as part of a very respectable middle-class estate and bore a deliberate resemblance to the Angel and Royal, the famous late medieval inn in Grantham (more calculated nostalgia: 1.13).[16] The Red Lion was later described, perhaps not entirely accurately, by Francis Goldsborough of Bateman's as 'the pioneer of the public house of today'.[17]

By this Goldsborough meant it was the precursor of the improved public houses that were springing up between the wars, especially in residential outer suburbs and were intended to exert a civilising influence on patrons and neighbourhoods alike. The movement was almost a benign form of social engineering. The principles involved can be readily identified from the illustrations and plans presented here. There are a number of common themes. In contrast to the Victorian street-corner local, these new public houses were freestanding on generous sites. They were surrounded by gardens, terraces, often a bowling green (or skittles, especially in the south-west), space for charabancs and, for the better-off middle-class clients they expected to attract, car parking. A large site permitted a large building and in turn this meant that customers were not crowded into the small, confined spaces which were felt to be such an evil in so many Victorian pubs. The gardens, perhaps seen as a vista through a loggia, could accommodate tables and chairs so that customers could sit outside to enjoy the fresh air: they might be able to order drinks at a hatch facing the garden without the need to go inside. Some pubs specifically included a place for children to play (see Pheasant, Wednesfield: 2.37); and certainly women were welcome. The First World War dealt a heavy blow to the pub as a bastion of misogyny; during the war respectable women visited public houses, often for the first time and, with peace, brewers were keen to include them in their plans.[18] The public bar might remain 'gents only' but ladies were welcome in the

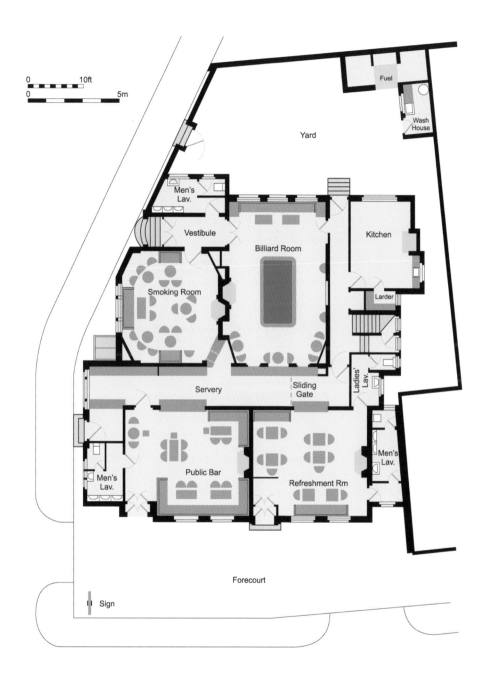

0 ___ 10ft
0 ___ 5m

Fuel

Wash House

Yard

Men's Lav.

Vestibule

Billiard Room

Kitchen

Smoking Room

Larder

Servery

Sliding Gate

Ladies' Lav.

Public Bar

Refreshment Rm

Men's Lav.

Men's Lav.

Forecourt

Sign

**3.59** The Crown, Stanwix, Carlisle, 1937, one of the Carlisle Experiment pubs, as built. The bar counter area is quite small and all rooms are provided with seating. Despite the desire to civilise the pub and broaden its customer base, ladies are only provided with toilet facilities adjacent to the refreshment room, suggesting that the smoking room was considered an essentially male space.

85

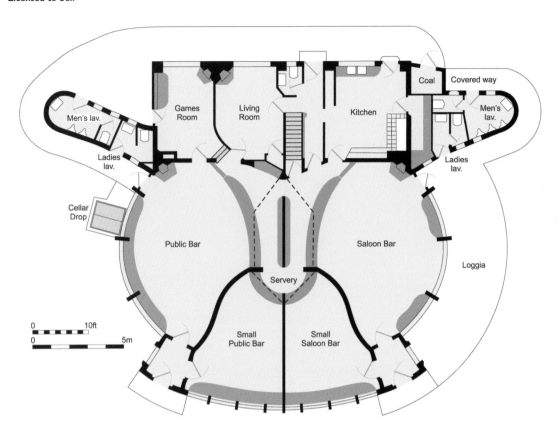

**3.60–3.61** The Prospect Inn, Minster-in-Thanet, Kent, 1939; architect Oliver Hill. One of the most individual pubs of its time with curving walls, and up-to-the-minute decoration. For all that, the result is a bleak drinking environment, as illustrated by the public bar. Its social status is reinforced by the representations in the rubber flooring of agricultural implements and ears of corn, everyday items of which Kent's farm labourers scarcely needed reminding if they popped in for a drink. After a long period of closure, now a hotel but the interior is totally altered.

lounge and saloon. Counters in the better rooms were much shorter than in the public bar or even non-existent as a deterrent to standing drinking. Customers in the Midlands and north were often seated and provided with waiter service. A large function room accommodated people for meetings, dances, concerts and other entertainments. Teas, snacks or more substantial meals were standard – plans often show the phrase 'lounge and tea room'. All this was a bold experiment to make the pub a major focus of local community life.

Improved public houses were built all over England but the movement was most vigorous in two places which were the focus of attention of brewers, architects and those desirous for social improvement – Carlisle and Birmingham. In its early years the Carlisle State Management Scheme Experiment (discussed on pp 46–9) and its chief architect, Harry Redfern, were mainly concerned to reduce the numbers of pubs in Carlisle and to reform those that remained. All this may have been morally uplifting but the results seemed artificial and unappealing, at least to those used to traditional pubs. In 1919 a party of thirty-six journalists visited a variety of Carlisle houses; the *Star* man found 'some of the better-class houses … remind one of an arts and crafts exhibition', while the *Daily Mail* reporter commented that one of the village pubs was 'as cheerful as a morgue'.[19] New pub building began in Carlisle in the mid-1920s producing sixteen between 1925 and 1939, all except the last designed by Redfern.[20]

Birmingham set to work building new pubs rather earlier, erecting the enormous Farcroft in Handsworth in 1921, and the British Oak, Stirchley, in 1923–4. Basil Oliver lists more than twenty pubs in and around Birmingham but this is only a small sample of the many that were built.

The uplifting facilities available to customers were housed in buildings of suitably architectural distinction. Carlisle provided an eclectic pattern book. There is everything in Harry Redfern's designs from the Vernacular Revival such as the 1930 Spinners Arms, Cummersdale (1930: 2.35), through Jacobethan at the Cumberland Inn (1929–30: 2.32–2.34), to Georgian at the Cumberland Wrestlers (1937). Redfern offered Art Deco at the Earl Grey (1934–5), and an exotic flowering of Hispano-Moorish at the Crescent Inn (1925). Around Birmingham there was huge variety too, starting with the gigantic, half-timbered Black Horse, Northfield (1929: 3.49) which turns into

Cotswold stone architecture at the rear. But there is also the quasi-Cotswold style at the Tyburn House (1930), by Bateman and Bateman; Elizabethan at the British Oak, (1923–4, by James and Lister Lea) and a basic interpretation of Art Deco (sometimes referred to as Moderne) at the Three Magpies, Hall Green (c1934). At the College Arms, New Oscott (c1930, by Holland W Hobbis), we find neo-Georgian, and there is even a Spanish hacienda-inspired design at the Court Oak, Harborne (1932, by Harrison and Cox). These Carlisle and Birmingham pubs, along with many others up and down the country that may, in part, have been inspired by them, relied on elegant design, the honest use of quality materials, fine detailing, and careful, intelligent planning, and may be seen as a late manifestation of the Arts and Crafts Movement.[21] This is certainly the claim that has been rightly made for Basil Oliver, designer of fine pubs in the vernacular tradition, and an influential writer about the improved public house. See 5.5 for an inn sign designed by him.[22]

The improved public house was based upon a vision that saw the pub as far more than just a place to drink, and a place that expected to draw in a wide spectrum of customers. Times have changed and, now, three-quarters of a century later, all this seems to have involved an overly genteel vision. Perhaps even more than their Victorian predecessors which were generally rather smaller and more homely, large inter-war pubs have suffered massive changes with the destruction of what we now regard as important historic fabric.

## Postscript – the late 20th century

In general, the architectural history of the post-1945 pub has not been a distinguished one. When work did get going again in the 1950s it still proceeded on traditional lines. Separate rooms were still in evidence, albeit without the extreme compartmentalisation found in many Victorian pubs. The public bar was still a distinct entity and much plainer than the other rooms. As before, customers paid a fraction more in the latter and often could still get table service while anyone planning an evening in front of their newly acquired television set could have their liquid needs satisfied from their local's off-sales counter. Many of the design

**3.62** The Margaret Catchpole, Ipswich. An improved estate pub of 1936 in the vernacular tradition by H R Cooper for the Cobbold Brewery of Ipswich. The interior is still as designed with three rooms and an off-sales lobby.

**3.63–3.64** The Doctor Johnson, Barkingside, London Borough of Redbridge, was built in 1937–8 for Barclay Perkins and is typical of large estate pubs of the time. Remarkably, it retains its four-room layout intact although the off-sales shop, connected by a passage from the cellar, is now an estate agents. Apart from the private bar the rooms are all very spacious: the lounge looks out on to a garden. The revolving door in the public bar was not installed. Johnson was a friend of Henry Thrale who inherited the Barclay brewery in 1758.

details were similar and, in the absence of documentary evidence, it is sometimes hard to work out whether features belong to the late 1930s or the 1950s. A common clue, though, is the quality of materials. In postwar 'austerity' Britain there was an inevitable paring back so that there is often a greater flimsiness than one encounters in the 1930s. On the wall, for example, plywood and hardboard masqueraded as wall panelling in cheap refurbishments through the 1960s and 1970s and are unlikely to acquire heritage or

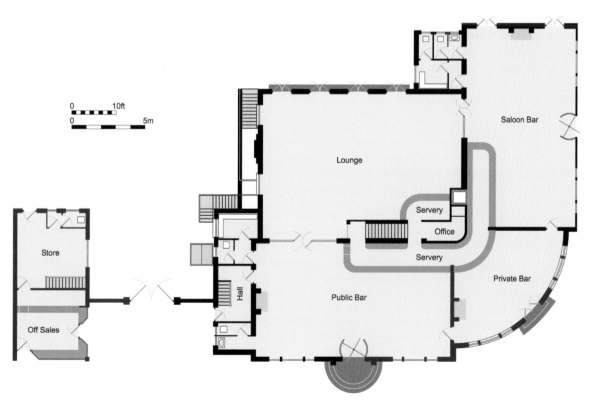

Store

Off Sales

0        10ft

0              5m

Lounge

Saloon Bar

Servery

Office

Servery

Private Bar

Hall

Public Bar

3.65 The private bar at the Doctor Johnson, Barkingside, and its
restrained fittings.

curiosity value for some years to come! It is a truism
in the history of taste that no age has such deplorable
standards as the one just preceding one's own. The
Victorians reviled the Georgians, the early 20th
century reviled the Victorians and so on. Nonetheless
we risk the view that a large proportion of the pubs
built and refurbished from the 1950s onwards are at a
low ebb in the history of pub design.

The years around 1970 represent something of a
watershed for the planning and, consequently,
character of pubs. There was a rapid escalation in
opening up existing pubs. This is graphically illustrated
by the sixteen pubs built between 1925 and 1939
under the Carlisle Experiment. Until they were
denationalised in 1972 the stock was virtually
unaltered; by the 1990s only the Cumberland Inn,
Botchergate (2.32–2.34), remained largely as built.
Looking at the national picture, the initiative by the

Campaign for Real Ale in 1991 to compile a National
Inventory of Pub Interiors of Outstanding Historic
Interest has found only 200 or so interiors in the
United Kingdom and Northern Ireland dating from
before 1939 that are intact enough to be included.[23]

In recent decades there has been a tidal wave of pub
refurbishments and wholesale gutting of interiors.
A good deal of it has happened under the influence of
the magistrates who have insisted on pubs being easily
supervised, with all parts visible from the servery.
Brewers and their successors in the 1990s, pub-owning
companies, have shown scant regard for heritage
interiors, unless forced to do so by statutory listing.
Huge amounts of money have been thrown at pubs,
almost, it would seem, with the aim of making one pub
look much the same as any other. All too often genuine
features have been discarded, only to have mock
heritage reintroduced a few years later. The rehabilitation
of things Victorian in the canon of popular taste has led
to bizarre results, such as installing Victorian cast-iron
fireplaces in 1930s pubs and old pictures and sundry

bric-à-brac into 19th-century pubs, which were purged of such things but a short while before.

As for new pubs, relatively few have been built since the 1970s. The tendency has been to design them as a single space or, where the conversion to pub use from a pre-existing building generated separate rooms or areas, the designers have usually aimed at a similar character throughout the building, in contrast to the hierarchical stratification that was *de rigeur* a century before. The J D Wetherspoon chain, founded in 1979, is an influential case in point whose buildings say much about late 20th-century pub design. Now numbering 760 outlets (at June 2011), the estate was built up mainly by converting redundant buildings to pubs but also adding some new builds. Each pub was planned as a far larger, higher turnover enterprise than was customary a century ago, open continuously from breakfast time until, usually, 11.30 pm or midnight (1 am Fridays and Saturdays) closing time, with interconnection between all parts of the pub and a generally homogeneous, contemporary character throughout. Although many of the pubs have similar characteristics, some of the designs have showed considerable flair and imagination with the firm winning several times in the CAMRA Pub Design Award scheme for its conversions.[24]

This is not the place to speculate in detail about the future of pub design. However, there seems no reason to suppose that, for the near future, the trend to large, open-planned outlets will not continue among the large operators, driven as they are by intense competitive pressures and expectations from the stock market. These need not, and hopefully will not, be the only way forward. Given the affection in which the truly traditional pub is held and given the fact that an important minority of people do appreciate and are willing to pay for good drink (and good food), smaller, intimate, genuine heritage-based establishments surely have a part to play. Trends since 2004 are discussed in chapter 8.

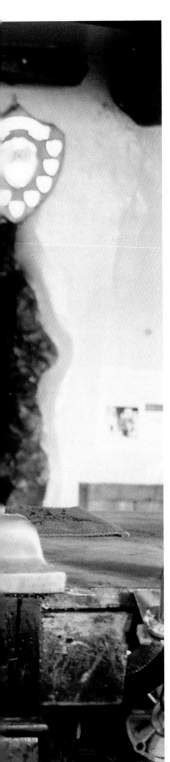

## Chapter 4

# Serving and Entertaining the Customers

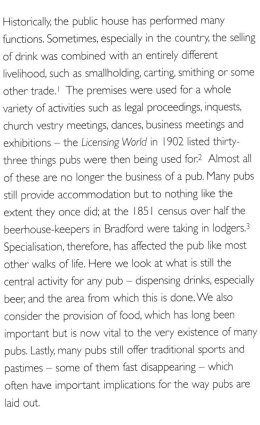

4.1 Hand-pumps at the Ship, Porlock, Somerset.

Historically, the public house has performed many functions. Sometimes, especially in the country, the selling of drink was combined with an entirely different livelihood, such as smallholding, carting, smithing or some other trade.[1] The premises were used for a whole variety of activities such as legal proceedings, inquests, church vestry meetings, dances, business meetings and exhibitions – the *Licensing World* in 1902 listed thirty-three things pubs were then being used for.[2] Almost all of these are no longer the business of a pub. Many pubs still provide accommodation but to nothing like the extent they once did; at the 1851 census over half the beerhouse-keepers in Bradford were taking in lodgers.[3] Specialisation, therefore, has affected the pub like most other walks of life. Here we look at what is still the central activity for any pub – dispensing drinks, especially beer, and the area from which this is done. We also consider the provision of food, which has long been important but is now vital to the very existence of many pubs. Lastly, many pubs still offer traditional sports and pastimes – some of them fast disappearing – which often have important implications for the way pubs are laid out.

### Serving the beer

At the simplest level, beer was and is kept in a separate ground-floor room and is drawn off by gravity dispense either directly into the customer's tankard or glass, or into a large jug. Such would have been the case in thousands of simple beerhouses and pubs throughout the country from time immemorial, especially in country areas. This procedure is now very rare indeed and will become even rarer as the most basic establishments cease to trade or fall prey to 'progress'. The Anchor, High Offley, Staffordshire and the Dyffryn Arms, Pontfaen, Pembrokeshire are two places where the beer is brought some distance from the cellar.

**4.2** Straight from the barrel. Beer is stillaged at the back of the servery at the Cresselly Arms, Cresswell Quay, Pembrokeshire. Landlady, Janet Cole, taps it into a jug.

**4.3** From the cellar. At the King's Head, Laxfield, Suffolk, glasses are filled directly from barrels kept in a ground-floor cellar.

**4.4** Caroline Cheffers-Heard, licensee at the Bridge, Topsham, Devon, brings filled glasses into the 'inner sanctum' from where they will be served through a hatch. Customers sometimes sit in the inner sanctum itself but strictly by invitation only. This is a survival of an old tradition in which a publican's close friends might be invited to join him/her in the bar parlour.

Sometimes customers are served at a hatch to the cellar, as at the King's Head, Laxfield, Suffolk, and the Cock, Broom, Bedfordshire. At the Bridge at Topsham, Devon, beer is brought to a hatch in the bar parlour. In a few other pubs, where there is no normal bar counter, staff pull beer from hand-pumps sited within the same space as the paying customers. Examples are the Red Lion, Ampney St Peter, Gloucestershire (1.23), the Manor Arms, Rushall, West Midlands and Tucker's Grave, Faulkland, Somerset.

Bar counters are now a near-universal feature in British pubs and make for the convenient separation of customers and unsold liquor within a single room.

A number of pubs continue to stillage beer behind the bar; most of them are in south-central and south-west England. But by far the most common practice is for beer to be kept in a below-ground cellar which offers the advantage of better temperature control, ideally at a constant 13–14°C for traditional beer. It is pulled through pipes which need to be cleaned regularly. Non-traditional pressurised drinks like lager, stout and cider require extra gas cylinders and cooling equipment which can be conveniently stowed away in cellars.

Tall hand-pumps are one of the prime symbols of traditional beer and the traditional pub but they are not the only way of pulling beer from the cask. Other

**4.5** When the Victoria Inn in Winchester was planned in 1913 there was no provision for storing beer in a below-ground cellar. Beer would no doubt have been drawn off and served as in the previous picture. Such 'gravity dispense' still takes places at various pubs, mainly in southern England (but not London). Note the tap room is far removed from the cellar.

traditional equipment is now extremely rare. At the Kimberley Club, Stacksteads, there are cask-pumps.[4] The only set of quadrant action, or 'cash-register hand-pumps' as they are sometimes called in regular use are at the Old Crown, Kelston, Somerset (4.14). They

appear in Loudon's 1833 illustration of a 'suburban public house' (4.12–4.13). A variant is the Autovac system, once common in west Yorkshire, where it appears to have become popular during the inter-war years (4.15–4.16). Here the pulling of a 'northern pint'

**4.6** (top) Wooden casks are now very rarely used, except by producers of real cider. These two are at the Rose and Crown, Huish Episcopi, Somerset. Former spirit casks are often used; recent spirit use can impart a distinctive flavour.

**4.7** The cask pumps at the Kimberley Club, Stacksteads, near Bacup, Lancashire, are thought to be the only ones still in use throughout Britain. The mild ale dispensed from one of them is now a great rarity in most parts of the country.

## Cider, cider houses and perry

The idea of the traditional public house is normally associated with beer and, to a lesser extent, spirits. But for large swathes of the country there used to be an alternative – cider. Cider, made from fermented apple juice, was the drink of choice for working people in apple-growing areas, taken into the fields to assuage thirst, and drunk in the pub among friends and fellow workers. When the French wars of the 1790s and 1800s cut off supplies of wine, good-quality cider became an acceptable replacement for the better-off.

Cider houses – ones selling cider and no beer – were once a feature of the drinking scene in southern England, and several existed in London until after the Second World War. Today there are only four, the Cider House, Defford (3.3), Ye Olde Cider Bar, Newton Abbot, Devon, the Cider House, Wootton Green, Shropshire, and the Cider Tavern, Brandy Wharf, Waddingham, Lincolnshire. In the heartland of cider drinking – the West Country, Herefordshire and Worcestershire – there are a number of other pubs where cider outsells beer. Cider, however, is made much more widely with producers extending as far as Yorkshire and the eastern counties. A big difference between western producers and those in the east is that the former use cider apples, rich in tannin, whereas the latter use a mixture of cooking and eating apples. The range of tastes is enormous, from very sweet to blisteringly dry, yet including some of the great pleasures of alcohol consumption in this country. It is thought that about 260 cider producers actively produce and retail cider and that some 750 pubs sell real cider on a regular basis, up from about 600 seven years ago.[5]

Most people are only acquainted with the modern, mass-produced variety of cider, made from concentrate, pasteurised, carbonated, and which comes from two producers who account for about 94 per cent of the UK market. The heavy promotion of such products has, fortuitously, also given something of a boost to real cider. So too perry, made from varieties of otherwise inconsumable pears, but this is still very much scarcer than real cider and is only available at CAMRA festivals and a few enlightened pubs. It is one of Britain's greatest gastronomic pleasures. Perry pear orchards take thirty years or so to mature, and some of them, up to 300 or even 400 years old, will soon reach the end of their lives. Fine, craft-made perry can, like good cider, be truly exquisite.

**4.8** A large, traditional hand-cranked cider press at Haye Farm, St Veep, Lerryn, near Lostwithiel, Cornwall. Over 100 years old, it takes one to two tonnes of apples. After pulping, these are layered in straw 'cheeses' (shown here). Building these is a time-consuming, skilful business and most farms now press through hessian sacking or terylene cloths. The juice runs into a stone trough before being pumped into oak barrels where it ferments. The spent straw and pulp are usually fed to livestock.

with its large foaming head produces abundant spillage into a drip-tray which is siphoned back into the dispensing pipes. Hygiene concerns led to the removal of most autovacs during the late 1980s.

Electric pumps dispensing measured half-pints were popular in the Midlands and north until the 1970s but have fallen out of favour, being all too easily confused with fonts dispensing keg beer. Similarly, the Scottish system of air pressure to dispense cask beer has largely disappeared, having been replaced by the ubiquitous hand-pump since the 1970s (see also p 160).

**4.9–4.10** The service of traditional beer is now most usually associated with the tall hand-pump. As this chapter shows, there are several alternatives but they have become increasingly marginalised. Gaskell and Chambers were one of the principal manufacturers.

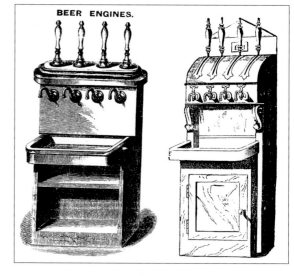

**4.11** Tall quadrant action hand-pumps and lever action pumps advertised in a catalogue of 1898 by Farrow and Jackson, suppliers of bar equipment. The beer was pulled up through 'best tinned lead pipe … 5d. per foot'.

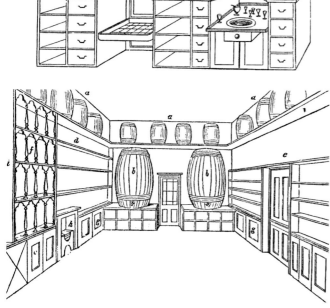

**4.12–4.13** (left) An early, model bar counter for 'a suburban public house' from J C Loudon's *Encyclopaedia of Cottage, Farm and Villa Architecture* (1833). It shows lever-action hand-pumps to draw 'the beer and ale of different ages and qualities from the butts in the cellar' and a bank of spirit taps. The drawers, Loudon tells us, are for 'tobacco, cheese, biscuits, sugar, lemons, &c'. He envisaged that the woodwork would be mahogany and any metalwork pewter. The spirit taps are connected by pipes to the casks marked 'a' ranged behind the counter: 'liquors … sold in larger quantities' are drawn directly from the large vats ('b').

**4.14** Quadrant action pumps were once as popular as tall hand-pumps. These ones at the Old Crown, Kelston, Somerset are thought to be the last ones in use in this country.

**4.15–4.16** (right) The vanishing Autovac, now confined to a handful of pubs in Yorkshire. Surplus beer is recycled down a tube back into the flow. This example is at the Shoulder of Mutton, Castleford, West Yorkshire.

**4.17** Three magnificent hand-pumps dating from 1887, but not now in use, at the Larkhall Inn, Bath: they are inscribed 'Nathaniel George Wilcocks City Iron Works Bath'.

## Cask sizes

A national standard for the size of beer casks or barrels was not adopted until the end of the 17th century, when the collection of the Excise demanded a standard measure. Until then, a variety of local standards had prevailed (the standard measure for the sale of ale in 16th-century York, for example, was the 'soo' of 7 gallons). Until the 1960s, casks were made from wood (usually oak) by specialist craftsmen called coopers, but wood has almost entirely been replaced by aluminium in the last forty years.

The standard cask sizes are:

| | |
|---|---|
| Pin | 4¹/₂ gallons |
| Firkin | 9 gallons |
| Kilderkin | 18 gallons |
| Barrel | 36 gallons |
| Hogshead | 54 gallons |
| Puncheon | 72 gallons |
| Butt | 108 gallons |
| Tun | 216 gallons |

Most beer is now supplied in 9 gallon casks (sometimes 18, and occasionally 36 gallons).

## Standard retail measures

Ale and beer have been drunk from vessels made from a variety of materials in the past – horn, leather, pottery and pewter have all been extensively used. Most beer is now served in glass, once an expensive material, which only came into general use after duties on it were removed in 1845. The general adoption of glass is said to have influenced the trend to lighter, clearer beers which became apparent in the 19th century.

Until the mid-19th century, ale and beer were typically sold in quart (two pint) measures, but thereafter the pint became the standard measure. Beer has also been sold in half-pints and gills (quarter-pints), although this was a measure more normally used for spirits (until the recent adoption of metric measures for spirits, they were still sold in fractions of a gill, typically one-sixth or one-fifth).

## Around the servery

Another prominent feature of the pub's serving area is the bar-back or back-fitment (or gantry as it is known in Scotland and Northern Ireland). It fulfils the very necessary function of housing glasses, spirits, other miscellaneous drinks, and all manner of snacks from crisps to pickled eggs, not to mention tills, collecting boxes and sundry clutter. At the simplest level there are just some basic shelves, at the most elaborate it can be a Victorian masterpiece in wood and glass. The majority of bar-backs are embellished by mirrors, often plain, sometimes very ornate. The lower part of the bar-back houses more shelves, or very likely now, one or more illuminated refrigerators for various bottled drinks.

Fully licensed premises, of course, sell spirits, sherry, port and other fortified wines as well as less potent drinks. Today they are dispensed from optics or from bottles via measures. Until the inter-war period, as well as being poured from bottles, spirits were served on

4.18–4.19 Advertisements in the trade press for items pictured at the Leicester opposite. A heater from 1880 and spirit urns from 1897.

BRASS & COPPER
**MULLERS,**
SAUSAGE WARMERS,
&c., &c.

Special Prices on application.

**G. FARMILOE & SONS**
SHOW ROOMS,
**34, St. John Street,**
WEST SMITHFIELD,
LONDON, E.C.

NEW    COX'S    REGISTERED
**SPECIAL WHISKY URN**
IN BEST CRYSTAL GLASS,
Containing 1 to 4 Gallons.
NOW IN USE IN ALL PRINCIPAL BARS IN THE UNITED KINGDOM.

**4.20–4.21** A fully-equipped grand Victorian pub: the Old Dover Castle, Westminster Bridge Road, Lambeth, London, by Treadwell and Martin, 1895, as photographed by Bedford Lemere.

Right – spirit barrels at two levels feed down to taps, a water heater stands on the counter, and there are the inevitable subdividing screens.

Below – a much more elegant setting. The counter front has more embellishment, its top is marble and carries decanters, snack containers, and a menu. Note also the glass spirit urns in the bar-back. In the background is a restaurant.

draught from bulk containers. Apart from fairly large numbers of ceramic containers which survive as ornaments in various pubs, England has very little evidence of this type of dispense (although more survives in Scotland and Northern Ireland). Small ceramic vessels would discharge directly to the glass but larger ones were linked by a pipe to a tap or, in some cases, a bank of taps. Full banks of these remain at the Haunch of Venison, Salisbury, Wiltshire, and Shipman's, Northampton. At the Queen's Head, Stockport, there are two banks of fourteen cocks which were supplied from an overhead room by pipes channelled down a hollow column. Vestiges of such pipes are found at the Travellers Friend, South Woodford, London, where they

are said to have conveyed port. A notice beside a tap at the Barley Mow, Marylebone, London, advertises Old Tom, a famous brand of London gin, which has star billing in George Cruikshank's polemics against the evil spirit (see 2.8). Customers could dilute their spirits from a brass water dispenser which can still be found on a few bar counters; in London at the Victoria, Bayswater, it still functions. More water dispensers survive in Scotland and Northern Ireland where there was a greater tradition of spirit drinking. Similar in scale to the water dispensers are cigar/cigarette lighters. An unusual one is at a Northern Irish pub, the Mandeville Arms, Portadown; a portly figure is labelled as the Tichborne Claimant, an impostor whose claims to be the vanished

**4.22** A bank of Victorian spirit cocks at the Haunch of Venison, Salisbury.

**4.23** Water dispenser at Hales Bar, Harrogate.

**4.24** (opposite) Cigar lighter at the Mandeville Arms, Portadown, Co Armagh, representing the Tichborne Claimant who fascinated the Victorian public. In a lengthy court case of over 100 days in 1871–2 he failed in his claim to the Tichborne fortune, and an even lengthier trial for perjury landed him in gaol in 1874. Behind is a now defunct spirit barrel and its tap.

Sir Roger Tichborne, the ninth wealthiest man in Britain, captivated public attention during two high-profile court cases in the early 1870s.[6]

Another overlooked feature of some bar counters is the doors in their fronts, recognised by disused hinges and keyholes. They have, so far, largely been noticed in London counters and date from the Victorian period right up until shortly after the Second World War. Whether they have a wider geographical spread is at present uncertain but their function, as reported by experienced licensees, was to allow access to the hand-pumps for servicing purposes when their mechanisms were more complex and bulky than they are now.[7]

GERARDIN & WATSON.

BEER ENGINES AND PEWTER POTS

**4.25** Behind the counter in the late 19th century. This advertisement ran in the trade press for years. Note the spirit barrels, lamps on the counter, and numerous drawers. The bar is probably divided into two by a screen behind the left-hand pillar. The counter is unencumbered with a pot-shelf which seems to be a relatively modern invention.

**4.26** Doors in the counter front at the Elgin, Notting Hill, London, to allow access to service the beer engines: this seems to have been a London feature – so far only one example has been identified outside the capital, at the White Lion, London Road, Heeley, Sheffield.

**4.27** A tiled spittoon trough in front of the counter at the Hope and Anchor, Hammersmith, London, c1930. An opening was left to enable the collected detritus to be swept through for collection.

## The changing landscape of the bar counter

The bar counter is the 'high altar' of the pub. It is the place across which most drink is served and where landlord and bar staff most usually interact with the customers. Its all-important long, flat top has been subjected to the vagaries of time. The top of the bar counter today differs in a number of respects from its antecedents. The Victorians made ample use of them to accommodate receptacles for snacks, heaters for mulling drinks, cash registers, water jugs and dispensers, soda syphons, and, in the smarter establishments, flowers and pot plants. But, apart from the occasional spirit or fortified wine taps (as in Loudon's illustration,

see 4.12–4.13), hand-pumps for beer were the only alcohol-dispensing equipment actually sited on the counter. Photographs of bar counters in the inter-war period and, indeed, up until about 1960, usually show a counter cleared of Victorian clutter, and sporting only a series of hand-pumps.

In the 1960s the 'keg revolution', serving beer under carbon dioxide pressure from the cellar, swept through the nation's pubs. It began with the arrival in 1955 of Flower's Keg and Worthington E, followed by Ind Coope Double Diamond, Courage Tavern, and that infamous icon of the movement, Watney's Red Barrel.[8]  Easy to keep and aided by the fact that much traditional ale was often sold in poor condition, keg's percentage of the beer market expanded from 1 per cent in 1959 to 8 per cent in 1966 and 17 per cent in 1971. Lager sales were also on the move although, even by 1971, they represented only 10 per cent of sales  (yet almost 45 per cent by 1986).[9] Gradually keg fonts for beer, lager and also stout and cider took

**4.28** The keg revolution comes to the Hero of Switzerland, Stockwell, London. A R Motion, Managing Director of Ind Coope (London) Ltd 'pulls' the first pint of Double Diamond flanked by the licensee, Mr Brett, and his wife, both of whom seem lost in admiration. Mild (left of the DD) has more or less vanished from London pubs. Photograph probably early 1960s.

4.29 Serving hatch to the corridor at the Loggerheads (formerly Shrewsbury Arms), Shrewsbury. The 'Gents Only until 1975' commemorates the politically incorrect days before the Sex Discrimination Act when many pubs had a room for exclusively male company. It was often spoken of as the 'G.O.' The Act came into force on 1 January 1976.

4.30 Women used to know their place (or lack of it) in room number 1 at the Old Cheshire Cheese in Fleet Street, London.

their place beside the hand-pumps and often ousted them. All that was needed for keg was a small tap to release the pent-up, fizzy liquid. Whereas the hand-pump had a more or less fixed size and shape, the opportunities were boundless for shaping the tap housing into an advertising tool. Whitbread Tankard, of course, had a tankard, Red Barrel a red barrel and so on. The drinks have multiplied and the result is a series of fonts of disparate shape and size, often illuminated and taking some exotic forms; they have radically changed the appearance of the counter. A prominent innovation has been the 'T-bar', a tall device shaped like the letter T and carrying a number of small taps. Rather like the old-fashioned spirit cocks, a cluster of pipes brings a range of drinks to the bar which can be poured with the flick of a tap.

## Children in the pub

Many food-orientated houses now have certificates to admit children accompanied by adults. However, the pub is widely regarded as an unsuitable place for children and their presence is often resented. But restrictions on children in pubs only go back to late Victorian times. The 1886 Intoxicating Liquor (Sales to Children) Act excluded any under 13 from on-sales areas of licensed premises. This was raised to 14 under 1901 legislation and applied to both on- and off-sales. It was known as the Child Messenger Act and thereafter sales of alcohol to children were to be in sealed containers only. The age was raised to 18 in 1923 and remains so today. The 18-year-old limit was extended to off-licences in 1953.

Today's pub-goers will also be familiar with structures standing on top of bar counters and which are primarily intended to carry 'pot-shelves' for storing glasses. In the absence of a recognised term for them we might call them 'gantries'.[10] Many are singularly ugly and all have transformed the appearance of the pubs containing them. Such features are now so much a part of the scenery in pubs that it is something of a surprise to realise they are a non-traditional item. They are absent in all the historic photographs (about nineteen of them) reproduced in Mark Girouard's *Victorian Pubs*. Examination of more than 250 photographs of pub interiors from the early 1950s to 1980 in the Brewery History Society's archive show hardly a single one.[11] Two dozen examples of shelves suspended from a low ceiling or canopy can be made out, but only a couple of the true, now-familiar gantries can be detected. The conclusion is that they must have spread rapidly from the 1980s onwards.

### Snob screens

Service at the counter obviously involves direct contact between the customer and the bar staff. Such contact was not always welcomed, particularly in Victorian and Edwardian times when there were finely differentiated gradations of social class and status.

The most well-known manifestation of this in pubs is snob screens, occasionally known also as shy screens. Their small square or rectangular etched and cut glass panels were mounted at eye level and swivelled so they that could be closed or open. In the closed position they prevented eye contact between either side of the counter while the drink could be passed beneath the bank of snob screens to the waiting customer whose anonymity was thus assured. Or so the traditional explanation goes. This relies on the idea that certain customers – masters – did not wish to reveal their identity to the bar staff – servants. It seems fairly improbable that such anonymity could be preserved, especially when identity could be established from the voice behind the screens.  Rather we should look to a simple desire for a degree of privacy among our class-conscious, better-class pub customers. Snob screens seem to have incurred the deep suspicion of magistrates at the end of the 19th century; in 1903, for example, the Portsmouth bench demanded the removal of all 'shy-screens', as they were called, from the town's pubs, despite protests from the brewers about the cost this would entail.[12]

We have to ask, how common were they? They are certainly known about by most pub goers who take an interest in historic surroundings. Peter Haydon wrote in 1994 that 'Examples of snob screens still abound' but this seems based more on theory than evidence.[13] After careful extensive investigation, we believe only about half a dozen original examples survive. Even allowing for the wholesale clearing out of such a vulnerable feature in the 20th century, the survival rate seems low for what is often thought of as a common item of pub furnishing. The only examples clearly surviving in situ seem to be in one of the compartments at the Prince Alfred, Maida Vale, London (4.31), and at the Bartons Arms, Aston, Birmingham.[14]

## Sash screens

There is plenty of other screenwork associated with the servery that has survived the depradations of the late 20th century, only because removal would involve cost and often be more inconvenient than keeping it. Much of it is to be found in the north where there was a tradition of having screens with vertically sliding sashes which were opened for service and closed at quiet times. Even where the sliding parts have been lost, the evidence of runners often still exists. Such screenwork was still being installed extensively in the inter-war period; at the Coach and Horses, Barnburgh, near Doncaster, the entire counter, throughout all the rooms, has glazed screens. Similarly the drinking corridors found in many a northern pub have screens with sashes separating them from the servery. Occasionally the sashes slide horizontally.

**4.31** (opposite) Snob screens at the Prince Alfred, Maida Vale, one of only two sets believed to survive in their original context. This well-known feature of pub-furnishing is now extremely rare.

**4.32** (above left) The Coach and Horses, Barnburgh, South Yorkshire, built in 1936–7, has a remarkable array of counter sash window screens, here being raised to allow service. The barley sheaf was the trademark of Whitworth, Son and Nephew, brewers of Wath-on-Dearne, who built the pub. Sash screens are found most commonly either side of the Pennines.

**4.33** (above right) Sash window screens to the servery at the Black Horse, Preston. They date from the building of the pub in 1898.

All pub-goers will have come across service hatches from time to time, especially outside London. Sometimes they are simply openings in the wall to the servery, sometimes they involve the upper part of a stable-type door.

## Table service

One of the things that helps make the British pub special is the way one obtains and pays for the drinks. In a continental café, one sits down, waits to be served, waits again for the drinks to appear, asks for the bill, and waits yet again, seemingly for ever, for it to appear (not to mention the wait for the change!). Not so in the British pub where the whole process is conflated into one at the bar. This has always been the case in the public bar but service at the table was once extremely common in the better rooms.

The evidence for this is widespread and easy to see. Many smoke rooms, lounges, saloons and so on still have bell-pushes on the wall or as part of the wall-mounting of the seating which were used to attract attention. A member of the bar staff or a dedicated waiter would come and take the order – hence the slightly higher price of drink in such rooms. The system worked much the same as the communication from upstairs to below stairs in great houses. Where there were several rooms to be served in this way, an indicator box would be mounted within sight of the servery, because, if the ringing of the bell had not been heard, then there was the safety net of a visible sign. The appropriate window on the box would have an oscillating tab to show where service was required. Very occasionally there are bells mounted in the centre of tables, such as at the Arden Arms, Stockport. By the 1960s, this system seems to have been defunct in the West Midlands, but it was still widespread in West Yorkshire and the north-west. It is still practised at a number of Merseyside pubs, notably at the Volunteer Canteen, Waterloo, and the Crow's Nest, Crosby, where it is used to attract the attention of the bar staff. At the Wheatsheaf, Knotty Ash and the Kensington, Liverpool, the still-functioning bells or buzzers do the job. The drinks usually carry a slight premium on the price and it is also common to give the server a small

gratuity. Elsewhere in the country we estimate that there are probably not more than a dozen isolated examples of table service.

Table service never seems to have been popular in London and at present the only known example of bell-pushes is at the Forester, West Ealing (4.35), built in 1909.[15] Here one room has them, yet this, oddly, has a proper bar counter too. Mark Girouard suggested the greater density of people per pub in London, the consequent need for speedy service, and generally higher costs may have militated against table service in the capital.[16] While this is no doubt true of the centre, it does not explain the situation in the

**4.34-4.35** (opposite) Bell-pushes for waiter service. The diamond-shaped one is at the Shakespeare, Farnworth, Greater Manchester. The other is at the Forester, West Ealing, which is the only pub in London presently known to have such a feature. Perhaps its unfamiliarity to London drinkers brought about the word of explanation.

**4.36-4.37** At the other end of the 'system' indicator boxes showed where service was required. A bell would ring and discs or flaps would show staff which room required service. The plain example is at the Commercial, near Bacup, Lancashire: one room was clearly intended for masonic meetings and there appears to have been a letting bedroom. A bell has been added for good measure. The ornate example is at the Crown, Belfast, and the letters refer to drinking booths (6.15).

**4.38** Waiter service survived most strongly in the north-west and was going strong in 1955 when this picture of the saloon bar at the Trafford Park Hotel, Manchester, was taken. The artwork is very much of its time.

suburbs where drinking life would have been more relaxed, and land values and costs lower. In 1896 St James's there was a pub for every 116 of the population (plus all the visitors to this central area) whereas Edmonton had a ratio of one to 727.[17] Surely it must have been feasible to provide table service in the north London suburb? Further research will no doubt confirm that table service was very much a Midlands and northern tradition rather than a southern one.

### Food in the pub

The public house, and often the beerhouse too, was usually a place at which customers could expect to obtain sustenance other than drink. Indeed, the authorities tended to take a dim view of establishments which did not offer at least some simple fare such as bread and cheese, a sandwich or a pork pie. Girouard notes how in the mid-19th century 'a glass of ale and a sandwich for four pence' was a popular offering by beerhouses.[18] Many pubs gave the working man the opportunity to bring in his own lunch and have it heated up for, say, a ha'penny provided he also bought a drink. Also, in the days of fairly rudimentary cooking facilities at home, the pub kitchen was a place where the family meal could be cooked for a small charge. This no doubt is the explanation that lies behind the name 'Public Kitchen' (3.25) which appears in door glass at the Victoria, Great Harwood, Lancashire, a pub which dates from the Edwardian years.

Food could be good business for licensees, even if it was still subsidiary to the business of selling drink. In Bradford, for example, town centre pubs catered for

**4.39** Food was clearly very much part of the repertoire at the Old Arcade, Cardiff.

**4.40–4.41** Whitelock's in Leeds is a famous local institution that has long done a busy trade in food.

### Seats – a civilising influence?

Pub-goers divide into two schools – those who like to drink standing up and those who prefer to sit. Although now both are considered as perfectly respectable, perpendicular (stand-up or vertical) drinking was viewed with some suspicion by the authorities, certainly up until the Second World War. This was because the upright posture was held to be more conducive to consuming greater amounts of alcohol. It also implied rapid consumption, as in the gin shops and dram shops of the early 19th century. Hence, in the improved public house, attempts were made to discourage it. Carlisle Experiment pubs had only short counters, and there was a general prohibition against vertical drinking in them. Customers were expected to be served at their seats by waiters, and were given as little opportunity as possible to drink excessively.

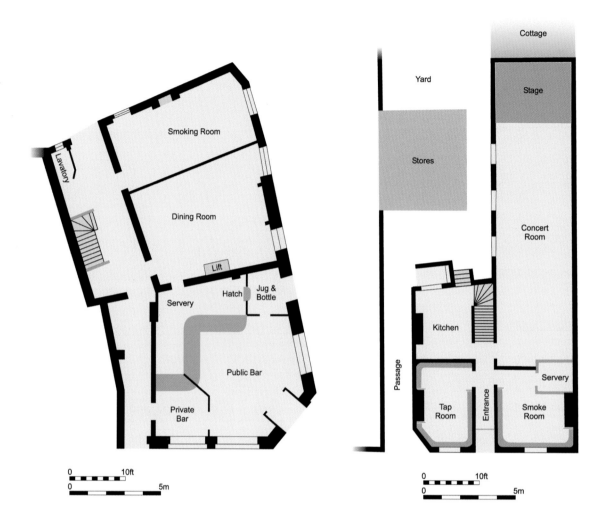

4.42  The dining room is prominent at the New Inn, Bedminster, Bristol, 1897. Note the lift which connected it to the kitchen.

4.43 (right) Entertainment must have been very important at the Albion Tavern, Sheffield. This plan from 1901 shows two small front rooms but a substantial concert room at the rear. The servery ('bar') accesses both the concert room and the smoke room.

traders, workmen and others. They offered set meals such as the 'good and cheap' ones purveyed by the New Inn in 1870. The Lord Clyde, in seeking a full licence, claimed to be serving 80 to 100 meals a day in 1873, a factor that presumably it hoped would weigh in its favour. Bradford food sellers also set up stalls outside pubs (as seafood vendors still do in London), offering anything from pigs' trotters through shellfish to fruit and gingerbread.[19]

The evidence of food service in former times can still be detected in present-day pubs. The most lasting feature – because it is a big job to remove it – is the dumb waiter which hoisted meals one way and dirty plates the other, since kitchens were often on the first floor. Occasionally old signage advertises the presence of former eating facilities.

## Recreation and the pub

Games, sports and other entertainments have long been intimately linked with the pub. Before the middle of the 19th century it was just about the only place away from the home where the poor could meet for indoor recreation and entertainment. Some unsavoury activities such as prize-fighting, cock-fighting (illegal since 1849), and ratting, where a dog competed to kill the maximum number of rats in a given time (and said to have survived into the early 20th century), have long gone. Others, like karaoke and quizzes, are fairly new arrivals laid on by enterprising licensees to attract custom. Yet various traditional recreational activities survive, some thriving, others on the wane. The following pages are not intended, for example, to catalogue all pub games as these are thoroughly

covered elsewhere, notably in Finn 1975 and Taylor 2009. Rather, the emphasis is on those recreational goings-on which have an impact on the layout of the pub and require particular equipment or fittings.

## Live entertainment

The sounds of live musicians or karaoke emanating from many an urban pub are only the continuation of a long-established tradition! After all, it was out of the pub that the music hall was born around the 1830s and 1840s and which soon developed as an independent institution. Such is the ever-increasing specialisation of building types since the mid-19th century. Many Victorian pubs, however, continued to provide musical entertainment and many plans for rebuilding and refurbishment indicate the intention to have a 'concert room' and 'singing room'. A few pubs, especially in London, still have theatres attached to them, such as the Horseshoe, Hampstead, the Tabard, Chiswick, and the Gatehouse, Highgate.

**4.44** Old Time Music Hall enjoyed a late flowering at Watney's Windsor Castle, Maida Vale, London. It was presented five times a week in 1964 when this picture was taken.

**4.45** An opulent London establishment like the Old Dover Castle, Lambeth, might be equipped with a couple of billiard tables.

**4.46–4.47** (below left & right) The scoreboard, the rules, spectators' bench, and the billiard table at the Commercial, Wheelock, Cheshire.

**4.48** (right) Billiards was an important source of income for late Victorian and early 20th-century publicans as these sale particulars for two pubs in 1892 make clear.

## Games inside the pub

Dominoes and card games, such as cribbage, require no special arrangements other than a scoring board. On the other hand billiards, when played on a full-sized table, requires an enormous investment of space and capital to accommodate tables occupying nearly seven square metres, quite apart for the space required by the players. The playing of billiards in fully licensed houses was legalised by an Act of 1845 (the same Act required beerhouses to obtain a separate licence for billiard tables), and it became very popular as a pub game in the late 19th and early 20th centuries, despite the legal requirement to lock any room containing a table to ensure it was out of use on a Sunday. When the two greatest Liverpool pubs, the Philharmonic and the Vines, opened, the tables and

£900 CASH. — FREE Suburban PUBLIC-HOUSE—bold corner position in thoroughly respectable neighbourhood—exceptionally good home—garden and stabling—easily worked at small expense—would suit a man with family—long lease—rent £100, cleared by billiards and stable—pays £160 a month.

EXCELLENT Fully-licensed Country PUBLIC—few miles out, Surrey—near railway main line—free lease at very low rent, more than cleared by billiards—exceptional home—full-priced trade of best description—cash required £800 to £1,000.

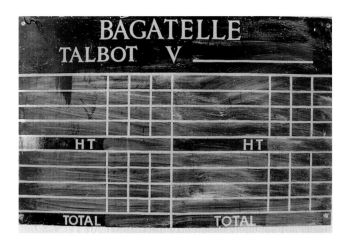

4.49–4.50 Bagatelle table and scoreboard at the Talbot in Chester. In the 19th century the game was popular enough to be grouped with billiards in the Gaming Act of 1845. Like billiards, a cue ball is used and the objective is to pot the balls in the cups.

4.51 Long-alley skittles at the White Swan, Chad Valley, Birmingham, in 1955. The game is no longer much played in the area.

players were taking up perhaps 40 per cent of the entire trading area. At the Crown, St John's Wood, London (3.32), the plan of 1898 makes clear the scale of investment; the billiard room housed two tables and had seating for thirty to forty people to watch the play. The grandeur of the billiard room was often enhanced by skylights with coloured glass such as that at the Salisbury, Harringay, London (3.28), and the Vines, Liverpool. Snooker only overtook billiards from the late 1930s when it was popularised by the great Joe Davis.

Now very few pubs have full-sized billiard tables. The Lamb, Eccles, is one good example and it even keeps its raised seating for spectators. Other full-sized tables are to be found at the Commercial, Wheelock, Cheshire, and the Douglas Arms, Bethesda in North Wales, where it is said to have been installed in 1930. Many pubs still have etched glass announcing 'billiard room' although the table(s) have long gone and, given their generous scale, billiard rooms have been pressed into other useful service. Those at the Salisbury and the Crown do duty as restaurants, those at the two Liverpool pubs as function rooms. The billiard table

has been usurped in pubs by the pool table which requires vastly less space. The game was invented in the United States about 1900 and is a relative newcomer to Britain. In 1960 there were no pool tables in Britain but by 1986 there were estimated to be around 45,000 in pubs and clubs.[20] It is now played in pubs all over the country.

**4.52–4.53** Hood skittles at the Queen Adelaide, Northampton.

Before the advent of pool, bar billiards arrived and offered a less space-consuming game than proper billiards (or, indeed, pool). The game was played in the 1920s under the exotic name of 'billard Russe' at cafés in northern Belgium and France where it was discovered by an English businessman, David Gill. [21] He brought it to England in the early 1930s and had tables made which were said to be improvements on their Flemish counterparts. The game was, and mainly is, most frequently encountered in the south of England. The first pub league was created at Oxford in 1936. The players aim to pot balls into holes, without knocking over strategically placed 'mushrooms'. It is an unusual game in that it is played against time with a bar coming down after a fixed period to prevent the return of potted balls. Bar billiards is probably a descendant of the much older game of bagatelle which was a very popular pub game from the late 18th century until well into the 19th. It is now only played in two places – Chester and Coventry (4.49–4.50).

As a pub game skittles is played in various forms. Most prominent and space consuming is long-alley skittles, a game which certainly goes back to the Middle Ages. A room between eight and twelve metres long is required, down which balls are bowled at the nine skittles. Our picture (4.51) was taken in a Birmingham pub but today the game is most flourishing in the south-west, especially in Somerset, Gloucestershire and Dorset. Long-alley skittles is also played in Leicestershire and Nottinghamshire. It was once very much more widespread, however, as 19th-century pub plans and inventories attest. There is a London game too, now played at only two places, including the Freemasons Arms, Hampstead: the 'cheeses', or bowling balls, are large and the pins taller than in other types of skittles.

A much more compact version is 'hood' or 'table skittles'. This is a table game which occupies a corner of various public bars in Northamptonshire and Leicestershire. The cheeses are hurled at pins set up on a table which has cushioned walls around the sides and back and, for the safety of bystanders, a hood over it.

Another type of table skittles which takes up rather less space is 'devil among the tailors' in which the skittles are knocked down by a ball swung on a chain (2.44).

Today the most widely played of all pub games is darts which, when in progress, takes over a defined space usually in the public bar.[22] The game seems to have had a long but rather shadowy history. It is often said to have originated as 'puff and dart' with the dart blown from a blowpipe and both were being played in Bradford pubs in the 1860s.[23] Darts was not an enormously popular pub game until the 20th century but by 1925 brewers were starting to organise leagues.[24] The game received a massive fillip in 1937 when King George VI and Queen Elizabeth were moved to throw darts at a board in a social club in Slough. There are various versions of the dartboard which is, in itself, suggestive of a long history. The standard or 'London' board has doubles and trebles and is numbered up to twenty but there are variants like the London 'East End' board with segments scoring multiples of five, and the Manchester 'log-end' board with tiny segments and no trebles.

4.54 (above left) Darts, played here with the standard or 'London' board.

4.55–4.56 Playing quoits at the Moon Inn, Mordiford, Herefordshire. The space is also used by darts players.

Less intrusive within a bar than skittles or darts are games such as shove ha'penny in which coins have to be shoved to land in 'beds' along the length of a slate slab. At the Star, Bath (4.57), the table is a permanent fixture, being screwed to the wall and hinged to drop down when not in use. In Dorset there is a localised form of the game played on the 'Swanage board', a very much longer version in which the coins should land in a scoring area at the far end of a mahogany

4.57 Shove ha'peny at the Star in Bath. The objective is to land three discs in each of the 'beds'.

board. An even more localised variant is push penny which survives around Stamford, Lincolnshire, and is also played on a mahogany board. Players still converge from yards around each September for the 'world championships' whose finals are held in the Jolly Brewer pub!

Tossing the penny is an East Anglian game which requires no more than a hole in a settle and a drawer beneath to collect successfully thrown coins. It is rarely played today but the permanence of the settles means a number of examples have survived. A South Downs variant is toad in the hole which requires a small table with a hole with a drawer beneath to catch flat weights, as at the Red Lion, Snargate, Kent, and the Lewes Arms in Lewes, Sussex.

Shooting is not a sport one would normally associate with the pub. However, miniature rifle ranges have found their way into pubs; several enterprising Bradford landlords erected them around the turn of the 19th century.[25] Indeed, in the Devizes, Wiltshire, area shooting is still carried on at pubs. The Lamb, Devizes, has a 25-metre shooting tunnel with the firing end in the snug (4.62). The George and Dragon at nearby Potterne has had a .22 shooting gallery for over a hundred years.

When people come together to play games and sports there arises, inevitably, the matter of betting. Gambling was illegal in pubs for centuries and the authorities took a dim view of it. Fines for landlords allowing gambling on their premises were regularly handed down and it was only in 1960 that the Betting and Gaming Act legalised bookmaking and allowed dominoes and similar games to be played on licensed premises for small stakes. The now almost ubiquitous fruit machines began to appear in pubs after the Gaming Act 1968 relaxed restrictions upon them. Earlier machines in pubs had offered attractions other than prizes; in 1904 Portsmouth's magistrates complained 'that certain licensees were permitting the exhibition of pictures of a suggestive nature in automatic machines', a practice which had to stop.[26]

## Games outside the pub

Skittle alleys, which were sometimes a little apart from the main pub premises, have already been mentioned. Quoits was a popular East Anglian game and extended to Northamptonshire where it co-existed with long-alley skittles. A plan for alterations at the Carpenters Arms, Northampton, in 1901 even shows two quoit grounds at the rear.[27] The game was also popular in north Yorkshire and along the Tyne valley.

The classic outdoor game associated with the pub is bowls, a game with medieval antecedents, in decline by 1800, but revived during the later 19th century.[28] The number of greens linked to pubs dwindled in the late 20th century as support for the game declined and licensees felt moved to turn them into car parks. However, they still exist in some numbers, especially in

4.58 (above) Tossing the penny is an East Anglian variant of pitching games – here the simple equipment is at the Cock, Brent Eleigh, Suffolk.

4.59 (top right) Toad in the hole at the Red Lion, Snargate, Kent. The grey surface is lead.

4.60 Ringing the bull at the Blue Ball, Grantchester, Cambridgeshire. A deceptively easy-looking game in which the objective is to swing a hook to land a ring on a hook (or real horn) during a given number of throws.

the West Midlands and north-west where the well-manicured swards greatly enhance the charm of the pubs to which they are attached. Two forms of bowls are played: the flat green game is played in the south but in the north and north-west Midlands a crown on the green introduces an extra level of complication. Some greens have a pavilion where equipment is stored and players can sit under cover.

**4.61** Gate Inn, Northampton. Plan of 1903 showing both a skittle room and a quoit ground.

**4.62** The shooting tunnel at the Lamb, Devizes, Wiltshire.

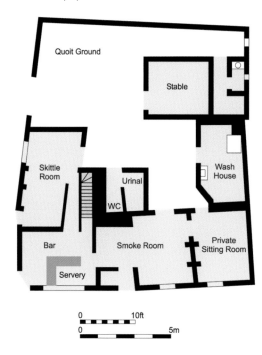

Quoit Ground

Stable

Skittle Room

Urinal

WC

Wash House

Bar

Smoke Room

Private Sitting Room

Servery

0    10ft

0         5m

**4.63** Nursery, Heaton Norris, Greater Manchester, a pub of 1939 with its own, well-used bowling green.

## The pub as museum and cabinet of curiosities

Any pub-goer will have encountered establishments bedecked with huge assemblages of bric-à-brac, collections of foreign currency notes, stuffed animals, pump-clips, clocks, suspended chamber pots and so forth. Yet all this is following in a great historical tradition! Victorian pubs were often stuffed with objects. In 1866 the Globe Tavern in Highbury Vale, London, was reported as having an upstairs museum with 'cases of tropical and English birds, curiously small dogs, … strange Chinese paintings, carvings, magnificent china-ware of unheard-of value, and vases'.[29] Other London pubs boasted amazing arrays of artefacts and creations of nature: the Bell and Mackerel on the Mile End Road displayed 20,000 stuffed creatures, and the Hole in the Wall, Borough High Street, held a collection of skulls. At the Edinburgh Castle, Camden Town, the licensee's

offerings, genuine or otherwise, included 80,000 butterflies and moths, the spear that killed General Gordon, the bugle that sounded the Charge of the Light Brigade, two pictures by Ruskin, and three great auk's eggs.[30] Charlie Brown's famous museum of objects from the four corners of the globe at the Railway Tavern, Limehouse, was a centre of attraction in London's East End. Most collections today are relatively modern but the beautifully displayed cabinets of birds' eggs at the Ship, Overton, Lancashire, seem to have been assembled in Victorian times.

**4.64** The pub as cabinet of curiosities. Charlie Brown built up his 'World Treasury' at the Railway Tavern, just outside London's West India Dock gates. Exhibits included Ming vases, stuffed snakes, human skulls and opium pipes. Brown (d 1932) took over the pub in 1894. This 'uncrowned king of Limehouse' was an unofficial banker to dockworkers and sailors who were, no doubt, the source of most acquisitions.

# Chapter 5

# Advertisement and Embellishment

Until the early 19th century, the alehouse and the public house – unlike inns – tended to be fairly simple affairs. All that was to change. Owners increasingly took steps to make their premises look distinctive, advertised them and the products on offer more aggressively, and fitted up their houses with more panache than ever before.

## External signage

The earliest sign indicating the existence of an alehouse was the ale-stake, as we saw in chapter 1. By 1600 or so, as alehouses adopted more permanent names, this was generally replaced by a pictorial signboard, and this remained a distinguishing feature until the 19th century. It was typically fixed to the building, either against a wall, or suspended from the building by a stake. Free-standing examples were also common from the 18th century onwards, particularly where the building was set back from the road.

**5.1** Bass makes a permanent mark at the Golden Cup, Hanley, Stoke-on-Trent. The Bass red triangle was the first registered trademark.

A pictorial signboard was essential when much of the population was illiterate, but during the 19th century it began to disappear as most people gained at least a basic education. By 1900, it had almost entirely vanished, being replaced by a simple lettered board advertising the pub's existence and its name. Such signs were not the only thing to appear in the 19th century. By the middle of the century, many pubs sported a variety of boards advertising the facilities available and the range of drinks to be found within. As breweries acquired ever-larger tied estates, it was normal to advertise their ownership so that discerning customers could be sure whose beers were on sale at a particular pub. Many photographs of urban pubs before the First World War (and this appears to have been largely an urban phenomenon) show the façade almost invisible under advertising signs. Many of these were mass-

123

**5.2** Britain's earliest pub sign, at the Swan Inn, Clare, Suffolk. The claim is slightly spurious as it probably began life at the base of an oriel window at Clare Castle some time before 1413 and was appropriated when the castle fell into disrepair after becoming a Crown possession in the late 15th century. The swan, gorged with a crown (a royal symbol) is flanked by the shields of Mortimer and de Burgh quartered and the royal arms.

**5.3** A number of inns erected 'gallows' sign boards: less than a dozen remain. This one is at Nunney in Somerset.

**5.4** Victorian urban pubs were frequently decked with large advertising signs. In this case the Vine Tavern on London's Mile End Road offers food in the form of 'chops & steak' as well as liquid sustenance. It appears in a sorry state and was demolished in 1903. Pubs, however, live on but public wash baths do not: the 6d would have bought about three pints of normal strength beer.

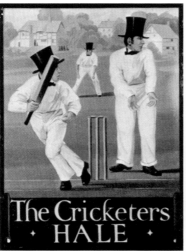

The Cricketers
HALE

THE SPOTTED COW

produced in materials such as enamelled sheet iron or steel, and often depicted the brewery trademark or bottles containing their product.

Excessive external advertising was one of the targets of the reformed public house movement in the years before the First World War, and of the promoters of the improved public house after it. One of the Government's first actions, on taking over the pubs of Carlisle, was to remove almost all the external signage, and this set the tone for much of the 20th century. Only in recent years have banners and placards advertising drinks and facilities become a familiar feature of the pub once again, despite the efforts of the planning authorities to control them.

While improved public houses were notable for the lack of external advertising, the pictorial sign enjoyed a renaissance during the inter-war years. The promoters of the improved pub, as we have seen, were influenced by a rose-tinted view of the Olde English inn, and the pictorial sign formed part of that vision. Brewers such as Whitbread of London, and Youngs, Crawshay and Youngs of Norwich began to commission artists to paint signs, or even to employ them as permanent members of staff, while signs in carved wood, sculpted stone or wrought iron, which harked back even more self-consciously to medieval models, also appeared. There was a very positive public response to the reappearance of the pictorial

5.5 (above, left) A lovely metal sign of the 1930s for the Fox, Bury St Edmunds, designed by Basil Oliver, architect, and an important promoter of the improved public house.

5.6-5.7 Two signs shown at the inn sign exhibition of 1936.
The Cricketers, Hale, Surrey, designed by Ralph Ellis for Watney, Combe, Reid & Co. Also by Ellis, the Spotted Cow, Littlehampton, West Sussex, for Henty and Constable, brewers, of Chichester.

5.8 Brewers developed distinctive trademark signs which stamped their identities on the areas where they traded. This plaque is at the Palace, Bristol. West Country Breweries was formed by a merger of the Cheltenham and Hereford Brewery Co and the Stroud Brewery Co in 1958. It was taken over by Whitbread in 1963. The pub companies which have arisen since the 1989 Beer Orders appear to have little interest in promoting visual corporate identities.

sign, and an exhibition of inn signs, held in London in November 1936, attracted widespread attention. The committee which selected the 400 or so signs on display included Sir Edwin Lutyens, Harry Redfern, Basil Oliver, Professor A E Richardson (a noted writer on the old English inn) and representatives of the Brewers' Society.

The continued appearance of the pictorial sign outside the majority of our pubs is arguably the single most enduring legacy of the improved public house, even if today it is as likely to be a computer-generated image as the work of a live artist.

### Internal signage

The interior of the pub was obviously a place to advertise the drinks on sale, and the facilities offered. Some of this advertising was permanent – such as fixed mirrors – but brewers (and other manufacturers of spirits, soft drinks and tobacco) lost no opportunity to put across their message to potential customers with a range of more ephemeral advertising material. Mirrors and posters (usually framed and glazed as a protection against tobacco smoke or accidental damage) were hung on the walls of even the most simple pub (2.4), whilst free-standing card adverts were placed on bar-backs or mantelpieces to draw the attention of customers to the latest bottled beer

or the choice of whiskies available. Early examples were quite plain but, from the late 19th century, many bore striking artwork, such as those produced by Guinness from the 1920s onwards. Although mid-19th-century mirrors, posters and card signs were typically the work of local printers, the majority of these later signs were the work of specialist firms such as Sir Joseph Causton and Sons of London, whose products decorated pub interiors all over the country.

### Other advertising material

The pub offered many other opportunities for advertising. Water jugs, normally pottery but occasionally of glass, advertised brewers or distillers. Waiter trays, usually circular but occasionally square or rectangular, could also be used in this way. In the 19th century, examples were typically made of metal such as copper or pewter, but during the 20th century many other materials (printed tin, wood, pressed papier-mâché or later plastic) were used. Early 19th century inventories suggest that even the smallest pub possessed dozens of spittoons, usually of pottery but occasionally of copper, brass or even cast iron. By the end of the century these were being replaced by metal or pottery ashtrays advertising drinks or

**5.9–5.10** Customers at the Olde Swan, Netherton, West Midlands, were left in no doubt about the virtues of what they were drinking or where they were drinking it. The ceiling is enamelled. Beyond the screen on the right is a tiny snug. The pub was rebuilt in 1863 and has brewed continually since, apart from a break between 1988 and 2000.

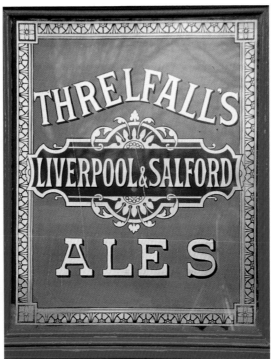

5.11 (above left) Glazed advertising panel at the Red Lion, Erdington, Birmingham, for Cragganmore whisky, probably dating from the building of the pub in 1899.

5.12 Glass advertisement at the Saddle Inn, Kirkdale, Liverpool.

5.13 (right) Advertisement at the Old Wine Store, Shotts, North Lanarkshire, suggesting medical approbation. The lockable drawer to the left would have been used for cash in the days before a till.

tobacco. Many of these, like the water jugs, were produced by major potteries: Doulton, for example, produced thousands of ashtrays for brewers such as Courage in the years before the First World War.

Other advertising appeared at the actual point of sale. It is not clear when the first pump-clips appeared, identifying the particular brew being dispensed, although it was probably sometime between the wars. Early examples were small and plain; more elaborate clips, typically incorporating the brewer's trademark, appeared during the 1950s. Even the barrels from which beer was dispensed on gravity could be used to advertise the product, either by using a printed insert attached to the barrel end, or a coloured jacket covering it. Spirit barrels and glass urns provided another advertising opportunity, as did their successors, spirit optics, which appeared during the inter-war years.

The motto of most drink manufacturers seems to have been 'if it is made, it can carry an advertisement'. Very few objects within the pub have not been used in this way. The different designs and advertising messages contributed immeasurably to the appearance and atmosphere of the pub. With the exception of a few pubs, which were noted for their 'museum' collections (4.64), there was very little decoration in the Victorian or Edwardian pub which was not related in some way to the products on sale. The miscellaneous collections of books, pictures and sundry artefacts which have been imported, seemingly by the cartload, into so many modern pub interiors without any reference to the building, its suppliers or

5.14 Customers enjoying a drink in one of the finest surviving pubs in northern England, the Garden Gate, Hunslet, Leeds. Built in 1903, it makes full use of the arts of the pub – ceramics, woodwork, glass, and plaster.

locale, would have been entirely out of place in pubs before the 1960s.

## Embellishing the pub

Massive changes took place during the 19th century in pub ornamentation and decoration, reaching a high-water mark around the 1890s. The rise of the richly treated 19th-century pub was heralded by the glitzy gin palaces of late Georgian and early Victorian England. These depended for their impact on 'gas and glass' which created a shimmering, febrile world through the brilliant effects of gas lighting on mirrors and plate glass. Such results were made possible by the products of the Industrial Revolution. New and improved materials were constantly becoming available and the combined effects of greater produc-tivity and economies of scale brought down prices in real terms. Cost reduction also came about through a series of tax concessions: duties on glass were repealed in 1845, the brick tax, introduced by Pitt in 1784, was abolished in 1850, and window tax, dating back to 1696, in 1851.[1] The price of plate glass came down by more than half.

The great boom in pub building at the close of the 19th century exploited this wide variety of materials to brilliant effect. Some of the most iconic images of Victorian pubs – scenes of, say, the Philharmonic, Liverpool (3.43, 5.47, 5.58), the Princess Louise, London (5.18), or the Crown, Belfast (6.1, 6.14–6.16) – are conveyed by the rich interplay and magnificence of glass, ceramics, woodwork, metalwork and plaster.

## Glass

Elaborate glasswork was used extensively in many secular building types other than pubs but so much of this has been lost. Now it is chiefly in the pub that we

can appreciate rich Victorian and Edwardian ornamental glass and, even here, there has been a huge amount of destruction over the years. All the techniques of treating glass are on show at pubs in many of Britain's major towns and cities, with the finest examples of all dating from the late 1880s and the 1890s.

Glass played a key part in creating the character of pubs and was used in various different locations. Window glass had a special role. The lower portions of windows both concealed and revealed. They were usually both etched and cut so that passers-by could not pry on the world of the pub within, yet it was possible to gain a sense of warmth and conviviality, of modest luxury and 'otherness' that set the pub apart from most people's daily lives.

**5.15** Mirrors at the Red Lion, St James's, London, make this tiny pub feel much bigger than it really is. The pub was probably refitted in the 1890s.

**5.16** (below left) Detail of glass in a screen at the Red Lion.

**5.17** (below right) Mirrors at the Assembly House, Kentish Town, 1896, by a local manufacturer, W James.

Techniques developed steadily during the Victorian period and included etching, cutting, embossing, enamelling or flashing, and gilding. Etching was carried out with dilute hydrofluoric acid; the parts to be left clear were protected and the acid attacked the unprotected ones. The embossed areas were ground with sand or emery powder to remove the transparency. Brilliant cutting was done by grinding followed by polishing the area that had been cut away. Enamelling involved applying a thin veneer of coloured glass onto clear glass. In gilding, gold leaf adhered to the glass by a coating of transparent size and was cut away to form the required letters or patterns.

The most impressive use of glass for late Victorian pubs is in the ornate mirrors which line the walls of London pubs such as the Argyll Arms near Oxford Circus, the Paxton's Head, Knightsbridge, or the Red Lion, St James's (5.15–5.16). The latter, particularly, is a most remarkable building that gives the impression of being of far greater size than its actual dimensions would suggest. It is all the mirrors lining the walls that achieve this effect. Occasionally, wall mirrors are back painted,

such as those at the Half Moon, Herne Hill, where
they are signed by Walter Gibbs and Sons of
Blackfriars, or at the Bunch of Grapes, Knightsbridge,
where the maker is named as W James of Kentish
Town. Walter Gibbs began work in the 1860s and also
worked at the Red Lion in St James's. His firm, along
with that of William James, was one of the most active
and well-respected providers of public house glass in
the capital. Other examples of painted glass are at the

## Embossing glass

A major step forward in beautifying the pub
from the 1880s was the advent of French
embossing which gave us some of the loveliest
of all pub glasswork, like that in the Princess
Louise, Holborn, and the Assembly House,
Kentish Town. Mark Girouard describes the
process: 'French chemists developed and
perfected a new procedure, involving the
application of "white acids". White acids result
from the mixture of hydrofluoric acid and
various other chemicals, and when applied to
glass form a dense white obscuration without
depth. If hydrofluoric acid is then applied to
these obscured portions it will reduce the
whiteness. By forming a block design with white
acid, coating parts of it with a protective and
applying an etch of hydrofluoric acid, two tones
can be obtained, known as "white" and "half-
tone".'2

Yet another tone could be obtained by protecting
the white and part of the half-tone and applying
another etch known as 'bright'. True French
embossing consists of these three tones but there
were cases of four or more tones being applied.
A factor which helps explain the profusion of
ornate glasswork from the late 1880s is that it
was possible to apply the French embossing
method to sheet glass, which cost about a third
the price of plate glass.

5.18 (opposite, top) Superbly detailed example of the late Victorian
glassworker's art at the Princess Louise, Holborn, London. It dates
from 1891 and is signed 'R. Morris & Son 239 Kennington Rd SE'.

5.19 (opposite, centre) Detail from the screenwork at the Half Moon,
Herne Hill, London, which was built in 1896.

5.20 (opposite, below) Door glass at the Red Lion, St James's, London.

5.21 (above) One of six back-painted mirrors at the Half Moon, Herne
Hill by W Gibbs & Sons, glass decorators, of Blackfriars, London.

Washington, Hampstead, and a tour de force by
James Carter of Gray's Inn Road at the Lord Nelson
on the Old Kent Road (c1888) depicting the admiral
himself. Painted glass of this type seems to have been
a feature of London, rather than provincial pubs.
Glazed advertising panels, often of considerable size
and incorporating mirror work, were sometimes a
feature of Victorian public houses. Their cost and the
fact that they were frequently built into the walls are a
telling reminder of their intended permanence and
hoped-for relevance – some of the products can still
be consumed today although others have long
disappeared. At their most spectacular such panels
seem to have been a feature especially of the London,
Scottish and Irish pub scenes. Fine examples in London
are at the Tipperary, Fleet Street, the Dog and Duck,
Soho (5.29–5.30), and the Prince Edward, Homerton,
the latter being a magnificent blue piece advertising the
wares of brewers Truman, Hanbury and Buxton.
A couple of notable Scottish examples are at Bennet's
Bar, Edinburgh, and the Old Toll Bar, in Glasgow, while
at the House of McDonnell, Ballycastle, Co Antrim, the
two bar-back mirrors attempt to persuade us to drink
the still-available Bushmills whiskey. Bar-backs are a
particularly rich location for the pub glazier's craft.
Not only is there advertising, but also every other
kind of glazed embellishment may be found, with the
Lord Nelson, Old Kent Road, probably taking pride of

5.22 (opposite) Flowers, fruit, ribbons and putti
at the Tottenham on London's Oxford Street,
and dating from 1892 when the pub was built.

5.23 (left) Lord Nelson, at the pub named after
him on the Old Kent Road, Bermondsey,
London, receives the surrender of the swarthy
Spanish after the Battle of Cape Vincent in
1797. It is the work of James Carter of Gray's
Inn Road and dates from c1888.

5.24 (above) Etched, gilded and painted glass
in the bar-back at the Lord Nelson.

place for its sumptuous gilded and coloured mirrors by Carter (5.23–5.24). An attractive feature of some bar-backs, as at the King's Head, Bristol, and, again, the Lord Nelson, is the presence of rectangular glazed panels on uprights (often with decorative motifs) or horizontals (often with advertising; 2.9, 5.53). The gold lettering on glazed panels was introduced in the 1860s.

5.25 (opposite) Stained glass window on the staircase at the Bartons Arms, Aston, Birmingham. The central monogram is for the Birmingham brewers, Mitchells and Butlers, who built the pub in 1900–1.

5.26–5.27 (below) This pair of windows in Pre-Raphaelite style at the Crown Posada, Newcastle upon Tyne, probably dates from 1880. Do we see the sexual politics of drink in times past? The subdued lady fills the glass, and a happier-looking gentleman raises it.

5.28 (right) Window glass of a type very common in Birmingham pubs in the early 20th century. This example is at the Bellefield in Winson Green (now closed).

## Ceramics

Glass is a permanent material, vulnerable only to accidental breakage (of which there is a fair amount in pubs!) and the vagaries of changing taste. Architectural ceramics are still more fortunate since, in most instances, they are difficult to remove. In many a modernised pub, tiles still line the walls or one can enter through a mosaic-floored former passageway. Such ceramics were expensive but offered the advantage of a very long, virtually maintenance-free life. They were also hygienic as they could be cleaned easily, a valuable feature in the smoke-filled pub atmosphere of our towns and cities whose air quality, in any case, left much to be desired.

Ceramics were used in various contexts, both inside and outside. External tiling on the ground floor, sometimes accompanied by ceramic lettering proclaiming the name of the establishment, its wares and their producer, are familiar sights which help define the character of many a pub. Very occasionally the work spreads further as at the Peveril of the Peak, Manchester, where the entire surface

of a routine pre-existing building has been covered with ceramics, probably in the 1890s. Sometimes the work can be very ornate indeed and was specially commissioned, as in the stunning brown façade of the Garden Gate, Leeds (1903), and the Stork, Birkenhead (c1905). Such work was highly visible and Lynn Pearson, who has charted the use of ceramics in the brewing

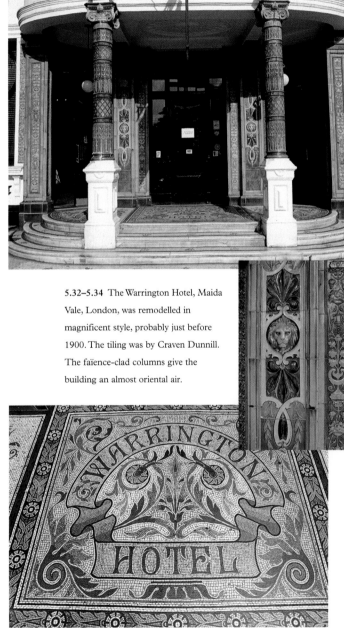

5.32–5.34 The Warrington Hotel, Maida Vale, London, was remodelled in magnificent style, probably just before 1900. The tiling was by Craven Dunnill. The faïence-clad columns give the building an almost oriental air.

5.29–5.30 (opposite) Wall tiling and advertising mirrors at the Dog and Duck in Soho. In the dado there are yellow tiles depicting the eponymous animals.

5.31 (above) The Peveril of the Peak, Manchester, was a humble street-corner building until it was entirely refronted with glazed brick and tiles, probably in the 1890s.

industry generally,[3] suggests that it was often a loss-leader to promote the work of the manufacturers involved, such as the Swan Tile Works, Liverpool, who kitted out the Stork. More rarely, lettered tiles appear within the pub – a spectacular example is the Marble Arch, Manchester, where a frieze just below the ceiling lists the range of drinks available.

In Birmingham and Portsmouth, ceramics were raised to especial prominence on pub façades. Around Birmingham it took the form of red tile and terracotta and was extensively used around 1900 by the prolific pub architects James and Lister Lea, and Wood and Kendrick. Much of the work was supplied by the Hathern Station Brick and Terra Cotta Company. In the streets of Portsmouth, the competing brewers, Brickwoods and Portsmouth United, were busy embellishing their pubs with ceramic frontages from the start of the 20th century. Brickwoods began this development and established a house style of dark red and brown glazed bricks or faïence (glazed earthernware) with white lettering. Portsmouth United favoured green faïence. Both brewers patronised Carter's of Poole.

5.35 Birmingham has a number of pubs with extensive ceramic decoration but among the finest is the Red Lion, Handsworth, rebuilt in 1901–2 by the Holt Brewery Company.

5.36 Detail of the tiling at the Prince Alfred, Maida Vale, London, c1898.

5.37 The smoke room at the
Red Lion, Handsworth,
Birmingham: tiled walls and
framed lithographs of comely
girls in idealised rural settings.

5.38 The Bartons Arms, Aston,
Birmingham. Tiled panel of a
hunting scene by Minton
Hollins, 1901.

Ceramics in the form of mosaic make a regular appearance at the entrance to many a pub. It forms the hard-wearing surface in large numbers of entrance lobbies and corridors and in rare cases such as the Salisbury, Harringay (3.27), and the Philharmonic, Liverpool, it continues further to become the flooring of a significant room. At the Philharmonic it even extends upwards to cover the main bar counter front (5.43).[4] In entrance lobbies, the name of the premises is sometimes picked out in a different colour from the rest.

The first known record of decorative ceramics in a pub context is in 1850 when the *Builder* noted the use of tiled pictures in the billiard room at Gurton's Tavern in Old Bond Street, London.[5] They showed fitting scenes such as 'Bacchus and Ariadne' and 'Jupiter's Cupbearer', and were made, perhaps, by Doulton of Lambeth. However, the widespread use of decorative ceramics at public houses did not start until the early 1880s. The date 1883 is a crucial one as this was when Carter's of Poole began to produce historical tile murals for pubs and other public buildings. Other makers followed. They were often placed in entrance lobbies or along corridors. Subsequent opening out of pub interiors has removed the original context but the murals frequently remain. London examples include the Ten Bells, Spitalfields (18th-century street scene by W B Simpson and Sons), the Shipwrights Arms, London Bridge (river scene/shipwrights at work, signed by Charles Evans and Co), and the Dolphin, Hackney (classical scenes, again by Simpsons).[6] Outside London notable examples are at the Havelock, Hastings (historical scenes painted by A T S Carter of London and made by Doulton), the Mountain Daisy, Sunderland (a fully tiled room of around 1902 by Craven Dunnill with various scenes of the north-east), and the Bartons Arms, Aston, Birmingham (hunting scene of around 1901, again by Craven Dunnill 5.38).

Pictorial tiling was expensive and, therefore, quite rare. Plain tiles and ones with a relief pattern are much more common. Usually they would have been chosen out of a catalogue but occasionally were made specially – a good example is at the Dog and Duck, Soho, where the dog and duck are depicted in relief. (5.30). Tiling as a dado is frequently encountered but it could also extend to full height. A particularly good example is the Waterloo, Smethwick, a landmark pub-cum-hotel of 1907, which has a subterranean restaurant with all-over tiling, including the ceiling and the facing on a large grill for steak, chops and so on.

**5.39–5.40** (opposite) Even the ceiling is tiled in the restaurant in the basement at the Waterloo, Smethwick, West Midlands. This showcase pub-cum-hotel was built in 1907 by Mitchells and Butlers whose brewery was nearby. The architects were Wood and Kendrick and the tilemakers Carter's of Poole. Quite why there should be a nautical frieze at a pub called the Waterloo is a mystery.

**5.41** (above) Craven Dunnill ceramics cover the basement bar at the former St Anne's Hotel, Lytham, Lancashire, and date from c1900. This is the longest of all ceramic bar counters. As at 2011 it is used as a function room.

**5.42** (right) Counter at the Black Horse, Preston, 1898, possibly made by Pilkington's Tile and Pottery Co. The floor is mosaic.

## Ceramic bar counters

Perhaps the most striking of all ceramic work in public houses is a very impressive series of bar-counter fronts. They were luxury items and were very expensive, thanks to the effort that went into producing them. The first known example (now gone) was installed in the first-class refreshment room at Newcastle upon Tyne station in 1892–3 and was made by Burmantofts of Leeds. The most active maker of such counter fronts were Craven Dunnill and it was they who made the one at the Crown, Belfast (6.16). The design here, with its delicate floral detail, is the same as the spectacularly long one at the former St Anne's Hotel, Lytham, Lancashire (open for functions: 5.41) and the Red Lion, Erdington, Birmingham. A different Craven Dunnill design features a grotesque mask and swags and can be found, in slightly varying versions, at the Gunmakers Arms, Birmingham (c1903), the Golden Cross, Cardiff (1904: 6.3), and the Mountain Daisy, Sunderland (c1902). Another manufacturer was Pilkington's and it is they who provided the heavily detailed and immensely tall counter at the Towler, Tottington, Greater Manchester (now resited within the pub). It has a family resemblance to the counter at the Black Horse, Preston (5.42), built in 1898, and Pilkington's might also have been responsible for this.

In all, some eighteen historic ceramic bar counters remain and it is likely that the number never exceeded this greatly. Their solidity and fine appearance mean they have stood a good chance of being retained. In addition to those already listed, they can be found at: Whitelock's, Leeds (4.41); the White Hart, Hull (a second such counter was removed); the Polar Bear, Hull; the Horse and Jockey, Wednesbury; the Waterloo, Newport, Monmouthshire (now a hotel and bistro); the Garden Gate, Leeds (5.14), and the Feuars Arms, Kirkcaldy.

There are also a few examples where the front is tiled. Pride of place must go to the Prince Arthur, Liverpool, and its striking red tiled counter: the same colour and patterns are picked up in the corridors. Whereas three-dimensional ceramic fronts do not appear after 1904, tiled ones occasionally crop up in inter-war contexts, such as the. Golden Ball, York (1929).

**5.43** (right) Mosaic counter front and floor at the Philharmonic, Liverpool, 1900.

**5.44–5.45** (below) Public bar at the Prince Arthur, Walton, Liverpool, with its unique red-tiled counter. The plan of this pub is the same as that at the Lion, described in 3.37. The screenwork in the L-shaped corridor is behind the screenwork in the background.

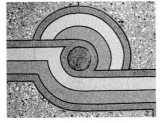

**5.46** (centre) Terrazzo flooring tended to take over in the early 20th century from mosaic as a hard-wearing, hygienic floor material for pubs. Small pieces of marble are set in a cement base, ground flat and polished. This fine Art Deco example is at the Vat and Fiddle, Nottingham, and dates from 1937.

**5.47** (left) Tiles, mosaic, and marble, both real (basin surrounds) and imitation (urinal surrounds), make the gents' at the Philharmonic the most sumptuous in any British pub.

**5.48** (above right) Even ceramics were not good enough for Frank Crocker, proprietor of the Crown, St John's Wood, London. The saloon has a fireplace and wall covering of various polished marbles. The counter top in this area is white marble.

143

## Woodwork

Ornamental woodwork was a feature of all but the most basic Victorian and Edwardian pubs. At the simplest level it may be just a little embellishment of the bar counter but at the other end of the scale it can involve a magnificently carved bar-back, rich fireplace, floor to ceiling panelling, and sturdy fixed seating. The wood may vary from cheap pine through to teak, walnut and mahogany which were consumed in huge amounts to furnish public houses a century ago.

The bar counter is a highly functional piece of equipment and there are definite limits to what can be done to embellish it. Indeed, the designs which evolved early on are mostly still with us. The most basic is tongue-and-groove boarding, either set

**5.49** Woodwork played a key part in defining the character of the Victorian pub. High Victorian decoration in the bar-back at the Victoria, Bayswater, London, 1864.

**5.50** Decorated wood and glasswork of 1896 at the King's Head, Tooting, London.

vertically or tapering away downwards from the customer. Moving up the scale, there is an unmistakable sub-Classical design that will be familiar to any pub-goer and was in use by the mid-19th century. The counter is divided up into bays by shallow pilasters, topped by console brackets beneath the counter. Sometimes the pilasters are omitted but the general effect remains. The intervening spaces are treated in one of a limited number of ways – perhaps tongue-and-groove boarding (sometimes upright, sometimes diagonally arranged), or fielded panelling. Different types may be found within a single pub and,

5.51 Advertisement for a stillion (a housing for shelves, barrels, bottles etc in the middle of a servery). The upright barrels, presumably for spirits, are features still found in many Scottish bar gantries. From the *Licensed Victuallers' Gazette*, 8 January 1892.

5.52 (below left) A richer-than-usual variation on a theme. The counter front at the Plough, Gorton, Manchester, 1893, with very elaborate console brackets and decorated panelling in between. But the basic elements of counter design established in the 19th century are still being deployed.

5.53 (below) Bar-back at the King's Head, Bristol. It dates from *c*1870 and includes glass advertising panels. 'Hollands' refers to gin.

145

### A unique pub

The Black Friar in the City of London has an unparalleled decorative scheme of the highest quality. The building went up about 1875 but thirty years later, its publican, Alfred Pettitt, turned it into a theme pub, the theme being the Dominican friars who occupied a site nearby in the Middle Ages. Pettitt's friars are not austere clerics. Instead, they are jolly, good-living ones of the sort reinvented in the late 19th century who could have shared a meal and a joke with Friar Tuck.

The work was done in two phases under architect, H Fuller-Clark. In 1904–5 the ground floor outside was embellished with mosaics and the distinguished sculptor, Nathaniel Hitch, provided caricatures of, among other things, friars feeding a pie to an ass, cutting into a cheese in front of two starving figures, and making music – not to mention a few gnomes. At the same time the interior was lavishly refitted with alabaster and marbles of various kinds lining the walls.

In the public bar (the front part), over the servery, are copper reliefs of friars on Saturday afternoon, showing them gardening. Over the saloon servery we have 'Tomorrow will be Friday' with the friars preparing for their meat-less day by bringing in eels and fish. Opposite, over the fireplace, they sing carols. The artist for these reliefs was Frederick T Callcott (see also 5.61).

The second phase was planned in 1913 but was delayed by the war, and involved creating an intimate extension to the saloon through a couple of arches. The work began in 1917 and the finishing decorative touches went in in 1923–4. The Saturday afternoon friars reappear over the arches and beyond them are humorous scenes with captions, for example 'Contentment surpasses riches' (a well-fed friar takes an outdoor snooze) and 'A good thing is soon snatched up' (four friars wheeling off a trussed pig). These copper reliefs are by sculptor, Henry Poole. The keystones and capitals illustrate nursery rhymes and Aesop's fables.

as in London at the Warrington Hotel, Maida Vale, can give valuable clues to the hierarchy of former spaces within a pub where the partitions have long gone.

Some kind of shelving is essential for any pub servery. In very basic houses one can still sometimes find completely unadorned shelving, as utilitarian as anything that might be found in a domestic pantry, but a pub with even modest ambitions aspired to a more ornamented bar-back (or 'gantry' in Scotland and Northern Ireland). By the mid-19th century the

5.54 (above) The Black Friar in the City of London. In the saloon contented friars go about their business. Over the fireplace they sing carols and over the arches to the 'small saloon' they occupy themselves with gardening on Saturday afternoon.

5.55 (left) Friars direct customers to the source of refreshment in the saloon.

standard form was a series of pilasters or arches supporting a cornice or entablature and perhaps pediments. Apart from accommodating bottles and glasses they also displayed advertisements, clocks, spirit barrels, measures, glass, and any other items necessary to service the pub. Before the advent of cash registers, money was kept in drawers in the bar-back (4.13): a few examples survive such as at the New Inn, Hadlow Down, East Sussex (1885): see also 5.13. A particularly early and magnificent bar-back is the one at the Victoria, Bayswater (5.49) which appears to date from 1864;[7]

it is signed by the maker, S Hill of Southwark. It incorporates some particularly striking mirrorwork decorated with green, red, blue and gold.

5.56–5.57 The Vines, Liverpool, has some magnificent decoration. The architect was Walter Thomas and his client Robert Cain, the same team that had built the Philharmonic. Here the base of a column and a female torso flank a fireplace.

## Metalwork

Ceramics, glass and wood are the most noticeable materials used to embellish the late 19th-century pub. Metalwork, in various forms, also has a part to play. Its most prominent usage is at pub entrances where richly swirling wrought ironwork fills the upper part of the entrances to some the grander pubs. At the Philharmonic, Liverpool, the doorway to Hope Street is filled with the

5.58 (opposite) A tour de force of Art Nouveau metalwork. The gates to the Hope Street entrance of the Philharmonic in Liverpool, the work of H Bloomfield Bare, working for architect Walter Thomas and client, Robert Cain.

5.59 Scrolly ironwork was often used about 1900 in the arch heads to pub porches. This example is at the Salisbury, Harringay, London. The floor is mosaic. The left-hand doorway leads to the grand saloon (3.27).

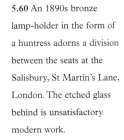

5.60 An 1890s bronze lamp-holder in the form of a huntress adorns a division between the seats at the Salisbury, St Martin's Lane, London. The etched glass behind is unsatisfactory modern work.

most sumptuous Art Nouveau metalwork, rivalling anything that Gaudí designed for Barcelona.

Light fittings were important in creating the presence and character of a pub. Large gas lamps illuminated the exterior of the grander establishments and some even had standard lamps rising from the pavement, such as still survive in front of the Star of the East, Limehouse, London (3.11), and the Prince Alfred, Maida Vale. In darkly lit streets or often ones that were not lit at all, such lamps must have made the pub look all the more inviting. Perhaps the most delightful internal light fittings are the bronze nymphs sprouting floral light-holders at the Salisbury in St Martin's Lane, London (5.60). They date from 1899 when electricity was coming into use for lighting as an alternative to gas and probably were electric from the start.

Other metalwork embellishing the pub may be found as door furniture, foot-rails in front of counters, ornamented structural columns, supports for inn signs, and water dispensers and cigar lighters.

5.61 (above) One of several copper relief panels at the Black Lion, Bayswater, London, depicting Shakespearean scenes. Here 'a Lord', who appears in the 'Induction' of *The Taming of the Shrew* announces his intention to play a trick on the stupefied tinker, Christopher Sly: 'Sirs, I will practise on this drunken man.' The artist was Frederick T Callcott who was responsible for some of the panels at the Black Friar (5.54).

5.62–5.63 (right) Plasterwork at the Vines, Liverpool. Viking ships set sail across a lunette over a fireplace and putti go hunting.

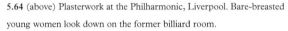

**5.64** (above) Plasterwork at the Philharmonic, Liverpool. Bare-breasted young women look down on the former billiard room.

**5.65** (right) Richly decorated wood and plasterwork of 1901–2 in the bar-back at the Dun Cow, Sunderland.

**5.66** (below) The highly decorated ceiling over the billiard room at the Crown, St John's Wood, London, inspired by Jacobean detail.

Chapter 6

# Over the Border

This book is primarily about English pubs. However, the pub is not an exclusively English institution and it seems desirable to say a little about drinking establishments in other parts of the United Kingdom. There are sometimes considerable differences and these point up the fact that the English have no monopoly on how to go about public drinking or building for it.

## Wales

Welsh pubs were influenced by much the same regulatory forces as their English counterparts. The temperance and teetotal movements were taken up more slowly than in England but, in the second half of the 19th century, they took on great vigour, especially in rural areas, supported by strong Methodist traditions and an association with nationalist aspirations.[1] 1881 saw the passing of the Welsh Sunday Closing Act and there were several attempts to introduce local option – allowing a local vote on whether to refuse new and renewed licences – but none ever passed into law.[2] It was Lloyd George who was a particular scourge of the drink interest in the early 20th century and, as Prime Minister, eagerly supported the stiff First World War measures to control alcohol sales. Until well into the second half of the 20th century, only *bona fide* travellers could purchase drink in some areas of Wales on a Sunday. Under local referenda established in 1961, dry areas were gradually whittled away. The last bastion of Sunday closing, Dwyfor, in Gwynedd, finally voted against it in 1996.[3]

The arrangement and hierarchy of rooms in the 19th and early 20th centuries, with basic public bars and better quality smoke rooms and lounges is the same as in most parts of England. The rural nature of much of the country and its relative poverty has not blessed it with many ambitiously planned or decorated pubs. The finest surviving is undoubtedly the Golden Cross,

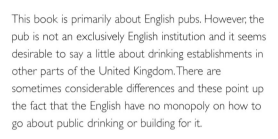

**6.1** The Crown Bar, Belfast, which vies with the Philharmonic in Liverpool as the most resplendent pub in the United Kingdom.

153

6.2 An unspoilt rural Welsh local, the
Dyffryn Arms, Pontfaen, Pembrokeshire.
A quarry-tiled floor, benches, domestic
table and chairs, and a hatch on the right
to the servery-cum-cellar.

6.3 Ceramic bar-counter at the Golden
Cross, Cardiff, 1904. It was made by
Craven Dunnill who supplied the same
design to two other pubs.

6.4 (opposite, top) The tiled frontage of
the White Horse, Aberystwyth.

6.5 (opposite below) Tiled mural of
Cardiff Castle by Craven Dunnill at the
Golden Cross, Cardiff.

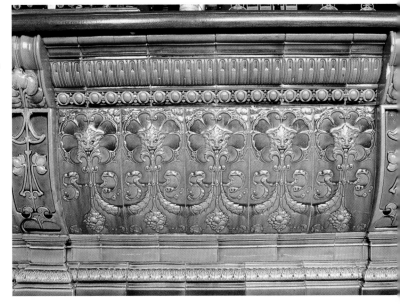

Cardiff, built by Brain's brewery about 1903. Craven Dunnill provided it with tilework that compares with almost anything in England. The ground-floor frontage is glazed, but the great feature is the interior tiling which includes a ceramic bar counter and two tiled murals (depicting Cardiff Castle and the owner's brewery). Wales has a second ceramic bar counters, at the Waterloo in Newport (now a hotel and bistro) although some years ago half of it was removed and exported to the United States. The other fine ornamental display is the ceramic exterior of the White Horse (now the Varsity) in the centre of Aberystwyth.

## Scotland

English and Welsh visitors to Scotland find that pubs look and feel noticeably different from those in their home countries. The cultural and legislative divide between Scotland and England in terms of pubs is greater than between England and the Principality, which is not surprising, given that Wales was forcibly united with England in 1536, long before the more peaceful union between Scotland and England in 1707. Also, historically, Scotland was closely allied with France, and the 'Auld Alliance' was reflected in its

architecture and its legal system, amongst other things. The great swathe of Border country between the sparsely populated, most northerly part of England and the densely settled area of the Scottish Lowlands has also served to reinforce the architectural and cultural separation.

The Beer Act of 1830, which had an enormous impact on the opening and subsequent development of public houses south of the border, never applied to Scotland. However, temperance and teetotal campaigners, allied to Sabbatarians and their desire to keep Sunday special, were highly active and effective. They secured an early victory in 1853 when the Liverpool MP, William Forbes Mackenzie, secured the passage of an Act banning Sunday opening throughout Scotland (*bona fide* travellers – those travelling three miles or more – could be served but, in practice, they would have relied on hotels). As in England there were efforts to crack down on new licences and to improve existing public houses, which were so effective that, despite the hard-drinking image of Scotland, there are many large, well-populated areas where pubs are few and far between.[4]  At one time in much of Aberdeen, for example, the only hope of securing a drink even now is at a hotel bar. In 1903 Glasgow's magistrates did what the English never managed to do – banning barmaids.[5] Furthermore, an Act to allow the local veto to close pubs without compensation was passed in 1913, although voting was delayed by the war until late 1920 (when most, but by no means all, parishes, burghs and wards decided to stay 'wet'). Nevertheless, nineteen areas were still 'dry' as late as 1969.[6]

6.6  Leslie's Bar in Newington, Edinburgh is part of tenement block and, like so many Scottish bars, presents an unassuming face to the street.

## A pub or a bar?

The term 'pub' is familiar to all. So too is that of 'bar' in the sense of a place where people go to have a drink. But is there a difference? The answer is yes, and the distinction is pointed up when we consider drinking establishments in England on one hand, and Scotland and Ireland on the other. Generally, the English go to the pub for a drink, the Scots and Irish to a bar.

The distinctions, of course, become blurred at the edges, but public houses, as they evolved in England, tend to be architecturally distinct and often very substantial. When passing a closed pub or one that has been converted to other use, its former function is usually unmistakable (3.2). Traditionally (and this goes with size) they had several separate rooms for public use. Bars, however, did not have the architectural pretensions of the pub. They tended to be smaller, often had just one room (perhaps with a built-in snug ('sitting room') or two), and if they changed to another use, the previous one would usually not be readily identifiable.

6.7–6.8 Unlike traditional English pubs, Scottish bars frequently had just a single drinking space. The Grill, Aberdeen, behind its plain, austere frontage, is one long room elegantly fitted out in 1925.

Restrictions on Sunday drinking were only eased in 1962, when the Licensing (Scotland) Act allowed hotels to sell liquor to the general public (not just travellers and lodgers) on Sundays. To ensure that there was no confusion with public houses (which still had to close on Sundays) a hotel was defined as 'a house containing at least four apartments set apart exclusively for the sleeping accommodation of travellers' if in a town, or 'at least two such apartments' in rural areas.

However, after decades of Calvinistic antipathy towards drinking, in the late 20th century Scotland proved itself far more enlightened than England and

**6.9** Spirit barrel at the Central Bar, Renton, West Dunbartonshire.

**6.10** The third spirit barrel at the Old Wine Store, Shotts, North Lanarkshire, still in action for its original purpose. The only other known 'working barrel' is in the Irish Republic at Thomas Fletcher's, Naas, Co Kildare. The word 'Store(s)' attached to a pub name is now rare but was quite common in the 19th century: for example, the Salisbury, St Martin's Lane, London, (5.60) was originally the Salisbury Stores.

Wales, when the Licensing (Scotland) Act of 1976 brought in all-day and Sunday drinking, and extended evening closing time. In many urban pubs drinking is now permissible to midnight and, in a few cases, beyond. The Central Bar, Leith, may hold the record, opening from 9 am till 1 am in the week and from 12.30 pm till 1 am on Sundays.

The most noticeable difference between Scottish and English pubs is that in Scotland pubs are less distinctive architecturally. They are often little different from the adjacent shop fronts. Even the magnificently appointed Central Bar at the foot of Leith Walk, Leith, of 1898–9, with its all-over internal tiling and fine woodwork, has a façade which scarcely attracts attention. The upper floors of most Scottish pubs look just the same as the upper floors of the other buildings in the block. Architecturally, they therefore look like shops which just happen to be selling drink rather than other goods.

Scottish pubs, then, often have no more architectural presence than most bars in, say, France or the Low Countries. And, indeed, they are often referred to as 'bars', with this term being applied in the title, as in the Central Bar, Leith, just mentioned, or Glasgow's finest late 19th-century pub, the Horseshoe Bar, to name but two. Given a weaker system of brewery-owned houses than exists in England, there is also a long tradition of naming the establishment after the person who founded it or a notable former owner. Hence in Edinburgh we find pubs called Bennet's Bar and Leslie's Bar, both of them notable for their intact interiors. Although one can refer to a 'bar' within an English pub, it is highly improbable that anyone would refer to the whole establishment in this way.

There is another way in which many Scottish pubs more closely resemble, say, French bars than traditional English pubs. We would suggest that to many people the term 'bar' – easier to use than define – often denotes a single space provided with a counter but with no real segregation of customers into different parts. And that is precisely what has

happened in many Scottish pubs for generations. There has been far less subdivision of the interiors than in England, and the ultra-compartmented London pub of around 1900 finds no place in the drinking places of Scotland's two great cities. Glasgow's pub historian, Rudolph Kenna, explains that in that city 'most pubs consisted of a single democratic drinking space' and cites the Horseshoe Bar as the finest surviving example.[7] Similarly the only intact historic pub interior in Aberdeen, the Grill (6.7–6.8), of 1925, is a single oblong space, stretching back behind an unprepossessing shop-like front. The reason for the openness of Scottish pubs was probably pressure from magistrates as far back as the late 19th century to ensure supervision by the bar staff.

Of course, not all Scottish pubs are single spaces. There are some that retain snugs, akin to those in England. In Scotland they are termed 'sitting rooms' and point up the contrast between respectable seated drinking that would take place therein, as opposed to the 'perpendicular drinking' to be expected in the rest of the premises. Good examples are at the Central

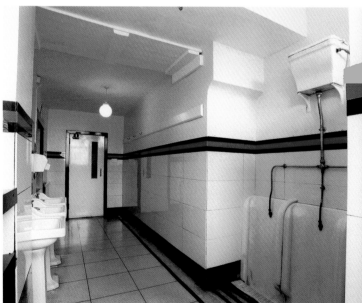

**6.11–6.12** The colour-coded toilets of 1936 at the Crook Inn, Tweedsmuir, are among the finest displays of Art Deco in a public house environment anywhere.

Bar, Renton (c1893), and the Clep, Dundee (1941), where each have two such rooms, and the 1930s Portland Arms, Shettleston, Glasgow, which has no less than four. The dates quoted suggest they enjoyed long-lived popularity at a time when England was starting the process of stripping out compartments.

A century ago many English pubs displayed prominent spirit or wine barrels. These are now almost all gone, although small porcelain ones can sometimes be seen. In Scotland, however, a number of pubs still retain barrels behind the bar, probably reflecting a more general spirit-drinking tradition than in England: Scottish beer production never exceeded 6 per cent of the UK output down to 1914, and this was an even lower figure than in Ireland.[8] Good examples of barrels in gantries are at the Auldhouse Arms, Auldhouse, near East Kilbride; Bennet's Bar, Edinburgh; Central Bar, Renton (6.9); Old Toll Bar, Glasgow, and the Bull, New Street, Paisley. Perhaps the most remarkable survival is at the Old Wine Store, Shotts, Strathclyde, where the no 3 barrel is still used for serving whisky (6.10), and is simply topped up as required. The fitting which houses such barrels is usually known by its own Scottish name – 'gantry'. This derives from 'gantress' or 'gauntress', old words to describe a wooden stand for barrels. The term 'back-fitment' is also used. In former times these barrels were filled with spirits raised from the cellar by water engines, which were also used to serve beer.

Scotland has its fair share of grand pubs dating from around 1900. The best and most complete examples are in Dundee (the Speedwell Bar, 1903); Edinburgh (Abbotsford, 1902–3, Bennet's Bar, Tollcross, 1891, the Café Royal, 1898–1901, and Leslie's Bar, Newington, 1899); Leith (the Central Bar, 1898–9, the bar for the former Leith Central Station); Glasgow (the Horseshoe Bar, 1885–7); Kirkcaldy (the Feuars' Arms, Edwardian), and Paisley (the Bull, 1901, with strong echoes of Mackintosh). In relative terms, Scotland has far more good surviving post-First World War interiors than England. This may be because they are in private hands, and have thus escaped the eternal desire for change on the part of brewers or large pub-owning

## A distinctive method of dispense

Until the 1950s almost all draught beer in Scotland was raised from the cellar by air pressure. Water engines were introduced from about 1880 and used mains water pressure to produce compressed air. They became more popular than hand-pumps although these probably did not entirely disappear. From about the 1950s water engines were replaced by electric compressors. Both, however, suffered heavy losses as lager and keg beer made massive advances from the late 1960s, and, in 1976, the second *Scottish Real Beer Guide* could find only 207 outlets for traditional beer in the whole country. 161 had electric compressors and a mere 26 water engines. From the 1980s real ale has made a come back thanks to the efforts of CAMRA but it is the hand-pump rather than air pressure which is the normal method of dispense. The number of pubs using air pressure is uncertain: none are believed to use hydraulic compressors and the estimates for electric compressors vary from as little as about a dozen to no more than four times this.[9]

The resurgence of the hand-pump has been dramatic. Only 9 pubs throughout Scotland used them in 1976 but the 1984 *Real Ale in Scotland* guide recorded 470 pubs with hand-pumps against 212 using air pressure (in addition 228 used electric pumps). The reason seems to be this. Traditional Scottish founts serving beer under air pressure were tall, had a tap at the top, and looked remarkably like the higher lager and keg founts we see today.[10] They were replaced by new versions from the early 1980s which were more compact but looked just like small keg founts. For brewers and publicans wishing to show they had real ale on offer, the hand-pump was an obvious solution.

companies. The best are in Aberdeen (the Grill, 1925: 6.8); Glasgow (the Steps Bar, 1938; the Portland Arms, 1930s); Dundee (the Clep, 1941, Tay Bridge Bar, with its 'Walnut Bar' of the 1930s), and Lochgilphead, Argyll and Bute (the Commercial, 1945–6). Special mention needs to be made of the Crook Inn, Tweedsmuir, on the Moffat–Edinburgh road: this, in fact, is a wayside hotel which was remodelled in 1936 and has a still-intact 'publican's rustic' public bar and sleek, vitrolite-lined loos (6.11–6.12).

## Northern Ireland

In the Middle Ages there was nothing to distinguish Irish drinking establishments from their English counterparts.[11] There were alehouses, taverns and inns but, given the relative poverty of the country, their numbers were far fewer than in England. As in Scotland, there was a long tradition of spirit drinking, and beer consumption never seriously rivalled that of spirits. Indeed, it was almost certainly the Irish who developed whisk(e)y, the earliest record of distillation there being in the *Red Book of Ossory* of around 1300 which predates by nearly 200 years the first Scottish record (1494). The term itself is of Irish origin – *uisce beatha* (or water of life). As for brewing, it was often a domestic business, intended for private consumption.

Although broadly following the English models, legislation on public drinking in Ireland was a separate affair; for example the 1618 English prohibition on Sunday trading did not descend upon the Irish until 1685, and the immensely important English 1830 Beer Act did not apply to Ireland, although many of its provisions surfaced in the Licensing (Ireland) Act of 1833. As in England, there was a proliferation in the number of beerhouses and beer consumption increased steadily from the mid-19th century. Recorded beer production, however, was low in comparison to England. It never amounted to more than 10 per cent of the UK output before 1900, even despite the phenomenal growth of Guinness after 1855 and which, by the 1880s, was the largest brewery in the world.[12] There was also a strong Irish temperance lobby, which campaigned against the sale of alcohol altogether; in 1878 an Act was passed which introduced Sunday closing, initially for a trial period of four years, although, as the major towns were exempt from the measure, it was not entirely

**6.13** Like their Scottish counterparts, drinking establishments in Ireland are generally much plainer than most English pubs. Many have frontages which would not appear out of place on a butcher's or a general stores.

**6.14–6.16** The Crown Bar, Belfast. Facing the counter across a tiled area are a series of drinking booths, a feature of several Northern Irish pubs. These provide for seating and waiter service. The tiled area is intended for stand-up drinking. The Craven Dunnill ceramic bar counter is the same as at two English pubs (5.41).

effective. Nevertheless, it was renewed annually from 1882, and was made permanent in 1906.

The long-standing tradition of whisk(e)y drinking is reflected, as in Scotland, in the survival of barrels in gantries: particularly good examples are Blake's Bar, Enniskillen; the Central Bar, Irvinestown; the House of McDonnell, Ballycastle, and the Mandeville Arms, Portadown. Ireland shares other pub traditions with Scotland. The idea of the pub as a bar is general, many of them taking the name of the proprietor. With this goes a generally modest architectural treatment with many pubs looking little different from neighbouring shops or houses. Although Scotland has its small sitting rooms and England a few remaining snugs, a handful of Northern Irish pubs have a feature which seems unparalleled (with one exception) in the former countries. That is rows of drinking boxes at some remove from the counter. It is true that London had small snugs in great numbers and, indeed, two survive at the Barley Mow in Marylebone (3.34–3.35). But these were/are linked to the counter and servery,

whereas the Irish ones are arranged in a line on the opposite side of the room from the servery. The unique English case is at the Cittie of Yorke, Holborn, London, but this exceptional pub is a one-off, of late date (1923–4) and follows no popular English tradition. In Northern Ireland, however, such boxes were widely popular in the late 19th century. There are examples at the Mandeville Arms, Portadown, the Fort Bar, Belfast, and, in rather fragmentary form, at Dan Magennis's, also in Belfast.

But for the grandest display of such boxes you need to visit the Crown, Belfast, where one of them sheltered the fugitive James Mason in the 1946 film classic *Odd Man Out*. This pub is arguably the most spectacular in the British Isles, thanks to a refit about 1885. It is a decorative tour de force, summing up all that is grandest and most lavish about the late Victorian pub – stained glass, rich woodwork, superbly decorated gantry (with spirit barrels) and even a Craven Dunnill ceramic bar counter.

A final point concerns spirit-grocers. In the 1980s and 1990s English high streets sprouted pastiche Irish theme pubs, which were recognisable from the outside by an assortment of sundry clutter in the windows – old packaging, bottles, advertisements for household goods and so on. This was a reference to the Irish tradition of the spirit-grocer, that is a combination of shop and basic

drinking-house. The spirit-grocer's licence was introduced in 1791, and allowed grocers, on payment of an Excise fee, to sell small quantities of spirits for consumption *off* the premises. The licence was much abused, with many spirit-grocers allowing drinking in their establishments. Typically, partitions were erected to divide the drinking area from the shop itself. Spirit-grocers were eventually brought under the magistrates' control in 1872. In 1877 there were 641 spirit-grocers in Ireland, 320 of them in Dublin[13] but their death knell in Northern Ireland came with the Intoxicating Liquor Act (Northern Ireland) of 1923. This was one of the first pieces of legislation to be passed by the Northern Ireland Parliament following Partition and abolished the spirit-grocer's licence altogether.[14] Occasionally one can still trace the vestiges of the dual functions. At the House of McDonnell, Ballycastle, for example, the partition dividing the two parts still remains. The tradition of the spirit-grocer survived south of the border but, with changing patterns of retail trade, their numbers have dwindled substantially and they may only amount to a few dozen: few have a very active shop business.

6.17 The Fort Bar, Belfast, is a smaller, but similarly planned version of the Crown with booths on the left. Note the fringe of tiles set in the counter and the spirit barrels in the gantry.

## Chapter 7

# Great Pub Myths

Pubs are fertile ground for tall tales. Secret tunnels, ghosts, dark deeds, and pubs of prodigious age all enrich the folklore of the pub. Where solid facts and hard evidence are absent, the resources of the imagination may amply fill in the gaps. However, once erroneous tales are born, they seem destined for a long and robust life because local tradition and those who write about pubs are all too prone to recycle the same information – each retelling adding a new stamp of authority. But why let facts spoil a good story, especially if it's good for business?!

## Ye oldest pub

Although it is difficult to say much definite about public houses prior to Tudor times, people certainly enjoyed a sociable drink long before then. It is very satisfying to identify places where they might have done so. Traditions have grown up around certain pubs which imbue them with a remarkable antiquity which pushes back the frontiers of history.

7.1 Fact, or more likely, fiction. Behind those pub doors, cheerful conversation, a lively imagination, and a beer or three, can create wonders. Even here we glimpse a ghostly spirit about to enter the world of credulous drinkers.

**Ye Olde Fighting Cocks, Abbey Mill Lane, St Albans**
A lovely pub in a lovely riverside setting, with an impressive timber-framed octagonal room for its core. It is, a notice outside proclaims, 'Reputedly the Oldest Public House in Britain'. A printed menu (as at December 2003) even specified 'an 11th Century structure on an 8th Century site' and cites the *Guinness Book of Records* as its authority for this architecturally amazing claim.

The tale of Saxon origins were common currency by 1909 as it was mentioned by Frederick Hackwood in his encyclopaedic *Inns, Ales and Drinking Customs of Old England* published that year.[1] Later authors have followed the same line.[2] However, when Offa founded St Albans Abbey in 793, there would not have been

"Ye Olde Round House Inn,"
*Abbey Mill Lane, St. Albans.*

THE quaint City of St. Albans, Herts, in addition to its distinction as the scene of the life and death of England's Proto-Martyr, lays further claim to having within its boundary the OLDEST INHABITED HOUSE IN THE COUNTRY. It stands in a sylvan valley on the banks of the River Ver. It is a curious structure —of octagonal shape—of early Saxon origin, having been built here as a boat-house to the ancient Monastery founded here by King Offa about the year 795, and is thus over 1100 years old. The basement has walls of great thickness, built, like the Abbey, of flint and bricks. There is a subterranean passage now blocked up running from the basement to the ruins of the Monastery, a distance of about 200 yards. The upper part is built of timber and bricks, the oak beams being of great thickness and as hard as iron. There is a shed at the back of the house where, it is said, Oliver Cromwell stabled his horse, himself once sleeping under its roof during the Civil War. The house stands in close proximity to the most picturesque and historical parts near the City, viz., the early British Dyke and Causeway, Verulam Woods, the walls of the Roman City of Verulamium, the Cathedral, St. Michael's Church, etc.

*Ales, Wines and Spirits of the Finest Quality. Luncheons and Teas provided. Good Accommodation for Cyclists, etc.*
Proprietor: T. MAGUIRE.

7.2 An early 20th-century postcard of Ye Olde Fighting Cocks, St Albans, advertising its marvels.

stone precinct structures in this position at so early a date. Unpublished excavations by Verulamium Museum prior to 1980 suggest the foundations of the present building date from no earlier than about 1600.[3] This would tie in with the likelihood that an octagonal pigeon house, perhaps of around 1400 and sited nearer the abbey church, was re-erected here in 1600, the year after a disastrous flood of the Ver.[4] It took the name, slightly erroneously, of the Round House.

So when did a pub emerge? Certainly not in Offa's day. The excavations suggested there may have been a monastic brewhouse on the site although this certainly does not imply the building acted as a pub. In fact the first recorded licensee does not appear until 1822, so maybe Oliver Cromwell didn't stable his horse here after all, despite what *another* legend relates. Before 1872, when the name Fighting Cocks appeared,[5] it had been called the Fisherman based on the idea that the monks would have stored their fishing tackle in this waterside spot. It did not obtain a full licence until 1951.

### Old Ferry Boat, Holywell, Cambridgeshire

The age of the Fighting Cocks is as nothing compared to this pub. An unfortunate article in the *Sunday Times* (1 September 2002) by a journalist with a page to fill on the oldest pubs in Britain regurgitated claims that it dates back to 560, that 'local records state 1100', and that locals believe it was built c1400 over the grave of a young woman who died in 1076. It goes on to state that archaeological digs show the 'foundations may date back to 460 [sic]'. The young woman is actually named at the pub as one Juliet Tewsley who took her own life after being rejected by a local woodcutter.[6]

Sadly, the Cambridgeshire Sites and Monuments Record has no knowledge of any archaeological investigations having taken place.[7] Equally unfortunately the building shows no evidence of dating from before the 17th century and there seems not a shred of evidence to support the imaginative claims for the antiquity of this fine riverside pub.[8]

7.3–7.4 The awesome antiquity of the Old Ferry Boat, Holywell, Cambridgeshire, suggests a triumph of marketing over historical fact.

### Eagle and Child (part of the Royalist Hotel), Stow-on-the-Wold, Gloucestershire[9]

Anglo-Saxon (10th-century) origins and thousand-year-old timbers are claimed here. The hotel's website declared (in 2004) 'In 949AD Saxon Duke Aethelmar founded The Royalist as a hospice that was to shelter lepers – one can still find a leper hole in the oldest part of the cellar.'[10] Another website says, 'Some evidence even suggests that The Royalist began as part of a Saxon community as long ago as 514.'[11] Then there is a tunnel to the church, a bear-pit, and witches' marks. A witches' brew indeed, but one which finds no place in the Gloucestershire Sites and Monuments Record[12] nor in the *Victoria County History of Gloucestershire (VCH)*.[13] There was a medieval hospital at Stow but its site is simply unknown, and there is no apparent evidence for the tradition that it was founded by Aethelmar before the Conquest. Worse still the *VCH* states that the earliest known inn at Stow was the Swan in Sheep Street which existed by that name in 1446 (closed around 1700). The Eagle and Child is not recorded until the 18th century, although the building itself dates from the 15th or early 16th century and was refronted in the 17th century. Some of the blame for all this may be laid at the door of the Rev David Royce who published a (very long) lecture

7.5–7.6 They can't both be right! Rival claimants from Gloucestershire and Nottingham.

as *The History and Antiquities of Stow* in 1861 where he noted that: 'Tradition reports that it was a Roman Catholic chapel. This tradition and the appearance of the house, particularly of the back of premises, led me to believe that this was Aethelmer's Hospital.'[14] Paradoxically he then goes on to identify 15th-century work! In a process akin to petrification, time and popular imagination have turned Royce's speculations into solid fact.

### Bingley Arms, Bardsey, Leeds

Another haunt of thirsty Anglo-Saxons. The pub's website as at April 2011 informs us it was the 'Priest's Inn' back in 953 and is mentioned in the Domesday Book.[15] All this is accepted by the *Guinness Book of Records*. But, as we churlishly point out on page 2, Domesday (1086) has no references at all to any alehouses or similar places of refreshment. What's more the West Yorkshire Sites and Monuments Record (SMR), which ought to know about these things, assures us it has no records to support the contention of 10th-century origins for the building. As far as this is concerned, the SMR has no reason to doubt that it is

7.7 The Bingley Arms, Bardsey, makes its claim in stained glass.

Nottingham's pubs, R S Tressider, after noting the earliest record of an inn in the city dates from 1483, rejects the 1189 date, pointing out that 'it was put up or rebuilt about 1680 when the first Duke of Newcastle was rebuilding the Castle above. … By 1760 there was an inn called the Pilgrim and by 1799 someone had improved the name suggesting that it implied a trip to the Holy Land!'[16] Another historic Nottingham pub, the Salutation, is painted up with the date 1240. Interestingly, old photographs in the Nottingham Local Studies Library include one showing the pub bearing the inscription 1280 – so as time goes on its origins seem to get progressively older. Both the Salutation and the Bell in Market Square have late medieval roofs but the first references to the buildings as pubs are in 1761 and 1638 respectively.[17]

### Skirrid Mountain Inn, Llafihangel Crucorney, near Abergavenny

Wales, too, has its myths. A 12th-century date is propounded here from 'local chronicles' of 1110 when a sheep-stealer, one James Crowther, was hung in the bar.[18] In fact the earliest record of the lordship of Abergavenny is a charter of 1086 but neither it nor the next records (which deal with castle building in 1255) have to do with pubs or the execution of sheep stealers.[19] As for the antiquity of the building, it goes back to the mid- to late-17th century.[20] The legend of hangings in the bar is compounded by executions ordered by Judge Jeffries. Jeffries did indeed secure a grim reputation for his 'bloody assize' which punished those involved in the Monmouth Rebellion of 1685. However, his activities were in the West Country, not south-eastern Wales, although a leaflet for the hotel notes an imaginative local belief that he might have done a bit of practising hereabouts around 1679. So how did the hanging stories come about? The answer lies in what appear to be rope marks on timbers in the stairwell which are probably the result of nothing more grisly than suspending sacks, bacon flitches or other heavy objects over the years rather than men. In any case early justice tended to be a public affair in order to demonstrate that it was being done, not hidden away in a hitherto unbuilt pub. The staircase itself is a fine, original, 17th-century example.

of 18th-century date, and entirely consistent with a surviving 1738 datestone. Bardsey church does have a late pre-Conquest church tower and the place is mentioned in Domesday – but it was probably going to be a very long time before the parishioners had the benefit of somewhere to drop in for a quick ale.

### Ye Olde Trip to Jerusalem, Nottingham

Part of this much-loved pub is cut into the soft rock on which Nottingham Castle stands. In bold black letters on the eastern wall the name is announced, plus the information: '1189AD' and 'the oldest inn in England' (7.6). The pub takes its name from the idea that it was a departure point for crusaders setting off to fight the infidel. However, the chronicler of

## Haunts of the highwayman

Being an 18th-century highwayman was thirsty work.
A book (2004) by James Sharpe explores both the real
and very different, mythologised worlds of England's
most famous highwayman – Dick Turpin.[21] This
unpleasant, pock-marked thug, one of many of his kind,
executed in 1739, and largely forgotten until the early
19th century, was catapulted to fame as a symbol of
adventure and daring. The cause of the transformation
was the now little-known William Harrison Ainsworth
and his blockbusting, three-volume novel *Rookwood*
which appeared in 1834. Ainsworth's invention of Black
Bess and the epic ride to York are not our concern
here but the appropriation of Turpin by numerous pubs,
anxious to claim a slice of history, is.

The Spaniards on the edge of Hampstead is the pub
with the strongest Turpin associations, with one
website informing us he was born in the pub (he
wasn't), had a tunnel built to another pub to escape
any pursuers (no), and that he stabled the (non-
existent) Black Bess at the nearby toll house. The
tunnel story turns up again at the Bell, Stilton,
Cambridgeshire, which was connected thereby to
another pub in the village known as the Angel.
Likewise Ye Olde King's Head at Chigwell in Essex was
thoughtfully provided with a tunnel from its cellar
which Turpin could use for unseen getaways. Turpin's
ghost haunts the George Hotel, Buckden,
Cambridgeshire while the sound of Black Bess's
hoofbeats disturbs the peace at the Crown Hotel,
Bawtry, further up the Great North Road in Yorkshire.
Scattered about the three dozen Turpin pubs, we also
find Turpin's pistols, a fireside seat where he rested, a
secret hiding place in a chimney, his clothes, his mask,
his spurs and so on.

## The tunnel to the church (and elsewhere)

Our forebears were much prone to excavating
tunnels from one building to another, often over
considerable distances. Invariably we find that people
are known to have entered them, walked part of the
way, but now, strangely, they have been sealed off. The
otherwise generally reliable Frederick Hackwood,

7.8 A place of Norman execution or just a 17th-century building?

dealing with the Fighting Cocks at St Albans, tells of 'A
subterranean passage, now blocked up, runs from the
basement to the ruins of the monastery, a distance of
about 200 yards.' At the Skirrid Mountain Inn there
was a tunnel to Llanfihangel Court (which must have
been useful to save crossing the main road): both
ends, unfortunately, are now blocked off. In
Abergavenny itself a 200-metre passage is claimed to
run from the Great George, Cross Street, to the
parish church.[22] In fact it is a passage with Tudor
doorways leading into the cellars of a row of houses
and could not have reached its supposed destination
without negotiating a now-culverted river. As we have
seen, more than one tunnel provided the heroic Dick
Turpin with a handy means of escape. If such tunnels

169

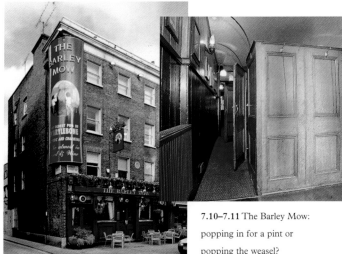

7.10–7.11 The Barley Mow: popping in for a pint or popping the weasel?

7.9 Did The Star, Netherton, miss the train?

led our highwayman to safety, the one from the Masons Arms in Upper Berkeley Street, London W1 did the very opposite. Those awaiting hanging at Tyburn, London's main place of execution until 1783, were shackled to the walls of the dungeons that now form the cellars of the pub, and then led up a tunnel to the gallows. In fact, the last journey by the condemned was a much more public affair made from Newgate gaol (on the site of the Old Bailey) in a cart on hanging days, which took place some three or four times a year in the 18th century with on average about five people being executed. As always, the Masons Arms–Tyburn tunnel is now blocked!

The examples of these mythical tunnels could, no doubt, be multiplied many hundred times. How, or indeed why, such tales have arisen is interesting in itself. Many town properties had cellars and vaults for storage and, if they point in the direction of the church, castle or similar prominent building, then … A vault was found under the Eagle and Child, Stow-on-the-Wold, in 1976 and no doubt merely reinforces the tunnel-to-the-church idea. Monasteries often come into the picture and the sophisticated water and sewerage systems of these houses probably fuelled notions about long-distance passages. There is always one vital ingredient missing in the tunnel tales – the real opportunity to actually walk from A to B.

## Pawnbroking

The two tiny drinking boxes at the Barley Mow, Dorset Street in Marylebone (3.34–3.35, 7.10–7.11) are now unique. They are so small they are incomprehensible to the average modern pub-goer and they cry out for an explanation beyond the fact that late Victorian Londoners liked drinking in highly compartmentalised pubs and small intimate spaces. So it is that the boxes at the Barley Mow are commonly said to have been for securing privacy for pawnbroking transactions. But, as Peter Clark in his classic study of the English alehouse notes, pawnbroking as an activity carried out by landlords, was pretty much dead by the early 19th century.[23] There were regulations by that time against taking pledges against drinking debts and furthermore there were specialist pawnbroking shops people could turn to – up to 300 of them in London by the 1820s. No – the Barley Mow customers were just after a very cosy drink or two.

## The wrong road

The Doctor Johnson, Barkingside, built in 1937–8 and seen in 3.63–3.65, has an imposing presence on the corner of two roads. Why? The answer, one learns from regulars and the staff, is that it was planned on a grand scale to serve as a substantial hotel-cum-pub on a major thoroughfare into London. But the plans for the road were changed and the great enterprise was left stranded.

7.12 Crocker's Folly – or was it?

The Doctor Johnson was actually built to serve some of the sprawling housing that covered swathes of Essex adjacent to London between the wars. It is an excellent example of the inter-war 'improved' public house. As discussed in chapters 2 and 3, these were often built on an epic scale, with a wide range of facilities to attract the upper working- and lower middle-class families who settled in places like this. After 1945 pubs were, and have continued to be, much more modest, and the Doctor Johnson, where the customers rattle around in the large spaces, became in need of an explanation – and it got one. True enough, the original plans allowed for seven guest bedrooms on the first floor,[24] but that was quite typical of many pubs and no more than many a guest house. And the great road? By the time the Doctor Johnson went up the main highway from London into Essex – Eastern Avenue – had been taking traffic for over a decade.[25]

### The train that never arrived

We turn finally to a couple of tales about pubs whose developers were woefully misinformed about local railway plans.

### Star, Netherton, Northumberland

According to local legend, the main part of the

building was put up in 1902 as an hotel to serve a projected railway – hence a rather imposing structure out of scale to what later people would think necessary for this quiet Northumbrian village. But the historian of the Central Northumberland Railway, Neil Mackichan, says that all the excitement of the final meetings for the CNR had simmered down by 1880–1 and the only line successfully promoted was the Alnwick to Cornhill line which was completed in 1887.[26] This got no nearer than Whittingham, some seven miles away, and although there was some talk of branches, for example, to Rothbury, there was not even the faintest suggestion after 1887 of a line to remote Netherton.

### Crocker's Folly, St John's Wood, London

Publican and entrepreneur, Frank Crocker, opened his magnificent Crown Hotel (5.48, 7.12) in 1898–9 in the sure knowledge that the Great Central Railway, the last main line into London, would bring great rewards by finishing at a terminus right by his new enterprise. But – ruin, disaster, despair – the railway ended up a mile away at Marylebone, and poor Frank ended his days by jumping from an upstairs window (or roof according to one account) of his fine new creation. A tragedy indeed or, at least, it would have been if there was a grain of truth in it! In fact, Parliamentary assent for the line was given back in March 1893 and the first trains steamed into Marylebone in July 1898, just five months after the foundation stone for the Crown was laid. As for the demise of Mr Crocker, this happened in 1904 when, as his death certificate records, he died of natural causes involving bronchitis and heart disease. He was only 41 and was buried in Kensal Green cemetery. The name 'Crocker's Folly' was adopted in 1987, and the pub sign sported a railway engine for twelve or thirteen years until the facts of the case were pointed out during a refurbishment to the then owners who tactfully depicted a crown but kept the name. It is ironic to think that, had he lived to a ripe old age, Frank Crocker is most unlikely to have become linked to the railway myth and would thus, like many thousands of other publicans before and since, have become consigned to obscurity. As it is, his name lives on for reasons for which he was in no way responsible.[27]

## Chapter 8
# Into the 21st Century

8.1 Prince Rupert, Newark, Nottinghamshire. The former locals' pub, the Woolpack, was extensively refurbished in 2010 and is an excellent example of new work grafted on to old, creating a pub which is welcoming both to drinkers and those wishing to eat. The untraditional pastel colours are typical of those adopted for 'gastropubs' towards the end of the 20th century, no doubt as part of the desire to differentiate them from traditional boozers.

A major theme of this book has been the ever-evolving nature of the British pub. The 'death of the pub' has been predicted by doom-mongers for decades but its survival is a tribute to the adaptability of the institution and resourceful owners. To meet the very real challenges facing pubs today, these qualities are as much needed as ever.

### A licensing revolution

When we went to press seven years ago, the Licensing Act of 2003, covering England and Wales, was still to come into force. This it did at midnight on 23 November 2005 when the responsibility for licensing passed to local authorities from the Justices of the Peace who had overseen it since 1495 (see p 6). There were widespread outcries about the loss of a time-honoured tradition and prophecies of chaos but the transition took place smoothly. The Act introduced 'premises licences' (replacing both the historic licence for the sale of alcohol and also those for cinemas, theatres, public entertainment, late-night refreshment houses and night cafés), supplemented by a system of personal licenses for persons selling alcohol. In a departure from previous regime, the premises licence does not need renewing annually but remains valid until either surrendered or confiscated. Premises already licensed when the Act came into force were entitled to unopposed 'grandfather rights', providing the application was lodged by 6 August 2005.

Other key measures in the Act included greater powers for the police and local residents to object to the grant of a licence or to influence the conditions attached to it, and a requirement for a licence for the playing of live music in any venue, however small.

### Apocalypse now! – '24-hour drinking'

The administrative aspects of the new legislation (unsurprisingly) made little impact on public consciousness. What did, however, was with the potential for up to 24-hour opening seven days a week. Sensationalist reporting by the press, aided and abetted by the anti-drink lobby, envisaged large swathes of the nation coming to resemble Hogarth's *Gin Lane* on p18.

8.2 Drinkers can enjoy the extended opening hours allowed under the 2003 Licensing Act. The rigid times demanded by the previous legislation are now more flexible, hence the 'til late' at the Sportsman, Huddersfield, where serving stops on Friday and Saturday nights at about midnight and customers are expected to leave by about 1 am.

We have not found *any* public house which regularly opens 24 hours a day. A Department for Culture, Media and Sport (DCMS) report in 2010 noted there were approximately 7,800 premises licensed for the 24-hour sale of alcohol – that is, just over 4 per cent of all licensed premises.[1] Over 50 per cent (4,400) of these were hotels, and 85 per cent of these could only serve residents. Another 1,700 licences were held by supermarkets and convenience stores, with only around 1,000 held by pubs, bars and nightclubs.

As the DCMS reported, 'The possession of a 24-hour licence does not necessarily mean that the premises will choose to open for 24 hours.' Most pubs and bars with 24-hour licences intended to extend their opening hours in specific circumstances, for example when hosting parties or wedding receptions, rather than opening around the clock as a matter of course. The vast majority of pubs and bars appear to have taken the opportunity to extend their opening hours by an hour or two, but other than in large towns it is hard to find many pubs open beyond midnight, even at weekends. A report by the Home Office showed that in 2007 pubs, bars and nightclubs stayed open for just under half an hour longer on average.[2] Licensees are not obliged to keep the full opening hours specified in their license but all customers must leave the premises by the latest time therein – the 'terminal hour'.

Nor, contrary to the claims of the tabloid press and alarmist television documentaries, has there been an increase in drunkenness and disorder. The DCMS report showed the number of incidents recorded by the police forces surveyed has remained constant, and there has actually been a small reduction in crimes involving serious violence. A survey of accident and emergency departments suggested that alcohol-related admissions have remained stable. The report found little sign of a '24-hour drinking' culture and the problems associated with it which had been confidently predicted by opponents of the new legislation, but nor was there evidence for the reduction in alcohol-related crime, drunkenness and disorder predicted by its supporters. Nevertheless, in a move apparently influenced by the increasingly vociferous tabloid press, the Government has recently announced plans to transfer the responsibility for licensing from the DCMS to the Home Office, and to give local authorities the power to charge significantly more for late-night licences. It is hard to see how such cosmetic changes will have much effect on Britain's youth determined on a good night out!

## No smoking

The other crucial piece of legislation affecting pubs since 2004 has been a ban on smoking in all indoor public spaces. Such a ban was introduced in Scotland on 26 March 2006 and was extended to the rest of the UK during 2007 – Wales on 2 April, Northern Ireland on 30 April and England on 1 July. It is not easy to assess the impact. There is anecdotal evidence suggesting the ban has driven some customers away from pubs, and that they have not yet been replaced by people who had previously avoided pubs precisely because smoking was allowed. Traditional, 'wet-led' pubs are said to have lost a greater proportion of customers than those offering food and facilities for families, but hard evidence is difficult to come by.

However, the ban has undoubtedly had a physical impact. The outdoor smoking shelter, carefully provided with open sides to prevent it being classed as 'indoor public space', is now a standard feature at most pubs: where space constraints preclude one, the

knot of smokers congregated around the entrance to the pub has become another standard feature. The

8.3 (above) A contradiction in terms. No smoking now in the Smoke Room of the Three Cups, Bedford!

8.4 The smoking shelter at the Royal Oak, Ockbrook, Derbyshire, is an ambitious affair which would look at home in the Arabian desert.

shelter may be a lean-to roughly cobbled-together from scrap wood and plastic sheeting, or a carefully designed and constructed freestanding feature. Few, however, can really be said to enhance the setting of the buildings they serve.

8.5 Flat-screen TVs have become standard fittings in pubs and can often be hard to escape. This one at the Jolly Sailor, Whitburn, Tyne and Wear, is even placed within an historic bar-back.

The only other recent physical change we would note has been the introduction of flat-screen television screens: prices of these slim-line units has fallen dramatically in the past few years and it seems there is hardly a pub in the land without one (or more).

## Other pressures on the pub

Supermarkets and off-licences now account for well over half of the UK's alcohol sales. Their prices for popular brands are well below those in pubs, and indeed the extraordinary cheapness of alcohol sold in supermarkets has led to Government plans for statutory minimum prices for drink. The 'binge-drinking' culture regularly documented and attacked in the media appears to be fuelled by the availability of cheap alcohol in supermarkets. Young people often 'pre-load' with supermarket-sourced alcohol before

hitting the pubs and clubs. Sadly, pubs as a whole are often damned by association.

For some years governments have capitalised on the alleged public concerns about alcohol use by raising duty above the level of inflation. Beer duty went up 5 per cent in the March 2010 budget and a further 7.2 per cent in March 2011 (in both cases 2 percentage points above inflation), thus making a total increase of 52 per cent since 2004. The tax on beer in the UK is 11 times higher than in Germany, nine times higher than in Spain, and seven times higher than in France.[3] Figures for 2010 from the British Beer and Pub Association (BBPA) show that beer sales fell 3.9 per cent with pub sales being particularly hard hit, dropping 7.5 per cent.[4] Overall, according to the BBPA, pub sales of beer dropped 20.2 per cent in the previous three years. Not surprisingly, the higher beer taxes have been self-defeating in terms of revenue, being down £257 million from 2009. The increase in VAT from 17.5 to 20 per cent from January 2011 has only added to the burden on drinkers and licensees.

Paradoxically, pubcos (see p 55) can also have a corrosive effect on the very fabric of the industry that underpins their existence. Apart from charging generally high rents, most impose a tie which requires their tenants to buy supplies through them at prices higher than in the open market. The result is a high turnover of tenants unable to make a decent living, and the closure of pubs which are increasingly sold for other uses.

8.6 A sign of the times at the Greyhound, Darlington. Unfortunately, similar (?)opportunities are available at all too many closed pubs.

## Pub closures

Anyone travelling around the UK today will have noticed numerous pubs which are closed/up for sale/ boarded up/open for rent or offering (to the unwary) 'a business opportunity'. The rate of closures has increased dramatically since 2004, reaching a peak in 2009 with an estimated 50 a week, but falling back to around 39 a week by mid-2010.[5] The latest survey, covering the second half of 2010, shows a further reduction although the closure rate was still a massive 25 a week.[6] Large numbers of bar and pub companies are going out of business with 130 doing so in the third quarter of 2010.[7] There is no reason to suppose the new Licensing Act is specifically to blame, although it has given police and local authorities stronger powers to suspend licences and even to close pubs altogether for breaches of the legislation. Furthermore the fees for licences from local authorities are much higher than those previously demanded by the licensing Justices.

The 1904 Licensing Act (see p 42) provided for compensation for owners whose pubs were to be closed, as it was accepted that a licence *added* value to a property. This is no longer the case. Pubs are now often worth more for conversion to other uses or as a cleared site for redevelopment than as a going concern. Many of the pubcos are in deep financial trouble: like many property companies during the boom around 2000, they borrowed heavily against their assets, but the value of these has fallen due to the deteriorating economic situation and the difficulties in the pub industry. Eager to reduce their burden of debt, pubcos have been selling off large numbers of traditional pubs: some have been leased back, but many have been turned over to private houses or other uses. Planning legislation is no barrier to conversion into cafés, restaurants or shops as no change-of-use permission is required for these purposes. Recently supermarket chains have been seeking out likely pubs in a drive to increase their presence through smaller, local stores. On the positive side, unless a good case for unviability has been made, especially in rural areas, local authorities are often reluctant to grant permission for change of use if it means the loss of a community amenity. The tendency of the pubcos and some pub-owning breweries to sell off closed pubs with covenants restricting their use has been much criticised. In campaigning against this anti-competitive practice, community groups and CAMRA have met with considerable support, and a Government consultation is being initiated to determine whether it should be outlawed.

There is little doubt that pub numbers will fall further, particularly in terms of wet-led premises in urban areas where the popular image of working men downing pints after a thirsty day's work in the steelworks or down a coal mine is largely a thing of the past. Similarly young people often meet now, not over a drink at the pub, but 'virtually' over the internet.

8.7 A pub no more. The Greyhound, Peterborough, is now the 'Mini Poli Express' minimarket, evidently hoping for custom from the city's Polish community.

### Ways forward

The pub market is highly segmented and its parts are not all equally affected. Although the wet-led local is suffering, pubcos and some breweries are investing hard in food-led outlets. In January 2011 brewers Greene King spent a princely £56 million on a small chain owning 12 carvery/restaurants with sites for ten more: development of the latter was planned for a further £25 million.[8] Likewise major food-led pubco

Mitchells and Butlers (turnover £2 billion pa) announced plans for 2010–11 to open 50 new pub/eatery sites across its many 'brands' and convert 70 more from within the existing estate.[9] In 2009–10 47 per cent of M&B's sales came from food.[10] Such pubs are a far cry from the traditional local but they undoubtedly meet popular demand with good-value food and a wide drink selection.

But Big Business is not the only success story. Most pubs now offer food and account for 35 per cent of the UK's eating-out market. In cities, the 'gastropub' has become widespread, with high-quality food and drink and a distinctive decorative style – bare-boarded floors, wooden panelling, pastel colours and an often eclectic mix of furniture (see 8.1). Some pubs allow customers to bring in food, assuming that increased drink sales will outweigh the inconvenience of washing up afterwards. A pub offering high-quality food will also provide a good choice of wines and beers and perhaps traditional cider too. A welcome trend has been the promotion of locally brewed ales, encouraged by CAMRA's 'Locale' scheme. After years of declining sales, real ale is now holding its own in a declining pub market for beer, as customers view it as a quality craft product and will pay a premium for it.[11]

An increasing number of pubs, particularly in rural areas, are being saved through community ownership. Pioneers such as the Old Crown at Hesket Newmarket, Cumbria, and the Jolly Farmer at Cookham Dean, Berkshire, both village-owned for years, are seen as models of community enterprise.[12] In March 2010 the Government announced a £3.3 million fund to help communities buy pubs under threat; sadly, in August it was axed, although over 80 community groups had already applied for assistance.[13]

Viability can be enhanced by new services. Providing facilities that might would otherwise be lost to a village can provide a lifeline for a pub which may itself be at risk of closure. Pubs now provide accommo-dation for shops, post offices, community centres, evening classes, and even religious services. 'Pub is the

Hub', initiated in 2001 by HRH the Prince of Wales, with support from the Countryside Agency, the British Beer and Pub Association, and Business in the Community, provides useful advice and many schemes are eligible for grants.[14]

In the 2004 edition of this book, we concluded that 'at the start of the 21st century, the future for the public house is less certain than it has been for decades'. That remains true; indeed, if anything, the situation has become worse. Excessive rates of beer tax, an increasingly bureaucratic and expensive licensing system, the equivocal attitude of the authorities towards drinking, the impact of a major recession, the smoking ban, the behaviour of pub-owning companies, the high value of pub sites for redevelopment, and increasingly hysterical attacks on a perceived culture of 'binge-drinking' in the tabloid press, all combine to make life difficult for pubs and their licensees. Nevertheless, there is much evidence to suggest that the public house remains as secure in public affection as ever, and that new models of ownership and operation are building on this to offer routes to survival.

8.8–8.9 'A pint of bitter and a bag of sugar, please.' Since 2008 the Sycamore, Parwich, Derbyshire, has, enterprisingly, incorporated a village shop.

# Notes

## Chapter 1, pages 1–25

1 Jennings, 19, who notes the phrase 'handy pubs' used by a diarist from the Bradford area on a journey in 1812: he adds that Bradford newspapers only used it from the late 1880s.

2 Ann Hagen, *A Second Handbook of Anglo-Saxon Food and Drink: Production and Distribution*, Hockwold-cum-Wilton, 1995, 246.

3 Ann Williams and G H Ann (eds), *Domesday Book*, London, Penguin, 2003, 716.

4 Martin Biddle, *Winchester in the Early Middle Ages: An Edition and Discussion of the Winton Domesday*, Oxford, 1976, 431–2 and fig 23(b).

5 Edward Miller and John Hatcher, *Medieval England – Towns, Commerce and Crafts, 1086–1348*, London, 1995, 329.

6 Richard H Britnell, *The Commercialisation of English Society, 1000–1500*, Manchester, 1996, 91, 94–5.

7 Colin Platt, *King Death: the Black Death and its Aftermath in Late Medieval England*, London, 1996, 9–16, 19–20, 34–5.

8 For a full account of the role of women in brewing, see Judith M Bennett, *Ale, Beer, and Brewsters in England: Women's Work in a Changing World, 1300–1600*, Oxford, 1996.

9 *Fyrst Boke of the Introduction of Knowledge*, quoted in *The Agrarian History of England and Wales*, vol 3, Cambridge, 1991, 304.

10 *Victoria County History of Oxfordshire*, 2, 261.

11 Derek Keene, *Survey of Medieval Winchester*, Oxford, 1985, 265–7.

12 11 Henry VII c2.

13 H S Darbyshire and G D Lumb, 'The History of Methley', *Publications of the Thoresby Society*, 35, 1937, 190.

14 F G Emmison, 'Elizabethan Essex Alehouses', *Essex Journal*, 5, no. 1, 1970, 30.

15 5 & 6 Edward VI c25.

16 3 Charles I c4.

17 These were Fridays and Saturdays, according to an Act of 1548, but Wednesdays were added by an Act of 1562. See Judith Hunter, 'English Inns, Taverns, Alehouses and Brandy Shops: The Legislative Framework, 1495–1797', in Beat Kümin, Beat and B Ann Tlusty (eds), *The World of the Tavern: Public Houses in Early Modern Europe*, Aldershot, 2002, 66–7.

18 Jennings 1995, 98: one lodger was usual but some houses took in several.

19 4 Edward III c11.

20 7 Edward VI c5.

21 Freemen of the Vintners' Company could sell wine without a licence within three miles of the City of London, and in cities and port towns down to the early years of the 20th century.

22 21 James I c28.

23 12 Charles II c25 (1660), and 32 George III c59 (1792).

24 Keene [note 11], 165–7.

25 W A Pantin, 'Medieval Inns', in E M Jope (ed), *Studies in Building History*, London, 1961, 188.

26 Ibid, 166–91.

27 Keene [note 11], 274–5.

28 Hugh Murray, *A Directory of York Pubs 1455–2003*, York, 2003, v.

29 William Harrison, *The Description of England*, Mineola, New York, 1994, 397–9.

30 Alan Everitt, 'The English Urban Inn, 1560–1760' in *Landscape and Community in England*, London, 1985, 156.

31 George Wilson, *Alcohol and the Nation*, London, 1940, 197.

32 1 William and Mary, Session II c4 (1689); 1 Anne, Session II c16 (1701).

33 The burden only began to be lifted with the provision of purpose-built barracks from the 1790s, although innkeepers and publicans remained liable to billeting for a further 150 years. The restrictions were eased in London from 1866. In the 1870s publicans were complaining they only got 2½d a night for a bed and 10d for sustenance which included a hearty 20oz of meat, 16oz of bread, 2 pints of beer and a candle (*Licensed Victuallers' Gazette*, 8 February, 1873).

34 12 & 13 William III, c11.

35 1 Anne c14.

36 P Sykes, *Inns, Taverns and Alehouses in King's Lynn, 1764*, King's Lynn, 1996, unpaginated.

37 'Report of the Select Committee on the Police of the Metropolis', 1817, quoted in Sidney and Beatrice Webb, *The History of Liquor Licensing in England, Principally from 1700 to 1830*, London, Longmans, Green, 1903, 90–1.

38 Andrew Davison, 'A Genuine and Superior Article: the Last Two Centuries of Brewing in York', *York Historian*, 10, 1990, 34.

39 16 George II c8.

40 24 George II c40.

41 2 George II c28.

42 17 George II c17 & 19.

43 26 George II c31.

44 Gambling and the playing of games of all kinds in alehouses had long been a concern to the authorities. The first Gin Act of 1729 confirmed earlier legislation against unlawful games, and allowed the Justices to

commit those playing them to prison without bail. An Act of 1757 (30 George II c24) ordained that licensees who allowed games to be played on their premises should be fined.

45 Sidney and Beatrice Webb [note 37], chapter 3.

46 5 George IV c54.

47 9 George IV c61.

48 11 George IV and 1 William IV c64.

49 Clark, 196.

50 Sidney and Beatrice Webb [note 37], 71.

51 Sykes [note 36].

## Chapter 2, pages 26–55

1 Harrison, tables 8 and 9, pp 328–9.

2 Sidney and Beatrice Webb, *The History of Liquor Licensing in England, Principally from 1700 to 1830,* London, 1903, 90–1.

3 R C Riley and Philip Eley, *Public Houses and Beerhouses in Nineteenth Century Portsmouth,* Portsmouth, Portsmouth Papers, 38, 1983, 7.

4 4 & 5 William IV c85.

5 3 & 4 Victoria c61: the rateable values were £15 in London, £11 in provincial towns, and £8 in rural districts.

6 32 & 33 Victoria c27.

7 Jennings, 162.

8 35 & 36 Victoria c94 (1872); 37 & 38 Victoria c49 (1874).

9 George Rudé, *Hanoverian London 1714–1808,* London, 1971, 70, quoted in Earnshaw, 167.

10 Lilian Lewis Shiman, 'Temperance and Class in Bradford, 1830–1860', *Yorkshire Archaeological Journal,* 58, 1986, 173–8.

11 James Ellison, *The Dawn of Teetotalism,* Preston, 1932, 31. Harrison, 119, 263 says he was a plasterer.

12 Norman Longmate, *The Water Drinkers,* London, 1968, 121–33.

13 44 & 45 Victoria c61.

14 Lilian Lewis Shiman, *Crusade Against Drink in Victorian England,* London, 1988, 130–3.

15 49 & 50 Victoria c56 (1886); 1 Edward VII c27 (1901): the latter came into force on 1 January 1902 and was known as the 'Child Messenger Act'.

16 David M Fahey, 'Liberal Party (United Kingdom)', *Alcohol and Temperance in Modern History: An International Encyclopedia,* Santa Barbara, Denver and Oxford, 2003, 367.

17 Girouard, 87.

18 Ibid, chapter 9.

19 K H Hawkins, *The History of Bass Charrington,* Oxford, 1978, 34.

20 J Trevor-Davies, *The Innkeeper's Handbook and Licensed Victualler's Manual,* London, 1893, 18–19.

21 *Yorkshire Gazette,* 7 September 1895 and 2 September 1897.

22 Riley and Eley [note 3], 20.

23 Crawford *et al,* 40–2.

24 2 Edward VII c28. The Act also stated that court sessions and coroners' inquests could no longer be held on licensed premises.

25 4 Edward VII c23.

26 In 1902 the Justices had asked the Chief Constable to survey all York's licensed houses, and his report guided the subsequent campaign of closures.

27 Girouard, 200–4.

28 *Licensed Victuallers' Gazette,* 37, 1892, 745.

29 Joseph Rowntree and Arthur Sherwell, *British 'Gothenburg' Experiments and Public-House Trusts,* London, 1900, 9.

30 J H Smith, *Grayshott: The Story of a Hampshire Village,* Petersfield, 1978, 70.

31 *Licensing World and Licensed Trade Review,* 19, 1902, 79.

32 Jean Wakeman, *Trust House Britain,* London, 1963, 13–16.

33 Henry Carter, *The Control of the Drink Trade in Britain,* London, 1919, chapter 2.

34 Quoted in Oliver, 21.

35 For Birmingham, see Ibid, 83; for Brighton and Portsmouth, see Philip Eley and R C Riley, *The Demise of Demon Drink?: Portsmouth Pubs 1900–1950,* Portsmouth, Portsmouth Papers, 58, 1991, 21.

36 Northampton Record Office, Northampton Building Control Registers.

37 The Seven Stars, Halfway House, Shropshire, until closure in 2005, was only licensed for beer sales. The last survivor in London, the Fox and Hounds, Passmore Street, Belgravia, went fully-licensed in 1999 (but had sold wine as well as beer).

38 At January 2004, 21,040 pubs (about one in three of the total) were owned by five pubcos. The situation was largely unchanged as at June 2011 when six pubcos owned almost 20,000 of the nation's (then) 54,000 pubs (Punch 7,675; Enterprise 7,399; Admiral 1,700; Mitchells and Butlers 1,600; Wellington 811 and Wetherspoons 760). However, Punch plans to split into managed and leased pub companies and to sell off about 2,500 pubs over the next five years (Iain Loe, CAMRA).

**Chapter 3, pages 56–91**

1  Other simple one-room pubs are the Cider House, Defford, Worcestershire and the Berkeley Arms, Purton, Gloucestershire.

2  Robert Kerr, *The Gentleman's House, or how to plan English Residences from the Parsonage to the Palace*, London, 1864, 358.

3  There are a few, very rare exceptions such as C F A Voysey at the Wentworth Arms, Elmesthorpe, Leicestershire (1895), and Norman Shaw at the Tabard, Chiswick (1880). The Drum at Cockington, Torbay (c1934), was part of an otherwise unexecuted scheme for a model village centre designed by Sir Edwin Lutyens as a commission for the Cockington Trust. The interiors of all these three pubs have been substantially altered.

4  A now very rare difference still exists between the two rooms at the White Swan, Broadstairs, Kent: as at June 2011 it was 4 pence a pint.

5  A rare collection of inventories of pubs owned or leased by the brewer Richard Bullard between the late 1830s and the mid-1850s is held by the Norfolk Record Office (reference BR3/13).

6  One correspondent (Julian Tubbs), commenting to us on the separation of tap room and servery at the Royal Oak, Ockbrook, Derbyshire, said he had been told that customers tapped on the furniture with a coin to attract the attention of the tapster. Well, perhaps!

7  *Licensed Victuallers' Gazette and Hotel Courier*, 41, 1897, 123.

8  Information from Peter Jackson.

9  We are grateful to Denis Funnell for information on this subject (personal communication, 1 August 2002).

10  Oliver, 58; Yorke, 21.

11  *Licensing World and Licensed Trade Review*, 11 February 1905, 88.

12  Andrew P Davison, 'A Good House, Fit for the Purpose: Public House Design in York, 1830–1950', MA thesis, De Montford University, Leicester, 1993, 80.

13  Northampton Record Office, Northampton Building Control Registers.

14  Crawford *et al*, 9.

15  Oliver, 131.

16  More details in Crawford *et al*, 43–4.

17  Quoted in Oliver, 86. This was no doubt said in the 1930s when Oliver was collecting material for his book. The other iconic pub that could lay claim to being the first newly-built improved pub is the Fox and Pelican, Grayshott, Hampshire of 1899 (see p 45).

18  For discussion of this important subject see David Gutzke, 'Gender, Class, and Public Drinking in Britain during the First World War', *Historie Sociale/Social History*, 27, 1994, 367–91.

19  *Licensing World*, 54, 1919, 360.

20  The last was by Redfern's colleague, Joseph Seddon: built in 1939–40 at Etterby, it was named the Redfern Inn.

21  This is convincingly argued by Angus Hutchinson in his MSc thesis, 'The Significance of the Public Houses designed by Harry Redfern and built between 1925–1939 under the Carlisle and District State Management Scheme', Heriot-Watt University, Edinburgh, 1996, esp 66.

22  See Stephen Oliver, 'Basil Oliver and the End of the Arts and Crafts Movement', *Architectural History*, 47, 2004, 329–60.

23  2003 edition.

24  Most recently the Winter Gardens, Harrogate and King's Fee, Hereford (2003), Gatekeeper, Cardiff (2002) and Sedge Lynn, Chorlton cum Hardy, Manchester (2000).

**Chapter 4, pages 92–121**

1  Until his death in c2001, the keeper of the Cupid's Hill Tavern, Grosmont, Monmouthshire, also ran a coffin-making business.

2  *Licensing World*, 19, 1902, 298: further uses included petty sessions (banned under the 1902 Licensing Act), church warden's meetings, depots for cyclists, pinfolds for stray animals, government enquiries and so on.

3  Jennings, 98; most took in just one but some houses had several.

4  Until 2009 they were used at the Case is Altered, Fiveways, Warwickshire.

5  Estimates originally provided by Victoria Gorman. Thanks for updates to Andrea Briers and Chris Rouse of CAMRA's Cider and Perry Campaign.

6  Tichborne was presumed lost at sea in 1854. Arthur Orton (alias Thomas Castro) emigrated to Australia, met the 11th baronet on whose death he persuaded his mother he was her long-lost son. His claim failed after 102 days in court and, after a 188-day trial for perjury, he was sentenced in 1874 to fourteen years hard labour. Released after ten in 1884, he died in 1898.

7  Explained to us by Will Williams of the Wenlock Arms, Wenlock Road, London N1, which has such doors. At the Haunch of Venison, Salisbury, the purpose is to allow barrels or crates to be passed to the other side of the counter.

8   Cornell, 205: the following statistics are from the same source.

9   Ibid, 222, 223.

10  Not to be confused with the same term which is the Scottish and Irish term for a bar-back.

11  The BHS material is held at Birmingham City Archives, reference M51865.

12  Philip Eley and R C Riley, *The Demise of Demon Drink? Portsmouth Pubs 1900–1950*, Portsmouth, Portsmouth Papers, 58, 1991, 4.

13  Haydon, 249.

14  Other examples, mostly displaced from their original context, are at the Lamb, Lamb's Conduit Street; Crown, Islington; Holly Bush, Hampstead; Bunch of Grapes, Knightsbridge; Travellers Friend, Woodford Green (all London); Posada, Wolverhampton, The Globe, Chagford, Devon, had them in the off-sales area. Given the presumed mass destruction of this Victorian pub feature, it is ironic that modern ones have been installed at a number of pubs (eg Andover Arms, Hammersmith, and several during excellent Victorianising refits by brewer, Samuel Smith as at the Champion, Fitzrovia, London: they are often mistaken for the real thing).

15  However, in the 1920s the saloon bar at the King's Arms, New King's Road, Fulham, was, allegedly, the largest in London, and had waiter service in the evenings (C Amies, *Images of London: Hammersmith and Fulham Pubs*, Stroud, 2004, 46). The bell push at the Camden Head, Camden Walk, London N1 are modern (possibly 1969).

16  Girouard, 245.

17  Haydon, 209.

18  Girouard, 10.

19  Jennings, 212.

20  www.tradgames.org.uk/features/pub-games.htm.

21  Taylor, 81–2.

22  Finn, 41–2.

23  Jennings, 100.

24  Taylor, 18.

25  Jennings, 204.

26  Eley and Riley [note 12], 6.

27  Northamptonshire Record Office, Northampton Building Plans, D158.

28  Finn, 38–9.

29  *Licensed Victuallers' Gazette*, 1 September 1866, 322.

30  Examples cited from Girouard, 11.

## Chapter 5, pages 122–51

1   J Mordaunt Crook, *The Architect's Secret*, London, 2003, 61.

2   Girouard, 170.

3   See bibliography. Much of the following information derives from this source.

4   Another fine mosaic front was at Throgmorton's, Throgmorton Street, London EC2.

5   *The Builder*, 23 March 1850.

6   Another example is at the Lamb, Leadenhall Market, showing Christopher Wren inspecting plans.

7   If, as seems likely, the date on the clock can be trusted.

## Chapter 6, pages 152–63

1   Harrison, 235.

2   The nearest it came was a bill introduced in November 1890 which failed at the committee stage the following year; the Sunday Closing Act was extended to Monmouthshire in 1921 (W R Lambert, *Drink and Sobriety in Victorian Wales*, Cardiff, 1983, 232–5).

3   Referenda on Sunday closing were abolished under the 2003 Licensing Act.

4   Rudolph Kenna, *The Glasgow Pub Companion*, Glasgow, 2001, 14 says that in the vast peripheral housing estates of Drumchapel and Easterhouse around Glasgow, each the size of Perth, pubs were not allowed until the 1960s.

5   Ibid, 15.

6   The Monopolies Commission, *Beer – A Report on the Supply of Beer*, London, 1969, 40.

7   Kenna [note 4], 13.

8   Gourvish and Wilson, 24 quoting G B Wilson, *Alcohol and the Nation*, London, 1940, 369–70.

9   At 2011 the system is thought to be only used at five Edinburgh pubs: Abbotsford, Athletic Arms, (Wee) Bennet's, Bow Bar and Thomson's (the latter two are modern bars).

10  It is sometimes said that the traditional Scottish bar tap tall to comply with 'ancient legislation' requiring glasses to be filled above the counter in full view. Although such visibility may have become custom and practice we have found no evidence of any legal requirement. Before the advent of the tall fount and since the modern rise of the hand-pump, a large proportion of Scottish beer was/is not dispensed within full view of the customer.

11  Various facts in the following are derived from Molloy 2002.

12  Gourvish and Wilson, 24, 99–102.

13  Molloy, 43.

14  See Elizabeth Malcolm, *Ireland Sober, Ireland Free*, Dublin, 1986, 207–11, for the attempts of the authorities to curb the abuse of the spirit-grocers' licence. She wrongly states that the licences were abolished in 1910 and this was followed by Molloy, 51.

## Chapter 7, pages 164–71

1  p 227.

2  Eg Charles Robert Swift, *Ye Olde Fighting Cocks*, St Albans, c1945, unpaginated.

3  We are grateful to Brian Adams of Verulamium Museum for information on the excavations (personal communication, 4 December 2003).

4  As made clear from a suit of 1622 by William Preston against his sister Anne Marston (widow) (Chanc Proc ser ii, 373/6 in the National Archives).

5  It was alleged to have been a venue for cock-fighting. This too seems dubious – the alleged cock-pit is a sunken area which it would have been impossible for people to stand around on all sides.

6  http://en.wikipedia.org/wiki/Holywell,_Cambridgeshire. Her ghost reappears every 17 March.

7  Information from Sarah Poppy of Cambridgeshire SMR, personal communication, 15 January 2004.

8  Our thanks to Bob Burn Murdoch of the Norris Museum, St Ives for advice on this case.

9  Thanks to Alan Brooks for his considerable help with this entry.

10  www.theroyalisthotel.com.

11  As note 6.

12  Thanks to Anna Morris of the SMR for details.

13  Vol 6, 1965, 148–9.

14  p 57.

15  http://www.bingleyarms.co.uk/history.php.

16  *Nottingham Pubs*, Nottingham, 1980, 5, 7.

17  Ibid, 7.

18  As note 6. The pub's leaflet, however, tells us James got nine months in gaol, and it was his brother John who was hanged.

19  We are grateful to Frank Olden for the sober facts about this pub.

20  John Newman, *Buildings of Wales: Gwent/Monmouthshire*, London, 2000, 287.

21  James Sharpe, *Dick Turpin: The Myth of the English Highwayman*, London, 2004 from which the following facts are taken.

22  Further information from Mr Olden who also told us he had heard a legend of a six-mile(!) tunnel from the Skirrid Mountain Inn to Llanthony Priory.

23  Clark, 318.

24  London Borough of Redbridge, Building Plans, 13986.

25  It was opened on 25 March 1925 (*Redbridge Recorder*, 27 March 1925). Having taken four years and £1.25 million to build there would not have been much appetite for another such road! The road into London from the pub is much narrower than the principal routes through Barkingside.

26  Personal communication 20 October 1999 from which the following details are taken.

27  A fuller account by Geoff Brandwood of the myth and the unpicking of it appears in *What's Brewing*, November 1999, 23. Thanks to Martin Bloxson, Len Bunning and Lance Potter for information about the Great Central Railway. As at June 2011, the pub has been closed for seven years and its future is, sadly, uncertain.

## Chapter 8, pages 172–179

1  Peter Antoniades and Victoria Thompson, *DCMS National Statistics Bulletin – Alcohol, Entertainment and Late Night Refreshment Licensing, England and Wales, April 2009 – March 2010*, DCMS Evidence and Analysis Unit, 29 September 2010.

2  Mike Hough, Gillian Hunter, Jessica Jackson and Stefano Cossalter, *The Impact of the Licensing Act 2003 on Levels of Crime and Disorder: an Evaluation*, London, 2008.

3  *Morning Advertiser*, 24 March 2010.

4  www.beerandpub.com/newsList.aspx (issued 25 January 2011). However, shop sales were up 0.6 per cent, reinforcing the point that it is pubs that are under pressure.

5  Research by CGA Strategy, quoted in Pete Brown, *Cask: the Cask Report*, vol 4, 2010–11, 44.

6  British Beer and Pub Association www.beerandpub.com/newsList.aspx (issued 16 March 2011).

7  Research by accountants and business advisers Wilkins Kennedy www.wilkinskennedy.com press-release 14 December 2010. The figure was up from 99 in the same quarter 2009.

8  *Evening Standard*, 31 January 2011, 39.

9  Interim Management Statement – January 2011 www.mbplc.com/newsandmedia/companynews.

10  www.mbplc.com/pdf/corporateprofile.pdf

11  Brown [note 5] 11–17.

12  Lucy Cavendish, 'Local Heroes', *The Guardian*, G2 section, 2 April 2008.

13  'In Praise of … Community Pubs', third editorial in *The Guardian*, 11 August 2010.

14  Advice and examples can be found at www.pubisthehub.org.uk.

# Illustration credits

All the photographs are by Michael Slaughter unless stated below.

Illustrations are reproduced by kind permission as follows:

Loral Bennett 3.57.

Bodleian Library 1.4 (MS Bodl 264, fol 158v – detail).

Geoff Brandwood 1.3, 1.25, 2.9, 3.2, 3.3, 3.11, 3.16, 3.55, 3.63, 3.65, 4.1, 4.62, 4.64, 5.6, 5.7, 5.39, 5.40, 5.42, 5.54, 5.55, 7.3, 7.4, 8.6.

Brewery History Society Photographic Archive (M51865) 2.44, 4.28, 4.38, 4.44, 4.51.

The British Library Board 1.2 (MS Royal 10 E IV, fol 114v).

Andrew Davison 1.10, 1.18, 2.2, 1.26, 2.4, 2.7, 2.8, 2.10, 2.13, 2.14, 2.18, 2.19, 2.26, 2.30, 2.31, 2.36, 2.38–2.42, 3.42, 3.56, 5.2, 5.5, 6.4, 7.2.

English Heritage (NMR) 1.19 (BB62/819), 3.46 (99/00744 AA 000347), 3.61 (6169/I), 4.20 (BL 13502), 4.21 (BL 13522), 4.45 (BL 13505), 5.4 (DD 57/129).

Victoria Gorman 4.8.

Lancashire Archives and Preston City Council 2.3 (CBP-2-18).

City of London, London Metropolitan Archives 1.22 (SC2/P2.WE/01/3264).

Norfolk Record Office 3.4 (BR 259/2 plan 2a).

Basil Oliver 3.59 (Oliver, 72), 3.60 (Oliver, 137).

Frank Taylor 2.11.

Robert Tims 7.1.

The University of Manchester 1.1, 1.7.

Wolverhampton Archives and Local Studies Service 2.37 (T-TPS/4/2/5).

The authors and English Heritage have endeavoured to ensure that full permission has been sought and given for all material used in this publication. Every effort has been made to trace the copyright holders and we apologise for any unintentional omissions, which we would be pleased to correct in any subsequent edition of this book.

# Bibliography

Bennett, Judith M. *Ale, Beer and Brewsters in England*, Oxford, Oxford University Press, 1996.

Blocker, Jack S, Fahey, David M, and Tyrrell, Ian M. *Alcohol and Temperance in Modern History: An International Encyclopedia*, Santa Barbara, California, ABC–CLIO, 2003.

Brandwood, Geoff, and Jephcote, Jane, *London Heritage Pubs: An Inside Story*, St Albans, CAMRA, 2008.

Clark, Peter. *The English Alehouse: A Social History 1200–1830*, London, Longman, 1983.

Cornell, Martyn. *Beer: The Story of the Pint*, London, Headline, 2003.

Cornell, Martyn, *Amber, Gold and Black: The History of Britian's Great Beers*, Stroud, The History Press Ltd, 2010.

Crawford, Alan, Dunn, Michael, and Thorne, Robert, *Birmingham Pubs, 1880–1939*, Gloucester, Alan Sutton, 1986.

Elwall, Robert. *Bricks and Beer*, London, British Architectural Library, 1983.

Finn, Timothy. *Pub Games of England*, Cambridge and New York, Oleander, 1975.

Girouard, Mark. *Victorian Pubs*, New Haven and London, Yale University Press, 1984 (reprint of 1975 first edition).

Gorham, Maurice, and Ardizzone, Edward. *The Local*, London, Cassell, 1939 (revised as *Back to the Local*, London, Percival Marshall, 1949).

Gorham, Maurice, and Dunnett, H McG. *Inside the Pub*, London, Architectural Press, 1950.

Harrison, Brian. *Drink and the Victorians: The Temperance Question in England 1815–1872*, Keele, Keele University, 2nd ed. 1994.

Haydon, Peter. *The English Pub: A History*, London, Hale, 1994 (re-published as *Beer and Britannia*, Stroud, Sutton Publishing, 2001).

Jennings, Paul. *The Public House in Bradford, 1770–1970*, Keele, Keele University, 1995.

Kenna, Rudolph, and Mooney, Anthony. *People's Palaces*, Edinburgh, Paul Harris, 1983.

Larwood, Jacob, and Hotten, John Camden, with additional material by Miller, Gerald. *English Inn Signs*, London, Chatto & Windus, 1951.

Longmate, Norman. *The Water-Drinkers*, London, Hamish Hamilton, 1968.

Mass-Observation. *The Pub and the People*, with a new introduction by Godfrey Smith, London, The Cresset Library, 1987.

Molloy, Cian *The Story of the Irish Pub: An Intoxicating History of the Licensed Trade in Ireland*, Dublin, Liffey, 2002.

Oliver, Basil. *The Renaissance of the English Public House*, London, Faber & Faber, 1947.

Pearson, Lynn. 'Decorative Ceramics in the Buildings of the Brewing Industry', *Tile and Architectural Ceramics Society Journal*, 8, 2000, 26–36.

Piper, John. 'Fully Licensed', *Architectural Review*, 87, 1940, 87–100 (reprinted in Piper, John *Buildings and Prospects*, London, Architectural Press, 1948).

Slaughter, Michael, (ed), *Scotland's True Heritage Pubs*, St Albans, CAMRA, 2007.

Slaughter, Michael, and Dunn, Mike, (eds), *Real Heritage Pubs of Wales*, St Albans, CAMRA, 2010.

Taylor, Arthur R. *The Guinness Book of Traditional Pub Games*, Enfield, Guinness, 1992.

Taylor, Author R, *Played at the Pub: The Pub Games of Britain*, Swindon, English Heritage, 2009.

Yorke, Francis W B. *The Planning and Equipment of Public Houses*, London, Architectural Press, 1949.

# Glossary

**Alcohol:** odourless and colourless but the chief intoxicating component of fermented and distilled drinks. Its formula is $C_2H_5OH$ which is common or ethyl alcohol (ethanol).

**Alcohol by volume (ABV):** a measure of the proportion of alcohol in a drink once fermentation is complete, generally given as a percentage (eg 5 per cent ABV).

**Air pressure:** beer dispense by applying compressed air on beer in the cask and mostly used now in Scottish pubs. Its use declined markedly as hand-pumps were reintroduced.

**Ale:** originally a fermented malt liquor, made without the use of hops. The term has been effectively interchangeable with 'beer' for at least the last 200 years.

**Ale-conner:** a person in the Middle Ages appointed to determine if ale was fit to drink.

**Alehouse:** originally, a house selling ale/beer, but not wine or spirits. From 1830 the alehouse licence allowed the sale of all alcoholic liquor.

**Ale-stake:** a wooden stake with a bundle of leaves at the end, displayed outside a medieval brewer's premises to advertise that ale was for sale.

**Art Deco:** a fashionable style between the two world wars in Europe and America. It relies on geometrical patterns and sleek lines. The name comes from the Exposition International des Arts-Décoratifs in Paris in 1924–5 which greatly enhanced its popularity.

**Art Nouveau:** a style relying on flowing lines and sinuous forms often based on nature and the human figure. It was popular from 1890 until 1914 but more in Europe than the UK. It does, however, crop up in pub decoration, especially on Merseyside.

**Arts and Crafts:** a late 19th-century English artistic and architectural movement that emphasised the value of handicraft and good design as against mass-production methods.

**Autovac:** a hand-pump with a return valve allowing spilt beer to be returned immediately to the flow. Introduced during the inter-war period, the autovac was particularly popular in South and West Yorkshire. The system avoided waste if beer was being pulled through a tight 'sparkler' to give a thick and creamy head. Hygiene fears led to the removal of most autovacs in the 1980s.

**Bar-back:** shelving, often very ornately treated and incorporating mirrors, at the rear of a servery. Also known as a back-fitment or (in Scotland and Northern Ireland) a gantry.

**Bar parlour:** as often, a term of some fluidity. In most parts of the country it implies a semi-public room where selected customers were admitted. In London it tended to serve as the publican's office and the restrictions on admittance were even tighter.

**Barrel:** a 36-gallon cask.

**Beer engine:** a device for raising beer from the cellar, nearly always referring to a hand-pump.

**Beer horse:** see stillage.

**Beerhouse:** from 1830, a house licensed to sell beer only.

**Beer Orders:** a shorthand term for the Supply of Beer (Tied Estate) Order 1989, which restricted the number of tied houses a brewery could own, and allowed many landlords the right to stock a guest beer of their choice. It led to vast sell-offs of tied houses (qv) by breweries, and the creation of large pub-owning companies ('pubcos': qv) which bought them up.

**Bell push:** a button that activated an electric bell or a visual indicator when there was table service in the better class rooms of many pubs in the Midlands and north.

**Big Six:** the dominant group of major breweries which emerged in the 1960s and which controlled 56 per cent of all pubs by 1972 (as against 24 per cent in 1960). They were Allied, Bass Charrington, Courage, Watney (Grand Metropolitan), Scottish and Newcastle, and Whitbread. They brewed 82 per cent of all beer brewed in the UK in 1972.

**Bitter:** a light, highly hopped beer, which appeared in the later 19th century and became increasingly popular in the 20th.

**Bottle and jug:** see jug and bottle.

**Brewers' Tudor:** a style, especially popular between the world wars, which drew nostalgically upon the half-timbered architecture of the Tudor period.

**Brewery-conditioned:** beer filtered and pasteurised at the brewery so that secondary fermentation cannot occur in the cask: to give it life it is served using gas pressure.

**Brewery tap:** a brewery's nearest tied retail outlet.

**Campaign for Real Ale (CAMRA):** consumer group founded in 1971 to campaign for traditional British beers which were under massive threat from the keg (qv) beers and lagers (qv) being promoted by the major brewers. Now numbering over 120,000 members, it campaigns for beer and cider quality and choice, and pub preservation and improvement.

**Carlisle Experiment:** a shorthand name for the pubs and breweries, chiefly (but not exclusively) in Carlisle, taken into state ownership during the First World War.

**Cask:** a barrel-shaped container for beer. Can be of various sizes whereas a barrel, strictly speaking, contains 36 gallons (see p 100 for cask sizes). Stainless steel and aluminium have almost entirely displaced wood.

**Cask-conditioned:** see real ale.

**Cellar:** a room where casks are stored, usually, but not necessarily below ground.

**Cellar drop:** a trap door in the pavement outside a pub or in the pub floor through which casks etc are passed to the cellar.

**Cider:** fermented apple juice with a maximum legal alcohol content of 8.5 per cent (above this it would be classed as a wine for duty purposes).

**Club room:** a room in many traditional pubs which was used for meetings. Often on the first floor.

**Coaching inn:** strictly, an inn on one of the main coaching routes, where horses would be changed and where passengers could obtain refreshment. Today, the term is applied indiscriminately to any inn, whether or not it was a calling-place for coaches.

**Coffee room:** a name occasionally used for a better room where, no doubt, coffee and other non-intoxicating refreshments were on offer to clients who had no wish to frequent the basic, public bar.

**Commercial room:** a room in Midland and northern pubs used by such customers as commercial travellers, and where some business might be transacted.

**Common brewer:** a brewer on a large scale who sells on beer through retailers.

**Console bracket:** a bracket with parallel sides and usually Classical details: commonly found on a bar counter front.

**Counter screen:** glazed screen on a serving counter, usually with a part that can be raised or lowered.

**Draught:** a drink served from a bulk container into a smaller measure. Misleadingly some suppliers label cans and bottles as draught.

**Drinking lobby/corridor:** an area for almost exclusively stand-up drinking. The lobby is usually an expanded corridor area with a bar counter; in corridors there is a hatch to the servery.

**Drinking-up time:** the period allowed after closing time for customers to finish their drinks.

**Embossed glass:** glass with raised and recessed areas formed by etching and grinding.

**Entire:** the original name for porter ('entire butt'). The term (in the form 'XXXX & Co's Entire') on advertising signs affixed to pubs in the late 19th century has been suggested (as in Whitbread's Word for Word of 1953) as meaning the establishment sold only that brewery's beer.

**Excise:** originally, in the mid-17th century, a duty imposed on goods, including alcohol. It eventually came to be applied to the official responsible for collecting customs (levied on imported goods) and excise duties.

**Faïence:** Blocks or slabs of earthenware, glazed after an initial firing. The name comes from Faenza, a major Italian centre of glazed pottery production in Italy.

**Fermentation:** the conversion by yeast of sugar into alcohol.

**Four-ale bar:** an old term for the public bar. 'Four-ale' was an old term for mild ale.

**Free house:** a pub not tied to a brewer, whose landlord is free to obtain beer from any source. The term is widely abused by modern pub companies, who do not brew themselves but insist that their tenants obtain beer from specified suppliers.

**Gallon:** the base unit for measuring bulk liquids, relating to the volume of a defined weight of liquid. By the 14th century there were separately defined gallons for ale (approximately 272 cubic inches) and wine (231 cubic inches). In 1824 'An Act for ascertaining and establishing Uniformity of Weights and Measures' (5 George IV c74) replaced both previous measures with the 'imperial gallon' of 277 cubic inches. The US gallon, notably smaller than that in use in the UK, preserves the pre-1824 'wine gallon'.

**Gallows sign:** public house sign spanning a road.

**Gantry:** Scottish and Northern Irish term for a bar-back.

**Gastropub:** a late 20th-century term for a pub where the main emphasis is on sophisticated food.

**Gin palace:** an early 19th-century term for a lavishly decorated premises emphasising spirits (especially gin) drinking. It is still sometimes used for ornate late Victorian pubs: this usage is, strictly speaking, inaccurate but no other term has arisen to encapsulate them.

**Glass:** term used in Scotland and Ireland for half a pint.

**Gothenburg system:** a system originating in Sweden in 1865 whereby those running pubs were given no incentive to sell alcohol. Profits over about 4 per cent or 5 per cent were ploughed back into the community. Several variants appeared in England and Scotland at the end of the 19th century.

**Gravity dispense:** beer or cider served direct from the cask into the glass.

**Guest ale/beer:** a beer not regularly on sale at a particular pub.

**Guinness:** a dark, bitter beer brewed by Guinness' brewery in Dublin, founded in 1759. The firm built up an extensive export trade, both to the rest of the British Isles and to the colonies, during the 19th and early 20th centuries; eventually, subsidiary breweries were opened in many parts of the world to maintain supplies, notably at Park Royal, West London, in 1936. Unusually for a major British brewer, Guinness has no tied houses, and sells its beer on the strength of its reputation (and its witty advertising) alone.

**Hand-pump:** the lever on the bar which operates a beer engine to draw beer from the cask in the cellar,

and now universally regarded as the standard method of dispense for real ale (qv).

**Hops:** flowers of a climbing perennial plant, *Humulus lupulus*, of the Cannabaceae family. They are dried and used in brewing to create bitterness and improve keeping qualities of beer. In England, cultivation has been concentrated in Kent, Sussex, Herefordshire and Worcestershire for many years; 'oast houses', with their conical-roofed kilns for drying the hops, are a typical feature of those counties, although most have now been converted to other uses. Two of the most famous English varieties are Fuggles and Goldings. For economy of space hops are often compressed into pellets.

**Horsing:** see stillage.

**Hush-shop:** an illegal, unlicensed outlet for drink.

**Improved public houses:** inter-war ones built with the aim of making the pub respectable. They tended to be large, had a wide range of facilities, and sought to attract a better class of customer, including women.

**India Pale Ale (IPA):** a much abused term. It referred originally to strong, highly hopped ales brewed to withstand the long haul to distant colonies, notably India. Today various brewers employ it for their ordinary bitters.

**Inn:** a house offering accommodation and refreshment to travellers.

**Jug and bottle:** small section of a pub, with a separate entrance off the street, where drink could be purchased for consumption off the premises.

**Keg:** originally a small cask containing drink (particularly spirits such as brandy and rum). Since the 1950s it has become a specific term for the pressurised containers used for brewery-conditioned beer.

**Lager:** a lightly hopped beer brewed using a 'bottom-fermenting' yeast (ie one which sinks to the bottom of the fermenting vat as opposed to the 'top-fermenting' yeast used for traditional British beer) which is then stored for a period of weeks or months to develop flavour and condition. The style comes originally from Germany (Lager is German for a store). The pale lager familiar today was first brewed in the Bohemian town of Plzen (hence 'pilsener') in 1842. Lager was introduced to Britain in the late 19th century but was not popular until the 1960s. Modern British lagers bear little resemblance to the German and Czech originals.

**Light ale:** a lower-gravity version of pale ale.

**Loan-tie:** see tied house.

**Local option:** a temperance proposal whereby licensing would be handed over to local councils and a two-thirds majority of ratepayers would allow them to close licensed premises without compensation. It became part of Liberal Party policy in 1889.

**Locale:** CAMRA's initiative, launched in 2007, to promote locally-brewed ales.

**Loggia:** an arcaded space, roofed, but open on at least one side, typically overlooking a garden.

**Long pull:** a serving above the legal measure, without extra charge. It became illegal in 1915, although the practice had been frowned on by magistrates for many years beforehand as encouraging drunkenness (and seems to have resulted in prosecutions).

**Lounge (bar):** the most comfortably furnished room in a public house. Beer was usually more expensive in the lounge bar.

**Malt:** barley that has been partly germinated and then heated to turn starch into fermentable sugars. These are then turned into alcohol by yeast.

**Manorial courts:** the manor was the basic unit of English medieval government and its court met regularly to hear minor cases of infringements of local or national laws. Nominally the lord of the manor presided but, in practice, his place was taken by one of his senior officials such as the steward or reeve.

**Market room:** a room name found in some pubs near markets and intended, presumably, for traders.

**Mash:** to extract fermentable sugars from crushed malt by running hot water ('liquor' in brewing parlance) through it.

**Mash tun:** a large vessel in which mashing is carried out.

**Matchboarding:** see tongued and grooved boarding

**Mild:** a low-gravity beer, normally dark in colour.

**Moderne:** an alternative term for Art Deco (qv).

**Misericord:** a ledge on the under side of a hinged choir-stall seat to support the occupant when the seat was upright.

**Muller:** a device for heating drinks and common in Victorian pubs.

**News room:** a term found especially in the north-west for a better room where a quiet drink and the perusal of the press went hand in hand.

**Off-sales:** sales of drink for consumption off the premises: the term sometimes is applied to the place in the pub where the sales take place (which also goes by other names such a jug and bottle).

**Old ale:** a strong, dark beer, normally stored for several months to condition, and sold during the winter.

**Optic:** a dispensing device for spirits. Usually inserted into the mouth of an inverted bottle, it delivers a standard measure.

**Oriel window:** a bay window supported on a bracket.

**Original gravity (OG):** a measure of the amount of fermentable material in a brew before the yeast gets to work. Water has an original gravity of 1000°, so a beer with an OG of 1050° has fifty parts of fermentable material to every 1,000 parts of water. As a rule, a beer with an OG of 1050° before fermentation would have an ABV of around 5 per cent afterwards.

**Outdoor department:** an alternative name for a jug and bottle department.

**Pale ale:** a dry, highly hopped beer, usually sold in bottles.

**Parlour:** see bar parlour.

**Pasteurisation:** so-called after Louis Pasteur who developed sterilisation through heat treating liquids. With beer and cider it prevents further fermentation.

**Perpendicular drinking:** drinking standing up (also known as stand-up or vertical drinking).

**Perry:** similar to cider but made from fermented pear juice. Production has declined severely since the 19th century.

**Pint:** the standard measure for the retail sale of beer

today: 20 fluid ounces (an eighth of a gallon) or 568ml.

**Porter:** a dark, strong, bitter beer popular in London and the south-east from the 1720s until the mid-19th century. It allegedly got its name from its popularity with the thousands of porters who transported goods around London.

**Porter room:** an alternative term for the tap room (qv), used in East Anglia until the early 20th century.

**Pot-shelf:** a shelf over a bar counter for housing glasses. They appear to be a late 20th-century development, and have profoundly and adversely affected the appearance of many pubs.

**Pre-Raphaelite:** in the style of the Pre-Raphaelite Brotherhood, founded in 1848, to produce art using principles and techniques as they were before the Italian painter Raphael (d 1520).

**Private bar:** a more select area than the public bar. The name implies occupancy by a group of regulars known to one another.

**Prohibition:** a policy pursued by the more extreme advocates of temperance, who sought to ban the manufacture and sale of alcohol completely. In the USA, the sale and consumption of alcohol was banned by the Volstead Act of 1919, which ushered in the 'Prohibition Era'. Prohibition was an unmitigated failure, and the Act was repealed in 1933.

**Pubco:** a pub-owning company with no brewing interests. They arose out of the Beer Orders (qv) of 1989. As at June 2011 just two companies own nearly 30 per cent of all British pubs.

**Public bar:** the most basic pub room (also known as the vaults and sometimes simply as the bar) where drink was slightly cheaper than in the better rooms.

**Publican's rustic:** a term used in this book for a nostalgic style of pub-fitting that began between the world wars, emphasising a consciously rustic atmosphere with large amounts of chunky woodwork and rough surfaces.

**Putti:** chubby male children, often winged, in Classical and Baroque sculpture.

**Quarry tile:** floor tiles, usually red and black, in square or lozenge patterns.

**Quart:** two pints. The standard retail measure for beer down to the middle of the 19th century.

**Real ale:** a term coined in the early 1970s to describe traditional beer, which undergoes a secondary fermentation and conditioning in the barrel (hence 'cask-conditioned' as opposed to 'keg' beers, which are brewery-conditioned). The term 'real' has since been ascribed to any number of other products, such as bread and cider; its use implies that they are traditionally made and additive-free.

**Reformed public houses:** those built from the end of the 19th century until 1914 which sought to improve the standard of the pub and attract a more respectable clientèle.

**Saloon:** a better-class pub room.

**Servery:** the area, almost always behind a bar-counter, from which drinks are dispensed.

**Shilling system:** a Scottish system of grading beers introduced in the 1870s deriving from the gross price of a barrel: 60s, 70s, 80s etc, the higher the price the stronger the beer.

**Sitting room:** a Scottish term for a small snug.

**Small beer:** very light, low-gravity beer, originally made from the final straining from the mash. It was the everyday drink until pure water became widely available in the 19th century.

**Smoke room:** a better-class pub room. In former times, when smoking was not a social issue, there is no reason to suppose that smoking was restricted to this area. It is likely that, being better furnished that the public bar, the room was somehow associated with taking one's ease, as in the smoking room of country houses.

**Snob screens:** a range of small, swivelling translucent glazed panels at eye level that provided customers with a degree of privacy.

**Snug:** a small, intimate drinking space.

**Spirit cock:** a tap from which spirits were drawn.

**Spirit-grocer:** In Ireland, a grocer licensed to sell small quantities of spirits for consumption off the premises. The spirit-grocer's licence was introduced in 1791, and abolished in Northern Ireland in 1923.

**Spittoon (trough):** A receptacle (or trough) for spit but no doubt accumulating cigar and cigarette ends, ash and other small refuse.

**Stillage:** a framework on which casks are mounted or 'stillaged' ready for service. Probably the name arises because of the need for traditional beer to remain still for a period to allow it to clear before service.

**Stillion:** a fitting in the middle of a serving area with shelves and storage facilities: sometimes called a wagon.

**Stout:** a dark beer brewed from roasted malts, usually highly hopped and bitter.

**Tap room:** a common pub room, but not, as the name might imply, connected to or within which drink was served or stored.

**Tapster:** the person serving drink in a medieval alehouse, inn or tavern.

**Tavern:** originally a drinking house serving expensive imported wine, as well as good-quality food.

**Teetotal:** refusing all drinks containing alcohol.

**Temperance:** a refusal to drink alcohol on moral grounds. The earliest temperance campaigners advocated moderation, and boycotted only spirits; from 1832, however, increasing numbers became teetotal (qv) and refused to consume any kind of alcoholic beverage.

**Terracotta:** very hard-wearing, unglazed pottery.

**Terrazzo:** Flooring consisting of small pieces of marble set in concrete, rubbed down and polished.

**Thrall:** see stillage.

**Tiddlywink:** a very basic beerhouse (see also Tom and Jerry shop).

**Tied house:** a public house which is committed to taking a particular brewery's beers, either because it is owned or leased by that brewery, or because the owner has accepted a loan in exchange for selling those beers alone (the so-called 'loan-tie').

**Tippler:** in the medieval period, one who bought ale in bulk from a brewer in order to sell it on in small amounts. Later the term came to mean someone who drinks slowly and repeatedly.

**Tom and Jerry shop:** a low drinking-house, normally licensed only for the sale of beer.

**Tongue(d) and groove(d) boarding:** in pubs, cheap panelling on walls and ceilings and consisting of

boards with tongues cut along one edge and grooves in the opposite edge and which are then joined together.

**Top pressure:** pressure of carbon dioxide to force beer from the cellar to the servery.

**Ullage:** waste beer, e.g. spillage, the residual beer in a cask, beer drawn through before commencing service.

**Undercroft:** a vaulted space wholly or partly underground.

**Vault(s):** as a pub room name, an alternative name for a public bar, especially in the north of England.

**Vertical drinking:** drinking standing up (also known as stand-up or perpendicular drinking).

**Water engine:** a traditional means of Scottish beer dispense in which mains water pressure was converted into compressed air pressure to raise beer to the servery. Now believed to be more or less extinct.

**Wet trade:** that part of a pub's turnover that derives from sales of liquids (as opposed to, say, food, hiring rooms, income from games etc).

**Wort:** the liquid produced by mashing and which goes on to be turned into beer by fermentation.

**Wrought iron:** iron which, because of its low carbon content, can be bent and twisted, hence its use, for example, for inn signs. Now virtually unobtainable, it has been superseded by steel.

**X:** some brewers produce beers with names including XXX, XXXX or XXXXX – the greater the number of X's, the stronger the beer. The origins of the system are unclear, although various theories are in circulation; medieval monastic brewers and the 17th-century Excise are both said to have been responsible for it.

**Yeast:** a single-celled organism, usually *Saccharomyces cerevisia* (meaning beer sugar fungus) which converts sugars (obtained by mashing crushed malt) into alcohol. The yeast used for British beer rises to the top of the fermenting brew (it is 'top-fermenting') whilst that used for lager (qv) sinks to the bottom ('bottom-fermenting').

# Pub index

Pubs shown in the illustrations or mentioned in captions are indicated in **bold**.

\* Indicates pubs believed to be closed (in a few cases temporarily) or demolished at June 2011.

n Indicates that the reference can be found in the Notes.

'Ye' is merely an old form of 'the' (and was pronounced 'the' until revived in modern times as a conscious archaism). Just as 'The Fox' is indexed under 'F', so 'Ye Olde ...' is indexed under 'O'.

# Geographical index

Successive reorganisation of local government over the past four decades has created a situation fraught with difficulty in compiling an index such a this. The areas and names of many of the new unitary authorities are unfamiliar to people living outside them. We have therefore opted to list pubs under their historic counties except for large areas like Greater London, Greater Manchester, Merseyside, and Tyne and Wear which do seem to have entered into popular consciousness. Hopefully, this hybrid approach will not cause too much confusion. For Wales and Scotland we list pubs under the names of the present unitary authorities as the areas are recognisable and easily understood. For Northern Ireland, and, for ease of recognition, we index pubs under the historic six counties.

Address details are given in the index of pub names.

Pubs shown in the illustrations or mentioned in captions are indicated in **bold**.
* Indicates pubs believed to be closed (in a few cases temporarily) or demolished as at June 2011.
n Indicates that the reference is to be found in the Notes

# General Index

Page numbers in **bold** indicate illustrations or a reference within a caption. References to notes are preceded by an 'n'.